About The Author

Ian Wishart is an award-winning journalist and author, with a 28 year career in radio, television and magazines, a #1 talk radio show and five #1 bestselling books to his credit. Together with his wife Heidi, they edit and publish the digital newspaper *TGIF Edition* and the news magazine *Investigate*.

Firstly, for Rochelle, and Arthur and Jenny, the Thomases, the people of Pukekawa, Vivien Harrison and for all those whose lives have been greatly affected by these tragic events. *For whatever is hidden is meant to be disclosed, and whatever is concealed is meant to be brought out into the open – Mk 4:22*

Arthur Allan Thomas:
THE INSIDE STORY

CREWE MURDERS: NEW EVIDENCE

Ian Wishart

HOWLING AT THE MOON PUBLISHING LTD

First edition published 2010
Howling At The Moon Publishing Ltd
PO Box 188, Kaukapakapa
Auckland 0843, NEW ZEALAND

www.ianwishart.com
email: editorial@investigatemagazine.com
Copyright © Ian Wishart 2010
Copyright © Howling At The Moon Publishing Ltd, 2010

The moral rights of the author have been asserted. *Arthur Allan Thomas: The Inside Story* is copyright. Except for the purpose of fair reviewing, no part of the publication may be copied, reproduced or transmitted in any form, or by any means, including via technology either already in existence or developed subsequent to publication, without the express written permission of the publisher and copyright holders. All Rights Reserved.

ISBN 978-0-9582401-7-8

Typeset in Adobe Garamond Pro and Ronnia
Cover concept: Ian Wishart, Heidi Wishart, Bozidar Jokanovic
Book Design: Bozidar Jokanovic
Cover images: front, Archive, and Ian Wishart
back, Ian Wishart

To get another copy of this book airmailed to you anywhere in the world, or to purchase a fully text-searchable digital edition, visit our website:

WWW.IANWISHART.COM

LEGAL NOTICE: Criticisms of individuals in this book reflect the author's honest opinion, for reasons outlined in the text or generally known at the time of writing

Contents

The Ultimate Cold Case	6
Darkness At The Edge Of Town	10
The Birth Of Arthur Allan Thomas	15
Scene Of The Crime	25
Closing In On Suspect No. 1	37
Did Norma Demler Feed The Baby?	71
Murder Suspect No. 2	84
Life On Remand	119
Push For A Retrial	148
The Inside Story: Prison Life	163
On The Cover Of The *Rolling Stone*	175
Shootout At The ICI Corral	189
Escape From Prison	204
The Icarus Agenda	222
Mystery Man	229
New Prime Suspect	252
The Jennifer Beard Case	266

PROLOGUE

The Ultimate Cold Case

"Juries are always told that, if conviction there is to be, the prosecution must prove the case beyond reasonable doubt. This statement cannot mean that in order to be acquitted the prisoner must satisfy the jury...it is the duty of the prosecution to prove the prisoner's guilt. If at the end of and on the whole of the case, there is a reasonable doubt, created by the evidence given by either the prosecution or the prisoner, as to whether the prisoner killed the deceased...the prosecution has not made out the case and the prisoner is entitled to an acquittal."
 – *House of Lords, definition of reasonable doubt in Woolmington, 1935*

It begins, as all good detective stories should, with a tip-off:
Letter to *Investigate*, 31st May 2008

Dear Ian
About June 1970 the Crewe murders took place at Onewhero. As you are aware, as at today's date no one has been convicted for this horrendous crime since Arthur Allan Thomas was released from prison with a pardon.
What would genuine new information about this mystery be worth, providing it is not absorbed, some idiotic fantasy or clairvoyant rubbish but undisputable facts, such as the name of the blonde woman who fed baby Rochelle? As you are aware, this has been the most asked question and one of the conundrums of this most infamous murder mystery and I firmly believe that I know who she was.
I have had information since 1970 that I have been far too frightened to release. I made an effort to inform the police in 1970 and spoke to

a Sergeant Johnston (I shall never forget his name) and outlined what I knew about some people that should be interviewed. Imagine my surprise when he went right off the rails and told me that if I ever rang the police with that information again or made any attempt to have it made known then I would be the next bastard found in the river, further now he had my name and I was to shut my bloody mouth forever over this matter.

Sergeant Johnston is now dead. However with the information that I have I am still a threat because all of his buddies aren't dead. The main threat is [Name suppressed] and what I believe I know about him could see him jailed for the rest of his miserable life..."

What you are about to read is the explosive new evidence in New Zealand's most perplexing and well known murder case, the culmination of a two year investigation, and a decision by the man at the centre of the mystery, Arthur Allan Thomas, to break a long silence and tell, for the first time, his complete story.

Because this book marks the 40th anniversary of the Crewe murders, many readers will not be familiar with the full background to the case. For that reason, we're covering it as if you've never read anything about it before. The last book to comprehensively document the Arthur Allan Thomas story was, in fact, David Yallop's *Beyond Reasonable Doubt* in 1978, so a re-examination is probably overdue.

First, an observation on previous books. There has been some sterling work done by the likes of Terry Bell, Pat Booth, David Yallop and Chris Birt. In many ways, this book rides on their shoulders, but to some extent that's an advantage. *The Inside Story* builds on 40 years of reportage on the Crewe murders. Pat Booth's first book, *Trial by Ambush*, was published in 1975 – partly as an effort to get Arthur Allan Thomas released. Chris Birt's offering, *The Final Chapter*, was released 2001, two years after Len Demler's death, and was primarily a book written to document Len Demler's alleged guilt. In the 26 years between Booth and Birt, pretty firm beliefs took hold that if Thomas didn't do it, then Len Demler must have.

The development of this dualistic, either/or, approach is fairly easily explained by the fact that Thomas' supporters were largely confined to working from the police evidence and court transcripts – what I call 'in the box' material. Within that police evidence, there were really only two suspects, Demler or Thomas. Thomas' defence lawyers worked to rebut the material 'in the box' or propose alternative constructions of it, but at a deep level they were confined largely to what was 'in the box'. The only other potential killer 'in the box' was Demler.

In my own investigative work, however, I've often found it much more productive to widen one's terms of reference to 'outside the box' material. In the case of the Winebox investigation, having circled the core documents I then went on a much wider information sweep, slowly working my way back into the centre but retaining intelligence I might otherwise never have collected. I did this kind of 'driftnet' fishing approach until I was confident I knew virtually all there was to know about the incident in question, and much more besides. I've adopted a similar wide-ranging approach to the Crewe murder investigation.

I have also in this book, where possible, sourced the earliest public comments by various witnesses, on the grounds that statements made closer to the time tend to be less corrupted by memory failings or the comments of other people. Of necessity, I'm indebted (again) to Booth, Yallop and Birt for gathering some of these original testimonies, and of course the various newspaper reporters before them who helped write the first draft of history in regard to the Crewe murders. Many of the key players are now dead, which further enshrines these early interviews as important historical material. They cannot be re-interviewed; their books are closed, their printed words effectively become their last words.

I am hugely grateful to Arthur and Jenny, who made available not just their time but their complete archives of documents, newspaper clippings, trial reports and notes on the case, spanning several decades. I'm grateful also to Ray and Des Thomas for their assistance over the past two years and for their tireless pursuit of the facts.

The one thing that struck me, reading the official documents, books and news articles on the Crewe murders, is how flawed the "either/or" approach of the police was, because it left gaping holes where other suspects might legitimately have been pursued.

Forty years after the event, I have the luxury of not having to prove Len Demler killed the Crewes in order to exonerate Arthur Allan Thomas. In fact, I have the luxury of seriously investigating, for the first time in a book, the case *against* Demler being the killer.

So who was it? As best I can tell, the killer was someone who wasn't 'in the box'. By assuming early on that the killer had to be a local – in the sense of a Pukekawa villager – police hamstrung their own investigation to the point where they couldn't make a case stick against suspect 1 and therefore had to fabricate evidence to nail suspect 2. Of course, there's always the possibility that someone in the police knew the killer, and had a reason to keep the killer's identity out of official records of the case.

CHAPTER 1

Darkness At The Edge Of Town

The blades slice across the glass, but they don't cut the blizzard of raindrops exploding ahead of me like golden starbursts in the oncoming headlights. An elderly schoolbus, young faces peering from behind steamy panes, rumbles past and I wonder how many of these Pukekawa schoolkids are aware that – 40 years ago this particular June day – a darkness fell on their town whose shadows linger still. It's a fair bet, I ponder as I throw the Toyota around another tight corner, that the answer to my silent question is 'none'.

The roiling stormclouds from the June frontal system battering the North Island retreat into the rear-view mirror as the car penetrates deeper into this north Waikato heartland and weaves through an interruption of late afternoon winter sunlight, dappling through dank roadside swamps and fens whose now azure pools are starkly punctuated by the reflections of lush cabbage trees and the wispy branches of the occasional native pine.

Fantails, regarded in Maori legend as harbingers of death, flitter and dip above the waters, diving into clouds of midges and emerging satiated.

The marshlands are still giving up their 20th century ghosts to this 21st century driver; decaying and abandoned farm sheds and homesteads dot the high ground, their ancient, scarred and often bare timbers now exposed to both the elements and the ethereal kiss of sunset.

It seems an oddly haunting moodsetter as the 70km/h speed-limit sign marking the edge of town flashes past. Ahead on the horizon another Everest-sized wall of tempestuous grey is rushing in from the Tasman sea and, behind, the equally squally system I've just confronted. Yet here, in the middle, the tiny hamlet of Pukekawa pauses to draw breath in the stillness that hides between thunderbands, and a rainbow crests over the village school.

"You're researching the Crewe murders?", the pump attendant ventures, semi-rhetorically, after discovering my interest in his village, but betraying no hint that he knows the significance of the date. I watch as the fuel gauge ticks over at speed, and momentarily marvel that the $106 I've just chalked up for a tank of gas would have filled up seven cars back on June 22, 1970.

"The community's still divided, even now," the attendant adds, clanging the pump handle back into its holster. "It's interesting to watch, see who won't talk to whom, who won't eat in the same room as someone else."

It's been forty years, and the events of a bitter winter afternoon still ricochet through time finding targets in the souls of villagers – some of whom weren't even born when the shots were fired. Yet, just as the countryside surrounding it, Pukekawa has changed little in that time. It still has one church, one shop, one hall, and the little, 100-pupil, settlement school established back in 1895 – behind whose wrought iron gates a boy named Arthur Thomas and a younger Jeannette Demler eventually shared a classroom together.

On June 22, 1970, however, those schoolyard connections were not at the forefront of anyone's mind. Instead, just as the clock ticked one in the afternoon, Jeannette's father Len was swinging open the creaky gate leading to the little brick and tile farmhouse Jeannette shared with her husband of four years, Harvey Crewe. Within the hour of that discovery, police cars would swoop and detectives be crawling across the property, as Pukekawa residents came to realise something unspeakable had happened to two of their own. It would be 144 days before the body search was called off, at a cost of 1,895,184 man hours of searching.[1]

In the just over 14,600 days since then, much has happened in the world. Colour TV arrived, replaced now by HD TV. Computers that in 1970 filled a large sized room and which could only do the work of an average desk calculator today, now compress 1,000 times the computing power into a chip smaller than your fingernail.

As the world turned, the Vietnam War ended, the China-Vietnam war began, and ended, crackly old 78 records and wind-up gramo-

---

1 *NZ Herald*, 18 April 1973

phones gave way to 33's, and then CDs, and now MP3 and iPod rule. The Beatles broke up. Elvis died. Abba came, and went, and came back again. Bowler hats and walking canes made way for baseball caps and skateboards, and New Zealand since 1970 has enjoyed the political leadership of Keith Holyoake, Jack Marshall, Norman Kirk, Hugh Watt, Bill Rowling, Rob Muldoon, David Lange, Geoffrey Palmer, Mike Moore, Jim Bolger, Jenny Shipley, Helen Clark and John Key.

Yet despite all this, two murders that took place in a little country farmhouse on June 17, 1970, and which weren't discovered until June 22 that year, have transcended everything else, like a cultural anchor-chain to the past that simply refuses to release itself and allow the dead to drift away peacefully to the land of the gradually forgotten.

The ghosts of Harvey and Jeannette Crewe still haunt the New Zealand Police force as a reminder of the day we began to lose our innocence; the first time that the public's faith in the integrity of the police and justice system was seriously shaken.

Today, public distrust in the standard of major police investigations is at an all time high. Regardless of one's views on individual guilt or innocence, few people would disagree that the police inquiries into the Bain case, Rex Haig or Scott Watson were less than competent. Yet in those cases and many others over the years, one investigation has served as a yardstick to measure them against: the arrest and trial of Pukekawa farmer Arthur Allan Thomas for the murders of David Harvey Crewe and Jeannette Lenore Crewe, on or about the night of June 17, 1970, at Pukekawa, South Auckland.

I remember, in the very early 1990s during my time as TV3's crime reporter, being briefed by Detective Inspector John Hughes on the Thomas case. Hughes had heard I was heading south to interview Thomas for a news story, and wanted to pass on his own wisdom.

"He's guilty, I can promise you," Hughes murmured conspiratorially over a coffee, as if letting me in on a major police secret. "I've interviewed him. It's in his eyes."

Hughes was an old-school cop. Eight years in the Navy, and a champion boxer, before joining the wharf police and rising up the ranks. His first big inquiry was the Bassett Road machinegun murders in the mid-60s, and he became one of the central figures in the Crewe murder inquiry. In my time on the police beat, Hughes was a regular contact and a seasoned pro who knew how to spin the news media in his favour. We worked closely in that symbiotic police/media relationship during the prosecution of David Wayne Tamihere for the double murders of Swedish tourists Urban Hoglin and Heidi Paakkonen in 1989.

An aspect of the case that still rings in my ears 21 years later is a memory of sitting in the courtroom, listening to a couple of police secret witnesses wheeled in by Hughes – fellow remand prison inmates who'd been celled up with Tamihere – regale us with lurid details of how Tamihere had confessed the murders to them, and described where he had killed them and how he had disposed of their bodies in certain locations. It would later emerge the secret witnesses – drug dealers – had cut special deals with prosecutors in return for testimony nailing Tamihere.

I remember, too, choppering across the dense, virgin Coromandel bush canopy during a golden sunrise on a crisp October morning two years later in 1991, landing atop a mountain bluff piercing through a cloak of mist, and then – buffeted by the helicopter's downwash – scrambling down the foggy escarpment to a clearing 100 metres below, where "police emergency – do not cross" tape surrounded the remains of a shallow grave marking the discovery of Urban Hoglin's body. My TV3 cameraman Pete Stones and I were there, waiting patiently with smug grins on our faces, when Detective Inspector Hughes and his entourage drove in an hour later on mud-splattered tracks accessible only by four-wheel drive.

Hughesy took our presence in his stride and, with an affable smile masking steely eyes and a mind like a bear-trap, he assured me the discovery of Hoglin's body dozens of miles away from where the secret witnesses had said it was – on the other side of a mountain range in fact and still wearing a watch police claimed they'd found two years earlier – did not materially alter the case against Tamihere.

It was only later that I discovered some equally dodgy jailhouse secret witness testimony had been trumped up against Arthur Allan Thomas as well[2], as Hughes and the rest of the police team attempted to fit the farmer up for the Crewe murders. You could say there was a little bit of a pattern to John's cases.

---

2 Ivan the Insane, a mentally-ill prisoner, was wheeled in by police at the Thomas Royal Commission hearings with testimony supposedly proving Thomas had confessed to him while they were in jail together. The Royal Commission, after hearing from psychiatric experts, told Crown lawyers the man was clearly barking mad and they were wasting the Commission's time. The police refused to take the hint and kept asking questions of the inmate.

I liked John Hughes. As a journalist, I enjoyed his company and his tip-offs. I later had good reason not to trust him further than I could throw him – he arranged for copies of my Winebox manuscript *The Paradise Conspiracy* to be stolen and given to Fay Richwhite & Co., who then attempted to stop the eventual #1 bestseller from being published. I did, nonetheless, come to forgive Hughes his sins.

One man who is not so forgiving of the police is Arthur Thomas.

"Dirty bastards," he mutters as he reflects on the events that changed his life forever.

I look into Arthur Allan Thomas' eyes, at the end of a long series of interviews – significantly more than police interviewed him for and much longer than John Hughes had face time with Thomas. As Arthur meets my gaze, there is the trace of a tear welling up. I don't see guilt, but instead the pain of a man who has kept it all inside for so long.

All that, however, is about to change...

CHAPTER 2

The Birth Of Arthur Allan Thomas

The New Year had just dawned when Ivy Thomas felt the first pangs. The tightening around her belly, and that low, deep contraction. It was different to the other twinges that had teased her these past days. This one meant business. She looked out across the meadow, soaking in those views to eternity across the rolling pastures of fertile Pukekawa, a sleepy rural community nestled in either South Auckland or North Waikato, depending on how you felt on the day. It's the settlement that sits on the southwestern bank of the Waikato river as it snakes its way out to the sea, marking a natural boundary between the Auckland region on the northern side, and the rest of New Zealand.

Ivy squinted, as a loud squawk from the towering macrocarpa was swiftly followed by the darting movement of two magpies screeching like a pair of fighter planes towards an encroaching hawk.

It was, she thought to herself, even as she winced when the second contraction hit, a beautiful day. One of those hot, languid New Zealand summer days where even the sun drips sweat and everyone is still trying to sleep off the effects of Christmas dinner a week earlier. The cicadas flitted everywhere as you approached, and down on the banks of the Waikato river children played in the shoals, drenching themselves in the cool sanctuary, as much to escape the sandflies as the heat.

It was 1938, the same year British Prime Minister Neville Chamberlain famously waved a signed agreement with one Adolf Hitler in front of the press and triumphantly declared, "Peace for our time". Ivy Thomas wasn't in peace, however, as the birth dragged on into January 2. Eventually, as was the custom in maternity units at the time, doctors knocked her out with chloroform, grabbed a pair of forceps and took over delivery themselves.

"I am sorry I cannot tell you the exact hour Arthur was born," she would later write,[3] "as his was a very slow birth. I can remember it was a beautiful Sunday morning, the sun was shining and locusts were singing as one landed on the window and was singing there. The date was January 2, 1938. The birthplace was Pukekohe. All I can remember after his birth was the doctor slapping my face to bring me around."

Arthur Allan Thomas doesn't remember much about his childhood now, either. He's seen 72 summers since being serenaded into the world by cicadas at the Pukekohe maternity annex, but sadly much of his life has come to be defined by the events of his 32nd winter.

The sound of birds whistling over the meadows makes for a lovely mental image, but it's the sound of jailbirds whistling in the showers that still rings in Thomas' ears. Little did he know, as a young boy, what the future had in store for him.

The family farm, which eventually grew to 272 acres (110 hectares) nestled at the northern end of Pukekawa district, just a hop, skip and a jump from the Waikato river, was last stop on the Mercer Ferry road before the ferry landing itself – a dead end. Beyond, the land just sloped gently down to the water, where the lights of Mercer township danced enticingly 500 metres away as the crow flies, and 40 or so kilometres away as the bus drives.

The schoolbus, incidentally, didn't come too close to the Thomas farm. The quaint little schoolhouse was at the southern end of Pukekawa, perhaps seven or eight kilometres away over gravel roads, and the nearest bus-stop to the Thomas farm was a mile away (1.6km). For the Thomas children, it was a round trip they made every day, in bare feet over the metalled backroads, hail or shine. On frosty winter mornings, Arthur would stand in fresh cow pats in the paddocks in order to keep his feet warm.

"Me old man and my mother didn't used to worry about us walking a mile there and back from the schoolbus," recalls Arthur, "and it wasn't until one of the other fathers said, 'Well, my kids are not going to be walking all that way, we're going to do something about it,' that the school committee finally decided to bring the bus much closer."

---

3 *NZ Truth*, October 15, 1974

The compromise was halfway, so the kids only had to walk half a mile to and from. Those walks, it seems, were a perfect opportunity for boisterous farm children to hatch nefarious schemes.

"There was one mate," says Thomas, a wry grin beginning to break out across his face, "a boy named Malcolm McArthur. We went to Pukekawa School together, and he ended up battling for me on the Thomas Retrial Committee, but anyways, we went to his parents' house, and he literally pulled out his old man's shotgun, grabbed these cartridges out of his bedroom, went out to the back of the farm. We were only 12 or so – only kids. Put the cartridge in, OK, and just put the gun to the post..."

I could finish the transcript of what Arthur Thomas said next by filling in the blanks from my own notes, but I think the official interview transcriber Melissa Harsant, who assisted with this book, captured the essence of what followed next beautifully:

"We knew that there was a kick, see? [Inaudible] A chicken... [Inaudible] flicked your gun up, [laughs] [Inaudible] bang! And you would see his red face. [laughs] [Inaudible] bloody [Inaudible] [laughs] And we laughed, laughed for hours!"

The chicken, as I understand it, survived, was never in any real danger in fact save for possible heart failure at the noise from the blast, but the recoil from the shotgun and its effect on a small 12 year old was something to witness. But it didn't end there. Malcolm McArthur apparently had more excitement up his sleeve:

"Anyhow, on the way back, we had some gorse on the farm, see, so he lit the stuff. I didn't say anything, and next thing, he has these shotgun cartridges and he threw them in the fire. Boom!"

The two 12 year olds scattered, ducking buckshot. McArthur, incidentally, never lost his mischievous streak or his fascination with fire.

"I remember one time, this is Jenny and I now," says Thomas with a nod to his wife Jenny beside him, "we went down to see him at Gisborne. He had a motel there and we were in the bedroom..."

"He must have had a key," grins Jenny.

"And anyhow," continues Arthur, he had a tin rubbish bin, he put some paper in and he lit the bin. And he came down to the bedroom – 'Fire. Fire. Fire!' He came into the bedroom with the rubbish bin on fire."

Thomas and Jenny begin to laugh again, although Jenny recovers her composure long enough to explain the possible motive. "I think he must've thought we were starkers in bed or something, and just for the hell of it he could get us running out of the room or something."

But watching Malcolm McArthur throw shotgun cartridges into a gorse fire wasn't the only mishap that befell the young Arthur Thomas. Just after starting school in 1943, five year old Arthur was in the the milking shed, watching his brother Ray fool around with some machinery.

"The war was on, I was five years old, and my old man was milking cows on the Pukekawa farm. He had a big long shaft going through to drive the separator, the vacuum pump, the skim milk pump – this big long shaft driving it from an electric motor.

"My brother Ray was feeding string onto this shaft from the hay bales, and next moment it catches and away she goes. There was a big heap of string going around this shaft and I thought 'I'd better grab this or my old man's going to get angry at us', but the string caught on my fingers – see?"

Thomas pauses in the interview to show me several missing fingers on his right hand, or more accurately the clear air where those fingers would normally be, gone in most cases from the first joint.

"Pulled the joints of my fingers – cut the fingers off!" he continues. "The war was on, and I knew I'd done wrong because my fingers were gone and there was blood everywhere, a hell of a mess, just about lost them right off down to the hand. I was crying, of course, and I went to tell me father who was milking the cows, and I yelled out, 'Dad, Dad, the rats bit them off!' because I didn't want to get in trouble, and we all knew there were rats in there.

"But of course there was hell to pay, we went to Dr Gray at Pukekohe and when I woke up in the morning I was in Auckland hospital. I was in Auckland hospital for a week. And the war was on and the aeroplanes – oh, I liked seeing the aeroplanes flying over – and from the hospital you could see the Domain, and the men training to go to war.

"Nobody visited me the entire week I was there. Punishment. I sussed that out pretty quickly. The old man would have seen the string spinning there and bits of my fingers everywhere, he would have known damn well the rats weren't guilty."

You get the feeling, looking at Arthur's face as he relives the experience, that being abandoned in a hospital 70 kilometres from home, without mum or dad visiting once, cut deeper than the loss of the fingers. Then Arthur leaves the moment, and that fleeting insight vanishes back into the past, an ephemeral memory that one day will live only on this page.

Perhaps the failure of his parents to visit was more due to his distance from them, and the fact there were other children at home to look after. "Ray was the oldest," he reminds me, "then me, Rita and Lynette." Richard, Lyrice, Margaret, Lloyd and Desmond would follow later. There was a tenth, but the child didn't make it.

It was at Pukekawa school that Thomas eventually met the woman who would change his life, Jeannette Demler. Jeannette was two years younger than Thomas, but ended up sharing a room in the older boy's final years as Arthur had been held back a class. Arthur was 13, Jeannette 11.

"I didn't go to high school," Thomas says softly. "The highest education I got was Standard Six (Form 2)". Instead, on his 14th birthday in January 1952, his father pulled him out of Pukekawa school to work on the farm. "I didn't get paid any wages, I was just expected to help the old man with chores, I think he really wanted things done on the farm."

Arthur's older brother Ray shared the same fate. Together, the pair of them did fencing, scrub-cutting and other dogsbody work on the property. They didn't have a ute or even a tractor, "just a horse and a sledge we hooked up to it to haul the hay", smiles Thomas. For the next four years, working the farm unpaid was Arthur Thomas' life.

At nineteen, however, Arthur Thomas felt the call of the wild or, more specifically, the call of an empty wallet. "I just wanted to make some money and buy a car. So I went to work for the Roose Shipping Company, right up there where the bridge is now. There was a big wire rope right across the river. And of course when the ferry's on either side, the wire rope would be on the bottom of the river. And I was working looking after, well repairing, drags, cranes and barges and boats and things."

Eventually, a young Arthur Thomas graduated to ferry captain, driving the ferry 'cross to Mercer' and back, all in the name of getting his own wheels – a 250 BSA motorbike first, "and then I bought a car."

The ferry job widened his social network. "I had to crank the handle to start me engine. On a Thursday night we'd all go to the pictures at Mercer, and quite a few people from our end would come down to the river so I had to crank handle to take them across this Mercer River to the movies, all the pictures on Thursday night at Mercer. And of course Mervyn Cathcart was the one that went on me rides, I remember."

Merv, who lived on a neighbouring farm, was a staunch friend. They attended church together, sang in the choir together, hung around together and, in 1959 – March 19 according to a diary[4] belonging to Cathcart's mother – began taking dance lessons together. Arthur was 21.

"Yes. I learnt to dance with Mervyn. He wanted to learn to dance and we, both of us, used our cars to go to Auckland and learn to dance in the late '50s I suppose."

Crown prosecutors would later try and build a case that Thomas was dancing at the age of 17 in 1955, but the diary tells a different story. The lessons were far away in Auckland city, and the boys couldn't afford to get there until they had jobs, and transport.

"We were both shy. Very shy. That's the trouble. You can't learn dancing unless you go to a dancing school. Cos we couldn't even ask a lady for a dance. That's why we thought well, that's the only way we can get some confidence".

"I can just imagine you two at dancing," quips Thomas' wife Jenny with a sly smile. I hit Thomas with a hard question of my own. "And so did you end up dancing with each other initially, or?"

"Oh no, no!! None of that!" laughs Thomas in mock horror. "Oh no! No way! No way! No. My sisters were good to me. My sisters. Yeah."

Surprisingly, the young girls of the day generally didn't attend dance classes – they learnt at high school. "Well, I missed out on that," says Thomas. Instead, eager young men were paired up with matronly instructors. Watching *Dancing With The Stars*, Arthur still thinks he has a little bit left in him. "I think I could pick up the odd step now, but no, I don't dance much now."

When he left Roose Shipping, armed with an excellent reference that he's retained to this day, it was for a job in forestry at Maramarua, about 40 kilometres away. "Forestry is good exercise. Had to be very fit. They showed me how to sharpen an axe, and my axe was – well, it would clip the hairs on my arm."

---

4 *Beyond Reasonable Doubt*, by David Yallop, Penguin edition, 1980, p83

It was there, in Maramarua, that Jeannette Demler's path would again cross that of Arthur Thomas. While Arthur was manning the Mercer ferry in the late 50s, seventeen year old Jeannette had applied for and been accepted as a teacher trainee at Ardmore Teachers College near Auckland. After graduating in 1958, she'd been posted for a year to Pukekohe North School, and then to Mangatangi School in the Firth of Thames for the 1960 school year. For 1960, 20 year old Jeannette Demler was living at an eight-bed teachers' hostel in Maramarua.

Occasionally the former classmates would catch sight of each other in the village, wave or say hello, but Thomas says they didn't socialise much. "With her? No, I just asked her out one time, went to look her up and I think that's where I found out she was staying overseas and I sent a present or two over. I told the cops the whole lot," he adds, "and the letter she wrote to me – I gave it to the cops".

"Yeah, you've got to hand it to him, he gave himself to the police on a silver platter," interjects Jenny.

For her part, Jeannette had decided her year at Mangatangi School would pay for her big OE in the UK and Europe. Although police would later try and claim Arthur Allan Thomas had an obsessive passion with Jeannette and never left her alone, the evidence on that point never stood up. Jeannette's roommates at the teachers' hostel in Maramarua say Thomas was never mentioned. One of those women, Grace Hessell, told David Yallop, "If any of the girls was going out the rest of us knew exactly where and exactly who they were going with. If someone called for one of them we would all know. As far as Jeannette was concerned there was no Arthur Thomas in the picture at all...Men were allowed to call at the hostel and visit. I never saw Arthur Thomas there."[5]

So by the time Thomas plucked up the courage to ask Jeannette out, sometime in 1961, she was already overseas. Arthur, far from suffering, went on to date a number of young women whose letters he also kept: Lorna, Gert, Margaret and Diana. He'd actually begun dating Lorna in 1960 while he was still working in forestry at Maramarua, while Gert's letter tells Arthur she loves him "with all my heart" and asks him to spend the weekend with her. Clearly, Arthur wasn't having trouble in the female department. He actually fathered a child out of wedlock during one relationship very early in the 1960s.

---

5 *Beyond Reasonable Doubt*, p26

No longer an axe-man, he'd graduated in 1961 to the world of aerial top-dressing after ingratiating himself with a syndicate of farmers near the settlement of Glen Murray, about 15km south of Pukekawa. Thomas wasn't flying the syndicate's plane, but he was learning how to load it and assist on topdressing runs. It turned into a paying job as a loader-driver for Barr Brothers Aerial Topdressing. "There wasn't much big money in it, but I enjoyed it because I was meeting farmers and flying."

As for the occasional gifts he sent Jeannette to "keep my options open", there were pleasant thank-you notes in return, later presented in court:

"To Arthur, Christmas cheer and best wishes for the New Year from Jeannette," was the introduction on a December 1961 card sent from England, before Jeannette continued, "Dear Arthur, what a surprise to find a present of beads and stockings at the O.V.C. Thank you very much. The beads were lovely and you were a good guess with the size of the stockings. You certainly seem to be seeing lots of different parts of the North Island with working at Barr Brothers. Life is still just as hectic as ever over here. I am stopping work to go for a skiing holiday in Austria early next year. Yours sincerely, Jeannette."

The final communication Thomas had with Jeannette was to send her a Christmas gift at the end of 1962, a brush and comb set. At that meeting, she told him she had a boyfriend, and that was the last time Arthur Thomas ever raised the issue again.

When she returned from her OE in London at the end of 1962, Jeannette made an appointment with the Auckland Education Board, seeking details of available positions in the greater Auckland region. One of the first Board staff she spoke to was Dianna Wishart. "She was quite beautiful, she could have married any man really," Wishart says. "As I recall we were able to find a temporary teaching position." Indeed, the AEB found Jeannette Demler another Maramarua placement, this time a relief teaching job at the Maramarua District High School. If Thomas had been harassing her as police later claimed, it's unlikely she would have returned to that area. As it was, the job was for a term, and then Jeannette travelled south to stay with schoolfriend Beverley Willis in Wanganui.

Again, given that the entire police 'motive' for Thomas hinged on him driving her nuts, Yallop's interview with roommate Grace

Hessell is instructive: "When she returned [from England] she was at a bit of a loose end and took this relief teacher position...The headmaster tried to persuade her to stay on because he liked her and she was a good teacher. She told him that she wanted to join her friend Beverley in Wanganui. It's absolute nonsense for anyone to suggest Thomas was pestering her and forced her to leave."

Thomas' topdressing work took him all over, from the Waikato through Auckland and Northland, and it would lead him into the arms of his future wife, Vivien Carter, a 21 year old English rose. It was January 1964, and Arthur Thomas was staying in Wellsford for some topdressing work. One afternoon, he and the pilot caught up with a local signwriter, Pat Vesey, to get a logo painted on the plane.

"One of the guys," explains Thomas, "said to Pat, 'Oh, have you got any sheilas up here? Arthur's just come up to stay'. Pat replied, 'I've got my niece out from England'."

When Arthur and the pilot called around to the Vesey house a little later, Thomas and Vivien Carter were introduced formally. They hit it off, despite Arthur's lack of wheels. "I didn't have a car up at Wellsford there, so I just used to go and meet up and socialise with her. Yeah, she was good to me."

The pair married on November 7, 1964, in Wellsford's Presbyterian church, Vivien just 22 and Thomas aged 26. Vivien, a wartime baby hailing from the town of Farnham in Surrey, had decided to do her big OE in New Zealand, mainly on the basis she had family here in the form of the Veseys, her aunt and uncle. It was a culture shock, coming from Britain in the swinging sixties, just as Beatlemania was breaking out, down to a cow-town two hours north of Auckland. Not only was she thrown into marriage, 20,000 kilometres from home, but she was thrown into farming too.

For his part, Arthur briefly continued working for Barr Brothers topdressing, but quit in early 1965.

The couple lived on several farms over the following year and a half, and were on a property at Clevedon, South Auckland, when Arthur Thomas' father Allan suggested the young couple lease the family farm at Pukekawa from him. At 272 acres (110 hectares) it was big enough but not too big. The operation straddled beef, dairy and sheep. They moved back to Pukekawa in June 1966, just coincidentally the same month Jeannette Demler married Harvey Crewe, the sweetheart she'd met during her three year stay in Wanganui. The

Crewes immediately moved onto the old Chennells farm Jeannette and her sister Heather owned through an inheritance – Harvey taking a $30,000 loan to buy out Heather's share.

It's true the Crewes and the Thomases lived in the same district, but when you say it that starkly it's a little misleading. The farms were 15km away from each other. To give that some perspective, imagine Arthur lived in Newtown, Wellington, and Jeannette lived in Tawa, north of Wellington near Porirua city. The families were not next door neighbours by any stretch of the imagination.

"I did see her once in the big outfit – Buckland & Sons (stock and station agent in Tuakau). I think she was walking out as I walked in. We just said 'hello' and carried on."

For Arthur Thomas, having control of his own spread gave him the chance to try new farming techniques he'd picked up. "I used to feed the calves skim milk. Big calves. *Big* calves drinking skim milk. The guys from Wrightsons and the supermarkets couldn't believe it. They'd say, 'Is this the right meat? Where are you getting it from?' And we'd sell it in the supermarkets, this beautiful meat, because they're drinking skim milk as well as eating the cut grass." He taps his nose, knowingly. "They had shiny coats and did very well there."

It seems idyllic, two sets of newlyweds making a go of the good old New Zealand dream. Little did Arthur Thomas or Jeannette Crewe know, but their lives were on a collision course.

CHAPTER 3

The Scene Of The Crime

What was the Demler family farm back then, on the corner of Sharpe Road and State Highway 22, has long since been in different hands and subdivided into lifestyle blocks. Children play with pet ponies and lambs, oblivious to the past. But the almost wild moorland feel of the original property remains. On June 22, 1970, farmer Len Demler was patriarch, father to sisters Heather and Jeannette and widower to the late Maisie (officially, May Constance) Demler.

Len Demler had taken possession of the farm back in 1937 and ended up marrying the girl next door, Maisie Chennells, whose parents owned the neighbouring farm. When Maisie's 39 year old brother Howard was killed by his tractor in 1950, ownership of the Chennells family property passed to his nearest relatives, Maisie and Len's children, Jeannette and Heather Demler, aged ten and eight respectively. Under the terms of Howard's will, the farm would be managed by others until the girls reached the age of 25, with profits being retained in a trust on their behalf until then. It's fair to say the Demler girls were independently wealthy as a result of the bequest.

Then there's the added complication of their father's financial woes. Len Demler had been pinged for tax evasion and in 1962 he was forced to sell half of his own farm to wife Maisie for the princely sum (in those days) of £9,540 – roughly equivalent to the £10,000 fine he'd incurred for the unpaid taxes.

According to British author David Yallop, in his book *Beyond Reasonable Doubt*, Demler tried to deny on oath during one of the Thomas hearings that he'd sold half his farm to Maisie, on the grounds that he never received the money. Yallop published a land transfer document where Demler had however signed as to the payment that "the receipt whereof is hereby acknowledged".

At first blush it looks as though Demler is clearly lying, which goes to his credibility. A more charitable view however is that the deal was probably a paper transaction, and money between husband and wife is unlikely, physically, to have changed hands and in that sense he was probably telling the truth as he saw it. But Demler, a farmer, may have misunderstood the legal significance: by signing the document he was signing over half the farm and making a sworn declaration that he'd been paid for it.

Legally, regardless of what Demler felt deep down, his wife officially owned half the property. And all of that came to a head in July 1969 when Maisie Demler drafted a new will, cutting out daughter Heather from any entitlement to a share in Maisie's half of the farm. Maisie was reportedly angered at Heather's decision to marry bankrupt divorcee Robert Souter, and didn't want her new son-in-law getting his hands on Chennells-Demler money. Instead, Jeannette was the main beneficiary of Maisie's will. Len Demler, in an attempt to restore balance between the siblings, reduced Jeannette's share of his own estate from half down to one third, leaving the rest to Heather.

Maisie died in February 1970 of a brain tumour, just months before Jeannette and Harvey Crewe were murdered. According to Yallop, this could have been the catalyst for the carnage of June 17, 1970:[6]

" Maisie Demler's will, which had only recently been probated, made it clear that not only had she cut Heather Demler off without a cent but she had also ensured that the entire farm would no longer be her husband's. He would only retain a life interest in her half of the farm which would then pass to Jeannette. Her will stripped him of his mana, and it would ultimately strip him of half the land that he'd worked and owned since before the Second World War.

"The police were also in possession of a number of statements that made it clear that before his death Harvey Crewe had wanted to buy his father-in-law out. Ian Spratt was one whom Len discussed this with prior to the deaths of the Crewes. Demler had commented that if he sold out to Harvey his son-in-law would kick him out and he would have nowhere to live. Len had treated it all as a big joke when discussing it with Spratt."

---

6 *Beyond Reasonable Doubt*, Yallop, p37

This, then, was the background to the Demler/Crewe relationship leading up to the day their house was found empty.

It was just after 8 o'clock on the morning of Monday, 22 June 1970, when stock agent Joe Moore and colleague John Dagg pulled into the driveway of the Crewe farmhouse. Swinging open the front gate, they hammered on the front door awaiting a reply that never came. Dagg saw the outside light was on but didn't try the backdoor. Moore had also tried the phone before he left the office, but no one picked up. If he'd peered through a window he might have seen the bloodstains, but he didn't. He might have heard baby Rochelle, but if he did it wasn't mentioned later. Instead, the two men left.

When he got back to town Moore rang Len Demler, asking if he knew where his daughter and son-in-law had got to. Demler replied in the negative. The crusty old farmer must have been getting frustrated, however, by the time Ron Wright from Tuakau Transport Ltd called, just before 1pm that day. Wright explained he had a load of sheep he was scheduled to pick up from the Crewes, but couldn't raise them. Demler said he would go and check.

According to police notes from 24 June, Demler found both the main gate and a smaller gate to the home's front garden shut when he arrived about 1pm. Although he didn't mention it, Demler would have walked past milk and newspapers lying uncollected at the main gate since the previous Thursday. He told police he walked to the rear of the house and found the outside light on, and the key in the back door's outside lock.

On getting no answer he entered the house, apparently noticing Harvey's slippers "placed close together just inside the door", and then seeing "stains of blood on the kitchen floor and then large stains of blood on the carpet in the lounge."

According to the man who would later head the murder investigation, Detective Inspector Bruce Hutton, Demler then explored the main bedroom for any sign of Jeannette and Harvey, without success, before entering baby Rochelle's bedroom where he found the 18 month old "in a distressed condition", as Hutton put it. "He said the child was unable to stand and smelt something terrible.

"He said that he had panicked as he thought someone might be lurking in the house and had hurried out and then driven home to phone the Tuakau Transport [company] to stop the truck from coming out to collect Harvey's sheep."

Why didn't Demler rescue his granddaughter from her cot, particularly if he thought someone might still "be lurking in the house"? The grandfather's actions in fleeing the scene, leaving a two year old alone and distressed in a bloodstained house, don't fit with what most of us think we would do in similar circumstances.

Nor did Demler ring Tuakau Transport from the Crewes' phone. He decided to drive home, without Rochelle, and ring Ron Wright from the Demler farmstead. Adding insult to injury, Wright was out of the office when Demler called to cancel the sheep pick-up, but rather than simply leave a message and immediately return to the Crewe house, Demler chose to wait for Wright to get back and return his call.

Only then did Len Demler return to the scene of the crime, by way of Owen Priest's farm just up the road from the Crewes. Priest has long since passed away, but he was interviewed in the 1970s by David Yallop:[7]

"I was working in a paddock between my house and the hatchery. Heard a car pull up on the road. When I got to the gate I recognised it as Len's red Cortina. He asked me to go up to the Crewe farm with him and said, 'I don't know what the hell's happened up there. But there's a terrible bloody mess.' With that Len turned and walked back to his car. On the way up Len turned to me and said, 'They're not there. I wonder where the bloody hell they've gone to.'

"He made no mention of any bloodstains.[8] Then when I went in and saw all this blood, it stopped me stone dead. Len was behind me. I recall him saying, 'I want to know what's happened. But I don't want to find them'."

Strange words, but they may indicate the simple fears of a man who could see the obvious, and didn't want to face seeing his dead child.

"I moved forward to search," recalled Priest, "not knowing what to expect. I comforted myself with the thought that if there was any funny business going on, Len was right there behind me. Although I was pretty composed and my mind was working clearly I was nevertheless apprehensive. I found Rochelle and then continued to explore the house. When I got to the bathroom and toilet I looked

---

7 *Beyond Reasonable Doubt*, Yallop, p6
8 Priest's memory is challenged in this regard. Police files from interviews taken immediately after the event in question reveal that Demler told Priest: "Something has happened over there – there is blood".

around to make some comment to Len. He was standing by the back door! I realised that I had gone over the entire house on my own. With perhaps some joker waiting to attack me. That rocked me a bit.

"Initially when we entered the house Len kept saying, 'The bugger's killed her and done himself in. I tell you Harvey's killed her'. It began to play on my nerves after he'd come out with this two or three times. I turned to him. 'Look Len, we don't know what's happened. It could have been a third party'. He was silent after that."

The men poked around the house and nearby farm buildings for around 20 minutes, finding nothing. Demler checked the haybarn, wondering if Harvey had driven the tractor somewhere; he hadn't, the vehicle was parked in the barn. While Owen Priest returned to his own home across the road to phone police, Demler took baby Rochelle to the home of Barbara Willis, a family friend.

Although hungry and distressed, the child showed no sign of being starved of food or liquid for five days. Police sought a medical report the following day from Dr Thomas Fox, a childcare specialist who'd been in medicine since 1940.

Fox's report, made available to the Thomas trials, records that "Rochelle had been found by her maternal grandfather Mr Demler in her cot at 1330 hours on the 22nd June, 1970. She was said to have been crying and whimpering as the grandfather approached the house, but to have stopped as he went to the cot side. Her eyes were said to have been 'sunken back'. Mr Demler took her by car to the home of Mrs Willis at 1430 hrs.

"On arrival at the residence of Mrs Willis, she was sitting on a blanket in the car. Mrs Willis noted 'a dreadful smell, that the child was very cold and shaking, that Rochelle just clung to her for the following two hours, that her eyes seemed sunken, that the white of her eyes were blood shot, that she was frightened and shocked, that she did not seem sick and that she was not desperately ill'."

Dr Fox noted that the smell was the result of a bowel motion, and that an unchanged nappy had left Rochelle with nappy rash and blistering in parts. As any parent knows, a nappy left longer than a few hours, particularly a teething nappy, can have similar consequences.

There is no doubt Rochelle was frightened. She had refused to let Barbara Willis out of her sight since waking up, and Fox records,

"During the interview, Rochelle appeared to be very apprehensive. She moved little, preferring to cling to Mrs Willis."

"On physical examination," he noted, "Rochelle was of good build and well covered. The tone of her skin and muscles suggested that she had recently lost one to two pounds (half to one kilo) in weight."

Fox concluded Rochelle was most likely to have been last fed before 2pm on the Saturday before she was found – meaning she was alone and unchanged in the cold house for around 48 hours. He did not think her condition was consistent with being left alone for five days.

"A child such as Rochelle, living under the conditions outlined above, might survive five days, but she would be seriously ill at the end of that time," said Fox.

Right from the get-go, then, police knew they were dealing with a highly unusual case – the killer, or killers, had returned to the scene of the crime to feed and care for the baby of the murder victims.

One of the first things police needed to do was try and re-trace the steps of Harvey and Jeannette Crewe in their final 24 hours on the planet. They had a fair idea the couple had vanished on Wednesday 17th, because Thursday's *NZ Herald* newspaper and Thursday's milk had not been collected from the box.

The evening of Tuesday 16th featured the weekly family dinner with Len Demler at the Crewe house. Demler, a taciturn – some would say "uncouth" – character, had got in the habit of dining with his daughter and son-in-law on a Tuesday ever since Demler's wife Maisie had died the previous February. This particular week had some unusual flavours in the mix, and they had nothing to do with the meal, which was corned beef and onions. Instead, it was overshadowed by legal work over Maisie's Will.

On the Monday, Len Demler had been to see his solicitor after receiving the final balance sheet tallying up the value of his late wife's estate – primarily her half share in their farm. At the lawyer's office he drafted that new Will of his own, leaving two thirds of his share of the farm to daughter Heather, and one third to Jeannette Crewe.

The following day, Tuesday 16th, Jeannette visited the same solicitor to finalise her share of her mother's estate. One outstanding item was higher than expected death duties, caused by a revaluation upwards of the Demler farm, and it was generally expected within the family that a Morris 1100 car accidentally inherited by Jeannette in the wash-up would be sold to offset the extra death duties. The lawyer later confirmed to police that Jeannette had agreed to sell the car, but had not finished the paperwork at the time she died.

Police speculated that this outstanding item was the cause of some acrimony at the dinner Len shared at Harvey and Jeannette's that Tuesday evening.

The next morning, Wednesday 17 June 1970, Jeannette hosted a local mother, Thyrle Pirret, to morning tea and biscuits. Thyrle, whose husband Hamish was a bowling mate of Len Demler's, had a three year old daughter named Virginia and wanted to take a gift – a little blue jacket – around for Jeannette's toddler, Rochelle. She was the last woman to speak to Jeannette.

"We'd recently bought a brand new Holden," a now elderly Pirret tells me. She still lives in the same property she did that day forty years ago. "And I remember telling my husband, under the excuse of 'running the car in', that I'd take this present around to Jeannette Crewe's. It was an awful day, as I remember, and we headed out about 11am.

"They were a very happy couple. I had morning tea with them. There was no element of any bad feeling, the atmosphere was very pleasant as far as I was concerned.

"I knew them through her father, because my husband was a bowling mate of Len Demler's. They were at our wedding actually. I'd met Jeannette's sister and her mother – Mrs Demler was a very sweet person.

"I had to be back at 1pm because my husband had to go to the chiropractor and have his back treated, and Jeannette had said, 'oh, stay and have a cup of tea', which I did. Then Harvey came in and we just talked for a little while. It was just before lunch and I think they were going out to the sale. I think one of the stock agents was going to be in after me, but I was there in the morning and I had no feeling of any bad atmosphere at all. It was a happy, welcoming morning tea. There didn't seem to be any ill-feeling or anything like that."

Pirret doesn't remember bills or the morning mail being scattered over the dining table when she was there.

"I don't remember anything like that. She just brought out cups of tea and we had biscuits, she just set the table, that was all. Everything was neat and tidy. Harvey and Jeannette seemed a very happy couple. That was the only time I'd been out there – that particular day. It was very sad."

Thyrle Pirret must have left some time around midday or a little before, to be back in time for her husband's 1pm appointment. At 12.45pm, John Lockhart remembered seeing the Crewes at the stock sale. Robin Dunlop, another attendee, reckons the Crewes arrived around midday at the sale, and when he left at 2pm he noticed Jeannette and Rochelle waiting in the couple's Hillman Hunter. It must have been a long wait with a toddler in the car, because Stuart Taylor and Henry Eyre both told police the Crewes were still at the sale at 3pm.

Alexander Irvine, a local farmer who knew the Crewes well, says he saw their car parked close to his own farmhouse, about 7km down the road from the Crewe residence on the southern border of the Crewe farm around 5pm. He told police he noticed a mob of sheep cresting a rise in the paddocks and guessed Harvey and his dogs were responsible, although he didn't physically see Harvey.

Now here's where the whereabouts of the Crewes get murky. Irvine, who knew them well and knew their car, reckons Harvey was working the sheep around 5pm on June 17 – just on sundown. Much later, and Irvine wouldn't have seen the sheep being rounded up in the distance.

However, police prosecutors building their case against Arthur Allan Thomas for an 11pm shooting relied on information from retailer Colin Massey and his 14 year old son Richard, who owned a fish and chip shop in Pukekohe. Leading QC Robert Adams-Smith was, in 1979 hired by Prime Minister Rob Muldoon to review the case and carried out his own investigation. Here's the story police spun him in their own clipped shorthand:[9]

"Massey (Richard) identified Jeannette Crewe from photo and described Harvey as the persons who called at the shop at about 6pm, 17.6.70. Jeannette purchased 2/3 flounders and chips. Saw them drive off towards Tuakau. The woman told Massey that they had a long way to go and wrapped the flounder and chips in extra newspaper."

Police Commissioner Bob Walton told the Government appointed investigator that the scenario of a late evening killing hung largely

---

9 Second confidential report of Robert Adams-Smith QC to the Prime Minister, 1979

on the fish: "The key...is that a flounder fish meal purchased on 17 June, was still on the table in the house when the murders were first discovered."

The investigator however, Robert Adams-Smith QC, couldn't get his head around why Harvey and Jeannette, if home at Pukekawa by 5pm, would go all the way back out to Pukekohe for fish at 6pm, then come back home again. If farmer Irvine was right, the Crewes were highly unlikely to be buying fish 30 km away, but if the Masseys were correct, then Harvey can't have been home at 5pm and dinner may well have been late. Adams-Smith writes: "Accordingly, I felt I should test the strength of the evidence as to the alleged purchase of fish."

He interviewed Colin Massey, and says, "Mr Massey told me that approximately 6pm on Wednesday 17 June 1970 a woman came into the shop and ordered a meal of flounder and chips. The woman was strikingly good looking and well dressed. She was followed into the store later by her husband and, according to what Mr Massey tells me now, one or other of the couple explained that they were running late because they had been 'at a stock sale'."

The Masseys explained how they'd seen photographs of the Crewes later, and remembered the couple from earlier visits to their retail premises.

"On the face of it," writes the QC, "what Mr Massey says today appears to clearly establish that the couple who purchased the flounder from his shop at 6pm that Wednesday evening, were in fact Mr and Mrs Crewe on their way back from the stock sale."

Forced to choose between conflicting evidence, however, the QC decided the Masseys were wrong – the flounder incident didn't happen.

"Unfortunately I cannot accept the evidence of Mr Massey today as being in any way accurate. I make that comment without any reflection upon Mr Massey; both he and his wife showed me every courtesy at my interview with them and clearly were only wanting to assist as best they were able.

"I feel, however, that over the years Mr Massey has unwittingly embellished the incident, which I have no doubt did occur just on closing time on the evening of Wednesday the 17th June 1970 but which was an incident which I am satisfied now had nothing whatsoever to do with Mr and Mrs Crewe."

This issue of 'unwitting embellishment' will arise again later in this book as we assess witness recollection on the mystery woman who fed baby Rochelle. But for now, it's clear Adams-Smith felt the Masseys' testimony was contaminated.

The QC went back to the Masseys' original police statement, taken on 29 June 1970. In it, the police had made no reference to the fact that the Masseys had already seen photos of the missing Crewes published in the newspapers. Instead, the statement records that Colin Massey was shown a police photo of Jeannette and positively identified her as the woman who'd been in his shop 12 days earlier.

Massey told police Jeannette was wearing a royal blue suit with a white blouse underneath. This was a red flag to Robert Adams-Smith QC, as no one had reported seeing Jeannette Crewe at the cattle sale in a premium royal blue suit jacket and skirt. Indeed, Harvey had been wearing "wet weather gear" at the sale making it unlikely that Jeannette was dressed much differently.

Both Massey and his son remembered the "strikingly good looking woman" was wearing dark sunglasses – 45 minutes after sunset. The son, Richard, didn't recall any discussion about a stock sale at all, and the QC suspects that's one of those "unwitting embellishments" that's crept in over the years. Both men were insistent, however, that the woman wanted extra newspaper to wrap the flounder and chips in to keep it warm, and Richard Massey saw her buy an *Auckland Star* newspaper to achieve this.

The QC notes, however, that the subsequent police search of the Crewes' house and car found only one newspaper on the property – the *New Zealand Herald* delivered each morning to the gate. Nor was Jeannette known to wear sunglasses much, let alone at night. Only a pair of men's sunglasses were found on the Crewe premises.

Perhaps even more significantly, police found a dirty frypan in the sink and flour and other ingredients normally used to prepare fried fish, suggesting the flounder cooked for the Crewe's final meal was obviously not purchased as a late takeaway at Pukekohe that night.

All of which means the police case built on a timeline of a late meal after returning from Pukekohe close to 7pm, was wrong. The last official sighting of the Crewes, then, was at 3pm at the stock sale, and farmer Irvine's sighting of Harvey's car, with sheep being rounded up, at 5pm. After that, nothing.

Len Demler gave evidence in the second trial of Arthur Thomas that stock and station agent Joe Moore had phoned him around

7pm that night, the 17th, complaining that he'd tried to raise the Crewes on the phone but got no answer. Demler told the court he wasn't worried at that point and didn't think about it any further until the phone calls rattling his cage the following Monday. If the Moore phone call story is true, it meant the Crewes were quite possibly dead by 7pm on Wednesday night, or they couldn't get to the phone right then because they had a gun pointed at them both. Either way, it would explain why dinner was still on the table.

There are several ways the killer could have approached the Crewe farmhouse. If it was Demler, for example, he could simply have ridden his horse across the fields in the night, if he'd wanted to avoid being seen. Another obvious option is the main road, either parking by the gateway about 30 metres from the house – with all the inherent risk of being spotted by nosy country neighbours – or parking further down the road. Then there's a more arcane approach – parking well down the road and approaching over the farm paddocks towards the back of the house.

But who was it that approached the Crewe house on a dark, stormy winter night?

For forty years Demler has remained prime suspect in the eyes of many people, accused of slaughtering his own daughter and her husband, smashing her face in with a rifle butt. If true, his motive was...what exactly? The will?

Let's examine that likelihood in a little more detail.

Demler still outright owned half his property. He'd known since 1962 – eight years earlier – that his wife owned the other half. Under his wife's will Len Demler was still entitled not just to the use of the entire farm for the rest of his life, but all profits from running it. In other words, there was no threat to his livelihood from the change in the will. Demler was 61, he'd made his mark and would soon be eligible for the pension, as well as the ongoing income from the farm.

Most people don't realise that Demler still owned half the farm. Even Arthur Allan Thomas has been labouring under the impression for 40 years that Demler slew his child because the Will left him penniless:

"I thought that Len Demler had done it, because of the Will. He was left with nothing. He'd worked his backside off but ended up with no assets at all! Jeannette had everything, she could say to him, 'I run the farm now, you can take off! He ended up with nothing. I think that's a pretty shocking Will myself," says Thomas emphatically.

Except, it wasn't like that at all. Jeannette wouldn't get control of her half of the farm until her father died, or unless she came up with nearly $50,000 to buy the remaining half off him. If Harvey and Jeannette bought him out of the half he still owned, he'd be cashed up, so no major loss there. These kinds of issues are fairly routine in families, personally it's hard to see this as the motive for murdering his daughter. If Demler did it, you'd want the motive to be a lot stronger than the non-event Last Will and Testament of May Constance Demler.

As you will shortly see, even the police files show and conclude that the Will provided no motive at all for murdering Jeannette and Harvey Crewe.

CHAPTER 4

Closing In On Suspect No. 1

Right from the moment the blood-spattered living room in the little brick and tile farmhouse was discovered around 1pm on Monday, June 22 1970, Lenard William Demler has been the bête noire of this tragedy – the man voted most likely to be the killer in the eyes of detectives and later named as an accomplice by *Auckland Star*'s Pat Booth, then implicated (without being directly accused) as possible killer by David Yallop, culminating in journalist Chris Birt going the whole hog with a well-researched *"J'accuse"* in his 2001 book, *The Final Chapter*.

The man who first nominated Demler as the killer, however, was a hard-bitten police officer named Bruce Hutton. A former farmer himself, hailing from the Dargaville district, Hutton made a career sea change by joining the police force in 1956. Two years later he was shoehorned into the gumshoe division, the CIB, as a junior detective, and quickly rose through the ranks to become top dog at the Otahuhu Police Station's Criminal Investigation Branch, with a jurisdiction covering the whole of South Auckland and into the North Waikato.

Dark-haired, with the face of a hawk, Hutton epitomised a certain breed of cop in the 1960s who would get the job done for his superiors, he liked closure on his cases and like the Canadian Mounties had a reputation for always getting his man, no matter how difficult the investigation. A clue to his belief in Len Demler's guilt was a reported comment from Bruce Hutton's wife, Dorothy, who'd told her local butcher about her surprise when Arthur Allan Thomas was arrested, because Bruce Hutton had been adamant Len Demler was guilty, "I sleep with the man and he told me it was Demler."[10]

---

10 Contained in affidavit of butcher Brian Duncan to the Thomas Royal Commission

Hutton, when he arrived at the Crewes' Pukekawa farmhouse that June 22nd, had a variety of possibilities to choose from, all of them fairly well documented now by the authors listed above.

Pat Booth argues that Jeannette was a battered wife who was beaten so badly by husband Harvey on the evening of Wednesday June 17 that several of her front teeth were knocked out. In the Booth theory, Jeannette snapped, grabbing a rifle and shooting Harvey in the head in retaliation. She then broke down and called her father Len Demler to help clean the mess and hide the body.

As Booth tells it, Jeannette had a further crisis of confidence a couple of days later and took her own life, forcing Demler to dump his daughter's body as well in order to save the family name.

"He then came and disposed of her body and later went through the pretence of discovering the house," Booth told the *New Zealand Herald*.[11]

In this scenario, then, Demler was an accessory after the fact to Harvey's murder, and then to Jeannette's suicide.

The way I see it, Pat Booth's theory has an ultimately fatal flaw.

Harvey Crewe was a big man. Sixteen stone, or around 102kg in modern terms. It was physically impossible for Jeannette, or possibly even one man acting alone, to shift a dead floppy weight of that magnitude. Booth's argument, that Jeannette called her father to help shift Harvey, is plausible in that regard.

But consider this: if Jeannette snapped and shot Harvey after a fight, she may arguably have been out of her right mind at that precise moment and incapable of making smart judgements. Len Demler, however, should and I argue would have instantly pointed out to his daughter that she could hardly hide the disappearance of her husband for very long in a small community where everyone knows your business.

For Demler to then hide his daughter's body after she shoots herself compounds the implied collective insanity: how does this lessen the scandal surrounding the family? The crime in this scenario escalates from tragic domestic murder suicide, to a full-blown international murder-mystery whodunit with a 40 year lifespan. Why would Demler dig a hole implicating himself?

If Demler was the accomplice, as Pat Booth believes, we are also required to believe he made not one, but two trips to the Waikato

---

11 "Campaigner disputes Crewe murders theory", *NZ Herald*, 8 September 2001

River to dump bodies on separate days, fortuitously unseen. Demler's car was a 1960s Ford Cortina.

Try lifting a floppy and heavy 16 stone man into a car boot or back seat and see how easy it is. Don't forget that while they were shifting Harvey, Jeannette was so badly injured that half of her face was smashed and six teeth were missing – she wouldn't have been in top condition to assist with the cleanup or lifting Harvey.

"It is obvious Harvey Crewe was shot on Wednesday night after a domestic in the house after he has assaulted Jeannette and caused her quite an injury," Booth told the *Herald* nine years ago when Chris Birt's book came out.[12] "My belief is that she and her father disposed of Harvey's body, tried to clean up the house and couldn't."

The idea that Jeannette killed herself after this also requires us to disregard the maternal bond with her baby Rochelle. What mother, having freed herself and her child from a violent partner, then takes her own life leaving her baby to the mercy of the world? While possible, in the Booth scenario it becomes yet another improbability to overcome, rather than supporting evidence.

Then there's the issue of motive for murder suicide. It is true Harvey Crewe had a temper in other instances, but according to those who knew the couple Harvey and Jeannette were close:

"Harvey and Jeannette were always open with each other, completely honest," said family friend Edith Judge back in the 1970s.[13]

"They had a real appreciation of each other and a deep respect for each other...A well-suited, wonderfully happy, strong and mature couple, completely capable of working out life in a harmonious, positive manner. Both intelligent, witty, fun to be with if they knew you well, otherwise reserved, but not awkward...Good as parents. Could be described as a very private couple."

The police files released under the Official Information Act disclose similar sentiment from Jeannette's sister Heather.

"She said as far as she knows Jeannette and Harvey have never had a word against each other or had words," recorded Detective Sergeant Mike Charles. "[Heather] said they were so attached to each other[14] in that way that it was slightly un-normal and cannot visualise what has happened."

---

12 "Campaigner disputes Crewe murders theory", *NZ Herald*, 8 September 2001
13 *Beyond Reasonable Doubt*, Yallop, p43
14 Always bear in mind, however, that Heather and her husband lived in the United States. They didn't have much contact with the Crewes.

Having said that, the instant reactions of both Heather Souter and Len Demler when they were asked about the tragedy by police was that Harvey Crewe must have nutted out:

"I thought Harvey must have gone beserk and killed Jeannette. I thought I might find them close by," Demler told police on one occasion.

When Detective Sergeant Mike Charles spoke to Heather he got much the same:

"The only thing she thought was Harvey had a fit and has carted Jeannette out of the house. I don't think she has thought about a third person, least of all her father."

Then again, given that most murders are domestic-related, perhaps it was natural for the Demler family to assume a spousal fight, regardless of whether the couple had seemed happy in the past. The closest we get to a domestic incident comes from neighbours interviewed by police, speculating as to a possible cause. Detective John Roberts has notes of his conversation:

"They point out that the death falls exactly on their wedding anniversary. Crewes could have had an Anniversary row. Mrs Crewe had hoped to go on expensive honeymoon to Australia [four years earlier]. Mr Crewe ruled it out as he was not prepared to be away from farm. Subject of holidays with Crewe family was a very sore point and they had rows from time to time because Mrs Crewe liked to go away on holiday. Mr Crewe prepared to be away for couple of days and no more.

"It seems it would be the subject of some tension. Mrs [name withheld by police] knew Mrs Crewe very well when she was younger and does admit that although not becoming slovenly, her standards have declined considerably."

So there you have it. The best evidence of a murder suicide is that Harvey and Jeannette might have been rowing over the fact that Jeannette didn't get a decent honeymoon back in 1966.

Don't forget the first-hand testimony from the last woman to speak to Jeannette, local mother Thyrle Pirret who'd visited the morning of the 17th to deliver a gift for Rochelle. She spoke to both Harvey and Jeannette and told me they seemed perfectly happy and friendly, with no "ill feeling" in the atmosphere.

Now, obviously the face that couples present to friends and family can sometimes be different from the one they present to each other, nonetheless there needs to be more evidence of family violence before we come even close to a motive for murder suicide.

Ultimately, in my view then, Pat Booth's theory fails. The Crewes owned a shotgun, so if Jeannette had grabbed a gun to shoot Harvey – the only weapon in the house was a shotgun in the laundry – she would have blown his head right off, not put a .22 bullet into it.

"Booth, having done sterling work in my view, just lost the plot," exclaims Ross Meurant, a former detective on the Crewe homicide inquiry, later to rise to the rank of Inspector before pursuing a parliamentary and then business career.

"She was clearly hit in the face with more than a fist – smashing teeth and all that sort of stuff," he adds. "She goes to find a rifle and shoots him, but there was no rifle in the house, then gets help or wheels him out. He was weighed down with an axle, and that means preparation – it wasn't just a spontaneous thing. Then she shoots herself and jumps in the creek, and the rifle is never found. It just doesn't hold together," says Meurant in a quirky turn-of-phrase.

The suggestion that Len Demler was an accessory after the fact can, pretty easily, be dismissed as fanciful, especially given the horrendous nature of the injuries to Jeannette inflicted prior to the fatal shot, such as to render her probably unconscious, possibly mortally wounded[15] from her smashed head (regardless of the finishing shot), and highly incapable of staggering past Harvey, grabbing an invisible .22 rifle and shooting him from behind with it.

But Len Demler's role in this saga has not been confined to mere observer or assistant in the clean-up. From the word go, police believed Demler was the prime suspect, the man responsible for the double killing. As early as 24 June – two days into the inquiry – Detective John Roberts says at the end of day conference: "My opinion is that Demler killed the two of them."

But remember what Owen Priest said of Demler's actions when they first arrived to search the property themselves?

"I moved forward to search," recalled Priest,[16] "not knowing what to expect. I comforted myself with the thought that if there was any funny business going on, Len was right there behind me."

But of course, Demler wasn't right behind him. Demler was

---

15 The autopsy later showed her skull had been cracked right around, like an egg, by the force of the blow.
16 *Beyond Reasonable Doubt*, by David Yallop, p6

evidently too scared to enter the house for fear the killer was still on the premises. If Demler had been the killer himself, it's likely he would have simply followed Priest through the house, knowing there was no danger of further carnage.

The grizzly farmer's state of mind when he approached the house with Priest seems to have been frenetic, as you'd expect. On the one hand he was worried the intruder was still there, but on the other he was voicing fears that maybe Harvey "killed her and done himself in".

Owen Priest himself recalled that the murder suicide theory was what Demler "initially" kept repeating "two or three times" as they entered. It was only after Priest retorted that it might "have been a third party" that Demler suddenly went quiet, seemingly processing this in his head. Priest was then "rocked" to find Demler had decided to hang back by the door leaving him to search the house alone – a response now appearing a little more understandable in the wake of what Priest had just said. On the strength of all that, I'd lean towards Demler's cowardice being genuine, and if genuine then he wasn't the killer.

Panic and confusion also go a long way towards explaining why Demler failed to rescue baby Rochelle when he first went to the house – a question that has long disturbed investigators. Demler told police he panicked, fearing the killer might be present, but he also told Owen Priest that he didn't really want to be the one who found Jeannette and Harvey's bodies if they'd been killed.

If Demler had been the killer, he would have known – when Ron Wright pressured him to check the Crewe house that Monday afternoon – what he would find and how he should handle it. Demler would have spent the previous five days preparing for the inevitable discovery of the crime scene and baby Rochelle. *He would have had a plan.*

Whoever killed the Crewes had carefully disposed of the bodies, left absolutely no fingerprints in the entire house, burnt evidence, tried to clean up and looked after the baby – tasks all suggestive of prior planning and organisation. Why would this cool, calculated approach suddenly fall apart? If Demler was really the killer, surely he would have grabbed Rochelle from her cot, dishevelled and stinking, and driven straight to Owen Priest's house saying "Call the police, I found blood all through the house, no sign of Jeannette and Harvey, and Rochelle alone in her cot!"

If he'd done that, Demler would have been the hero, quashing all speculation about his bizarre actions on the day. The difference between the cool chutzpah of a killer and accomplice who hung around the scene of the crime for days (and to this date have gotten away with it) – and the bumbling panic of Demler, are too much of a sharp contrast. Demler's actions instead made him an automatic suspect in the eyes of police and his neighbours – a magnet for attention that was so strong he was almost prosecuted. Heck, his actions have seen him portrayed in books and documentaries as either the callous killer of his own daughter or an accessory after the fact. Demler has been thoroughly convicted in the court of public opinion. Yet his behaviour does not actually fit the psychological profile of the very careful killer we know must have murdered the Crewes.

The weight of public opinion about Len Demler can be measured in the testimony of Arthur Allan Thomas to me: "Demler didn't help with the searches, he kept out of it. It's a bit bloody strange, I tell you what – if my daughter went missing I'd be out there daylight to dark, looking," exclaims Thomas, accusingly.

Aye, there's nowt queer as folk, down on farm. But did Demler really stay away? Detective Inspector Bruce Hutton challenged Len Demler on this very point in early July 1970:

"Why haven't you been over to help the searchers? You must know, surely, that all of the local farmers have come along to search for your daughter and son-in-law."

According to Hutton's notes, Demler "remains silent. Didn't appear to have an answer at all".

It's true Demler didn't form part of the official search roster, but as police were to discover, it's not true that he wasn't with search teams all the time. Being winter, the mornings were fog-bound, "with visibility down to 10 feet" according to police notes.

"We were not particularly happy about this...we kept coming across fresh hoof marks and it subsequently turned out that Demler on his horse had been tracking us all day. We finally caught up with him right down in the valley as we turned to sweep back up to the house and finish our search. He had been with us all day, and in the fog we did not see him."

In fact, police conference notes from early July 1970 record:

"Although Demler has not turned up for searches he has been seen daily moving about on his horse watching the searchers at work, and not working at all on his farm, apart from occasionally yarding the stock."

At a police interview with Bruce Hutton on 16 September 1970, Hutton again asked Demler why he didn't help with the police search. This time, Demler was more forthcoming:

"I didn't want to when I knew the police and some of the others thought that I had done it. I got my back up...I didn't want anything more to do with any of you."

This could explain why Demler shadowed the search teams like a ghost – he wanted to be there, but didn't feel he could take the eyes boring into his back. You also need to remember he had lost his wife of more than 30 years to cancer just months earlier. For the last forty years (and Demler was alive for nearly thirty of those), the man's reputation has endured whispered slings and arrows from people who say he never even bothered to search for his daughter, and that he murdered her because the Will left him nothing. As you've now seen, those widely held beliefs are not true – he did search, and the Will didn't affect him.

There is a further aspect to Demler tracking and spying on the police search teams that's worth bearing in mind. If Demler had killed Harvey and Jeannette, and dumped their bodies in the Waikato river, what could he possibly gain from following the searchers around every day, at the expense of doing his regular farm chores? If he truly knew where the bodies were, then he also knew police had no chance of finding them on the Crewe and Demler properties. Yet here he was, metres away from police search teams, unseen in the fog, awaiting their discoveries as keenly as Bruce Hutton was.

It's yet another piece of the growing jigsaw of evidence that suggests Len Demler wasn't involved in the murder of his daughter. His actions don't match the profile of the killer. They instead fit better with that of a grumpy old farmer with dodgy people skills, who wanted to know where his dead daughter was but didn't want to be the one to find her body, and who wanted to help police but became furious about being treated as a suspect.

There's another reason why Demler didn't join the searches: legal advice. It was clear within 72 hours that he was a suspect, and it appears to have coloured his response. "I understand Demler went to Lloyd Brown QC very early," Arthur Allan Thomas reveals one afternoon, "and Brown told him, 'Do nothing, say nothing, don't help with the searches, stay out of it'."

It's interesting that one of the very first police file notes on Len Demler found he was initially very cooperative:

"I started off by interviewing [Harvey Crewe's] old dad-in-law," the officer in charge of interviewing relatives recorded on June 24 1970, just 48 hours after the house was found empty. "Covered most aspects of the matter to date. I am convinced that he is well above board and I stake my reputation on him. He is a good, solid type of bloke, I would say. I don't think he has really realised what has happened yet, don't think shock has hit him. Sort of putting on a bit of a front at the moment. Story he told me today ties up well with what he told Murray [Jeffries] yesterday."

Another police file note from June 23rd contains what may be the only reference in police records portraying Demler as a grieving human:

"The child was taken by the grandfather to a Mrs Willis who says that when [Demler] arrived he was crying and appeared very distressed, and in her opinion was quite cut up about it."

All references to Demler crying as he delivered Rochelle into the care of a neighbour vanished as police instead began to paint him in the role of villain. How did Len Demler manage to rub police up the wrong way so soon after one officer said he would "stake my reputation" on Demler's innocence? The best answer is probably 'personality clash', or what police refer to as 'failing the attitude test'. In the context of a murder inquiry, detectives instinctively hunt for behaviour that's out of the ordinary, that's "suspicious". Demler had already fallen into that pigeon-hole with the way he'd handled the discovery of Rochelle left alone, so when he started to get his "back up" over the perfectly natural requirements for the police to investigate his movements, that was like sticking a flashing light on his head whilst holding a sign, 'Pick Me!' as far as police were concerned.

It's interesting, as a crime reporter, to see how behaviour comes to be seen as 'suspicious' and directly relevant, even though it later turns out to be utterly irrelevant. Consider this example.

Detective Craig Duncan visited Demler at the Crewes' farm on the morning of July 9, 1970, where he engaged him in conversation with the help of Demler's house-guest, Graeme Hewson, who'd been secretly feeding police information about Demler.

"After morning tea," Detective Duncan writes, "Hewson shifted some sheep from the holding yard; I made a comment about the sheep getting rid of the grass in no time and Demler replied by saying, 'there's nothing better for packing the ground down'. Hewson said, 'yes, you could bury something in there easy enough and you would cover all trace of it'. Demler made no comment.

"I said, 'well, we are only waiting for a couple of good days' rain and we will find what we are looking for'. Demler turned to me and said, 'why?'. I said, 'the ground will sink a bit, won't it'. Demler turned and walked away," records Detective Craig Duncan in his file note of July 10.

What a fascinating yet ultimately trivial interplay. The way police describe it, the conversation was cat and mouse, hunter and hunted, an interchange redolent with unspoken guilt and fear of discovery. Yet as we now all know, the bodies were not on the farm but in the river, no amount of rain on Demler's grass was going to make a blind bit of difference, and Demler's apparent silence and apprehension in the face of police jibes meant nothing, if he was indeed the killer, because he would have known the bodies weren't there. In journalistic terms, we call the style of notations in this police report, 'interviewing your typewriter'.

In police terms as far as the Crewe inquiry was concerned, it appears to be called 'detective work'. It's an excellent illustration of what happens when you fail the police attitude test – everything, even a twitch, suddenly becomes the smoking gun that will bring you down. In Demler's case it wasn't a twitch, but drool, that aroused Detective Duncan's suspicions.

"At 9am while moving sheep from one holding pen to another Demler got wild with his dog 'Tip' who would not obey any command given by Demler and was in a pen full of sheep, worrying them. Demler threw a large sod of dirt at the dog and swore at it continually. By the time the dog got out of the pen and went to Demler, Demler was frothing at the mouth and spitting saliva. This was not controlled spitting but spitting in the form of dribble."

Now, I don't want to take anything away from Craig Duncan's creative writing talents, but if you were an elderly farmer, and your dog was in the middle of a crowded sheep pen giving the flock merry hell and ignoring your every instruction, and you – unable to move – were trying to rapidly bark orders (including, apparently, the f-word) in a futile response to every move the dog made before you had the chance to draw breath, I'm pretty sure you'd be left with your tongue hanging out your mouth as well, and every f-sound sending fleck flying.

Don't forget, Demler by this stage had been repeatedly accused of murder. Another example of interviewing your typewriter came from Detective Sergeant Phil Seaman, who'd found it strange on 24 June that Demler didn't mention the Crewes.

"I had just come to tell him that the statement [he'd made to Det. Sgt. John Hughes the day before, 23 June] was not ready at this stage. Demler told me that he would be around the house until midday. Again, he never mentioned the Crewes."

To Seaman, this implied an unwillingness to talk. But on the other hand, Demler clearly knew the police were there because of the Crewes, and he may not have felt the need to state the obvious. Demler was then hauled in for questioning that afternoon, June 24. First, police showed him his initial statement made before Hughes, then at 4.15pm Demler was questioned for an hour and a quarter by Detective Inspector Hutton.

The following morning, at 8am, police staged a search of Demler's home, vehicles and farm buildings, looking for "anything which could tie up with the disappearance of the Crewes". Det. Sgt. Seaman says Demler seemed grim.

"I said to him, 'How are you this morning', to which he replied, 'I am still alive'. He did not appear to be in a very pleasant frame of mind."

With his daughter missing and police searching his own bedroom and car, perhaps Len Demler just wasn't feeling very jovial. Police found two cars, Demler's red Ford Cortina, and his late wife's near new Morris 1100. Detectives noted the boot of the Morris was "very small", and they couldn't find blood or "anything that would point to the fact that the vehicle had been used to transport bodies." Inside the house, police took away clothing for forensic analysis, and a "wooden handled knife which Demler said he used to kill sheep".

"We searched the garden thoroughly, fowl house, barn and woolshed," reported another officer, "and could not find anything there that looked the slightest bit suspicious. There was a bit of paddock turned up but it was only a rabbit burrow."

If he didn't feel like a suspect during his interrogation the previous evening, he certainly did that morning as he watched half his wardrobe disappear out the door. The next day, 26 June 1970, was little different. Demler was transported to Otahuhu Police Station for further questioning at the hands of Bruce Hutton.

"I...questioned him as to why, since the disappearance of his son-in-law and daughter, that he had shown no interest nor had he offered in any way to help the searchers," recorded Hutton on the police file. "He said that on the Monday when he had discovered Mr and Mrs Crewe missing, he had gone out with the searchers for a little while, but he did not have any explanation to make as to why he had not offered his services since then."

Let's look at the timeline for a moment. Empty house discovered Monday 22 June in the afternoon. Police called, rest of day a complete write-off, although Demler did join a search briefly[17]. On Tuesday June 23, Demler spent more time "helping police with their inquiries" courtesy of Det. Sgt. John Hughes. On Wednesday, June 24, police turn up around 8.45am and tell him to be ready "about 9.30am so that he could sign the statement which he had made to Det. Sgt. Hughes". Except, police weren't ready at 9.30am, so Demler was left hanging all morning. Finally, after lunch, Det. Sgt. Phil Seaman told Demler to come with him to the police Base HQ to sign the statement and be interviewed by Bruce Hutton. Demler wasn't dropped home by police until 6pm, after dark.

Then, as you've read, Thursday June 25 was a wipeout thanks to the police search of Demler's farm that began first thing and took most of the day, and now here was Demler being dragged into Hutton's office on Friday 26th to be accused of failing to help with the search! It's a little bit like trying to answer the question: "Have you stopped beating your wife yet?" Little wonder that Demler stared at Bruce Hutton incredulously across the desk and asked:

"You think I did this, don't you?"

Bruce Hutton met his gaze and played his card:

"I think you are the person who removed Harvey Crewe's body from the Crewe household. In fact, I'm quite certain you've done this."

Demler, according to Hutton, "made no answer whatsoever but just continued looking at the floor, and he offered no objection whatsoever in being accused of doing this act."

The possibility of 'shock and disbelief' as a reason for the silence

---

17 Hutton subsequently admitted at a 15 July 1970 police briefing conference that Demler had indeed joined the very first police search on the evening of June 22nd.

appears to have escaped Hutton. There's no record of Demler being read his rights and cautioned as a suspect at this point. So, within four days of the discovery of Rochelle, Demler had been left in no doubt that police thought he was guilty of having a hand in the disappearance of the Crewes. Nor were police keeping their suspicions secret in the district – David Yallop alleges they would often pester Demler's neighbours with questions like, "What does it feel like living next door to a double murderer?"[18]

Owen Priest's wife Julie was on the receiving end of one of those, and she told Yallop of the impact it had on Demler.

"Two days after their disappearance, Len told me he was the number one suspect and with tears running down his face said: 'I honestly did not do it'. What upset him so much was that nobody would believe him," recalled Julie Priest. Even the local vicar took a swipe at Demler from the pulpit, while Demler was in the pews.[19]

Demler's people skills were famous in his hometown. You could almost call him the 'anti-Dale Carnegie of Pukekawa' – how to lose friends and influence people in a bad way. If the police wanted people to point the finger at Demler, they had only to knock on a door, any door.

"They did say that Demler was extremely callous at the time his wife was dying," Detective John Roberts quoted neighbours. "He was absolutely steaming drunk at times and they detested Demler… they said he is inclined to be very mean, tried to defraud Income Tax. They hate Demler."

Fred Hoskins, the 66 year old farmer (who'd be 106 if alive today) whose 700 acre property bordered both Crewe's and Demler's spreads, told police that "everyone…crossed swords with Demler about the grazing on the roadway on Sharp's Road". Hoskins called Demler "hot tempered" and prone to "swearing profusely while on horseback".

Detective Sergeant Mike Charles raised the issue of how Demler behaved during his wife's terminal illness with Jeannette's sister, Heather Souter.

"I spoke to her about the way her father reacted to her mother dying," writes Charles in the police files, "and she said that in the first instance he was a good and loyal husband, went fairly regularly to see her [but] as time went on he went more to bowls.

---

18 *Beyond Reasonable Doubt*, p38
19 ibid, p38

"Comment was made by various people why he was not going so often to the hospital She said she thought him a typical farmer in that he treated death in the way of animals the same as humans, and she thinks well it may be [similar in the Crewe case] as well, that he apparently is accepting the fact that they are both dead and if that is the case, that is the case," concluded Det. Sgt. Mike Charles with one telling observation:

"Her father bitched to her about the way he was spoken to the other day, and he was told, well, we are doing our job."

Another Demlerism that did him no favours was to constantly refer to everyone else – including his missing daughter – as "bastards". Police records show farmer Owen Priest – who accompanied Demler in searching the Crewe house initially – remembered Demler repeating the words, "Where are the bastards?" and "Where have the bastards gone?"

"Priest tells us," said Bruce Hutton in one briefing, "that Demler was quite upset when he first went to speak to him but by the time he had got to the house he had recovered his normal manner and even laughed at times. I might add that this man Demler is known to be a person who does laugh nervously."

Harvey Crewe's friend Graeme Hewson – who was staying with Demler – told police "that Demler did make such remarks about the police as 'there go the bastards', when he heard us leaving to go home [from the crime scene] at night." Police began to wonder whether Demler, to paraphrase Everest-conqueror Sir Edmund Hillary, had "knocked the bastards off".

But despite all the, "ooh, he's a strange one, guv'nor" comments, the one thing eluding Hutton was a plausible motive. "The likely motive appears to be that it is tied up in the Will of Mrs May Demler, now deceased, previously the wife of Len Demler," Hutton told his troops at a strategy session in late June.

Hutton explained how Jeannette had inherited her mother's half of the farm and that "as a joint trustee" she would have had "a considerable say" in how the farm was managed. This, he argued in June, was probably why Demler killed her. Additionally, the death duties on wife Maysie's estate were higher than anticipated, meaning Demler might not have had sufficient money to pay them.

On July 2, however, police spoke to John Handcock, the former manager of the Crewe farm. "He would probably know the two and

Mr Demler as well as anybody else," noted Det. Sgt. Lin Sinton. "He does not think Demler is capable of this."

A few days later, Det. Sgt. Mike Charles was bringing disappointing news to his boss on the killed-because-of-the-Will theory:

"It appears that Demler would have had no financial gain by disposing of these two. The death duties would have been adequately met by cash in Mrs Demler's savings account plus a Morris car."

Detective Sergeant Murray Jeffries added that he'd visited Demler's solicitor in Hamilton, grabbed copies "of previous Wills of both Mr and Mrs Demler" as well as mortgage documents. He'd then interviewed Demler's accountant, who said he'd told Demler "that he is neither losing and was gaining very little as a result of the new Will his wife made out."

Jeffries told Bruce Hutton: "Most of the action that Demler has carried out recently as far as a new Will is concerned was done on the advice from his accountant. *As far as motive goes we have not found anything.*"[my emphasis]

Bruce Hutton, in a police conference to discuss progress in the case in early July, was forced to concede to his assembled team, "Demler [still] has half [the farm], and he has got use, occupation and income". In other words, what looked like a promising motive a week earlier – the alleged financial destitution of Demler because the Will stripped him of everything (a belief which has remained embedded in popular culture for 40 years), was now a motive shot full of holes and sinking rapidly.

All the police attention on Demler, however, was beginning to have shocking consequences. On 11 July, 1970, someone electrified his front gate. "He found this when he arrived home about midnight [from the pub] on Saturday night, and was very upset about it," noted John Hughes wryly.

"He seemed very weary," continued Hughes. "I put it to him in no uncertain terms that the case was building up and he said he was innocent. He would appear to be suffering from lack of sleep and looked very drawn."

Hughes' quaint phrasing – "I put it to him in no uncertain terms" – should actually have read, "I told him, 'we're closing in, you're guilty and you are going to go down for this, Len'."

At an evidence-assessment conference involving Hutton and police top brass like Assistant Commissioner Bob Walton on 15 July 1970

— four weeks before the discovery of Jeannette's body with a .22 gunshot wound — there was detailed discussion about Demler possibly shooting the Crewes with a .22 rifle:

"What firearms has Demler got?" queried Bob Walton.

"Shotgun," fired back Hutton, "which belonged to his mother and father who are still alive here in Auckland, and an exhaustive firearm check of Crewe and Demler and his people has come up with the fact that way back the old Demler [Len's father] had a .22 and this is the subject of an enquiry at this time. They have to be seen as to what happened to that firearm."[20]

"Nothing found during the search of his house?" asked Walton. "[Was it] searched to that degree?"

"Well and truly. No trace of any .22 ammunition. Harvey Crewe's shotgun was in his house," confirmed Bruce Hutton.

Why did Demler take the bodies? That was the question bugging the Assistant Police Commissioner.

"I think his mind worked like this," said Hutton after a moment. "He would remove the bodies as his one thought would be to remove possible tracing of evidence — say the .22 and the bullets in the bodies. If he moved the bodies and the weapon and cleaned the scene up there would be nothing to point to him."

It was an interesting discussion for police to be having four weeks before they found the first body and confirmed death by gunshot, because in fact the medical opinion provided by police forensic expert, pathologist Frank Cairns, had earlier ruled out the involvement of firearms.[21]

"Having studied the condition of the entire house," writes David Yallop, "Dr Cairns discussed with Hutton and his fellow officers his view of how the Crewes had been killed. He considered death had been caused by a blunt instrument, a heavy piece of wood that had been subsequently burned on the fire, an axe or a tomahawk. There was some discussion about the possibility of bullet wounds but Dr Cairns ruled this out on the grounds that no weapon was in evidence and there was no indication in the room that bullets had been fired."

Did the police have some inside information that a .22 rifle was

---

20 The police job sheets show the .22 and some ammunition was picked up from Demler's father in Auckland city.
21 *Beyond Reasonable Doubt*, p9

involved, or were they simply hedging their bets, considering all angles? Ordinarily I would opt with the latter every time, but for reasons that will become apparent later in this book, we can't automatically rule out the first scenario.

Then there's the issue of how the bodies were disposed of. Police forensic checks failed to find any hint, apart from Harvey's wheelbarrow, as to how the bodies had been removed. It was done without trace. Not one fibre, hair or any other forensic detail was found in Harvey's car, Demler's cars or any other vehicles they checked. Whoever had transported the bodies had apparently used technology from the 1960s TV show *Star Trek* to beam away Harvey and Jeannette to a place unknown by means unknown.

This is something that journalist and author Chris Birt spent quite a bit of time on in his 2001 book on the Thomas case, *The Final Chapter*. Birt argues the bodies were removed by horse, and his main evidence for this is the hearsay testimony[22] of Alexander (Sandy) Fletcher, an engineer at the Kawerau timber plant who in 1970 had been working as a casual farm labourer in the Pukekawa area and its surrounds.

On Easter weekend, 1972, Sandy Fletcher made contact in Auckland with Thomas Retrial Committee chairman Pat Vesey's brother, Doug, offering some information on the case. Fletcher explained how two years earlier he'd gone looking for a whitebaiting spot, even though it wasn't whitebaiting season, in June 1970. It was an old metal road going down to a stopbank on the Waikato, and he was surprised to find two people, two horses and some farm dogs milling around in the willow trees near the river's edge. On the ground were two bundles.

"Fletcher," writes Doug Vesey in a statement,[23] "said the pair, dressed in wet weather gear, appeared to be surprised at seeing him. It was a cold drizzly day and late in the afternoon in June."

The pair, described as an older man wearing an oilskin and trilby hat, and a "past middle-aged" woman, in a raincoat and hat, explained when questioned that they were "just getting rid of some rubbish".

Fletcher explained to Vesey that he'd approached police with this information after hearing appeals for help from the public, and a

---
22 Fletcher died in a workplace accident before his evidence could be tested or verified.
23 *The Final Chapter*, by Chris Birt, Penguin, 2001 p152

Detective Inspector named Bruce Hutton personally took a statement from him for the police file.

"Hutton...had expressed the view that this was the break the police had been looking for," Vesey recalls Fletcher saying.

However, and this is interesting given what you read at the start of this book, when Fletcher later contacted police to see whether his information was useful, he got told "in no uncertain terms that if he did not forget the incident and shut up he would find himself in serious trouble."[24]

Unfortunately, there is no record in the parts of the Crewe murder file released publicly so far, of the statement taken by Bruce Hutton from one Alexander Edwin Fletcher. However, I'm sure that it exists somewhere and that the police officer in charge of the file could be held responsible if it isn't.

Fletcher was shown photos of Len Demler by Doug Vesey, and made a positive identification that Demler and the "past middle-aged" woman were the people he saw on the riverbank with two horses, two bundles and their dogs.

Unfortunately, the description of an old farmer wearing an oilskin and a trilby hat and riding a horse with a white blaze could fit a number of farmers, even today. In an ideal world, Vesey would have shown Fletcher a range of photos of old farmers in trilbies and riding horses with white blazes, so that Fletcher's identification would more closely resemble a 'line-up'. He didn't, however. And it's a well known psychological fact that the human mind gravitates towards finding order and meaning. Faced with a photo of a likely suspect three years after the fleeting event in question, did Fletcher really positively identify Demler or was it wishful thinking?

Cast your own mind back to a fleeting meeting with a stranger three years ago in a shop, or somewhere else, where the person was doing something a little memorable: can you really recall their face? Really?

Chris Birt suspects the road – Fletcher never gave the name of it – could have been Churchill Road in Pukekawa. As the crow flies, its riverbank section comes closest to the Crewe farmhouse at the northern end, about six kilometres by bird, much longer by road. As the photos from Google Earth show, however, that's six

---

[24] For reasons that will later become obvious, I'm pretty sure Fletcher must have spoken to Detective Len Johnston.

CLOSING IN ON SUSPECT NO. 1

kilometres up and down hills, through bush and across other district roads and the village of Orton. Now, if you were making such a trip on horseback with two bodies, including that of a 183cm tall, 102kg monster[25] like Harvey, you'd be fairly conspicuous in a broad daylight trip, which it was.

I also suspect that if you saw two bundles on the ground the size of bodies, all wrapped up, you'd probably describe them as "the size of bodies" rather than just bundles.

On the face of it, I'm prepared to concede that Fletcher saw Len Demler and his new girlfriend out riding. However, am I prepared to accept that the couple chose to transport the bodies of Harvey and Jeannette Crewe across land, including past other people's farmhouses who knew Demler, and past the settlement of Orton and across other public roads, in broad daylight? No.

The police files, if they tell me anything at all, tell me Hutton wanted to nail someone – anyone – for the Crewe murders, and his best suspect right up until mid October 1970 was Len Demler. The files, as we've seen, reek of wanting Demler's head on a plate.

So, in the wake of those comments, Fletcher's horseback sighting was literally a gift-horse for Hutton to carve up and serve Demler to a jury as dog tucker, another strand of circumstantial evidence in the rope of conviction that police wanted to tie Demler up with. The fact that they didn't hit Demler with this suggests that either it was another farming couple based much closer to the river than Demler, or it was Demler but it really was just general rubbish.

There's no hint of this in the police notes about Demler, so I'm guessing it turned out not to be him. Incidentally, the police search of Demler's farm on 25 June found only one horse, not two:

"He has also got one horse which was examined by myself but no blood spots were visible on the horse," recorded Detective Sergeant Phil Seaman.

If Demler was riding with his girlfriend to remove the bodies, where did they ship in the second horse from? Perhaps more to the point, why bother? After all, they had use of the Crewes' car or indeed Demler's, and there were easy access roads to the Waikato River in much better dumping spots just a few minutes away by vehicle. Why on earth would you mount a two hour cross country

---

25 About the size of an All Black front rower.

trek with two horses each carrying a live rider and a dead body, in broad daylight, going past a settlement and over public roads? As a rider myself, I know too well how a change in the gait of a horse over interesting terrain can dislodge a good rider at the best of times, let alone a dead one. An excursion of this nature with bodies draped across horses seems like the plotline from a British funeral comedy or *Some Mothers Do 'Ave 'Em*.

But if we assume Fletcher is correct and Demler was actually dumping bodies there, four things come to mind. Firstly, as the Google Earth photos show, the Waikato river runs shallow over sand banks in that location – not ideal if you want your bodies to disappear from view. Secondly, the bodies were found many kilometres down river, having supposedly floated through numerous bends, twists and double-backs without being seen or snagged anywhere else. There are much better dumping points much closer to where the bodies were eventually found, easily accessible by car within minutes.

Thirdly, Harvey Crewe's body was supposedly weighed down by a cast iron trailer axle. You can't tell me it floated 20 kilometres in such circumstances.[26]

The fourth aspect is that much has been made, by author Chris Birt and others, of a swipe of Jeannette's blood being found in Demler's Ford Cortina. Was it disposal of bodies by horsepower, or by horse power? It can't have been both.

Don't get me wrong – I'm not criticising Birt for raising this line of evidence. I would have done exactly the same, and some when they get to the final chapters of this book will accuse me of it, I'm sure. I'm just approaching it with different eyes, and don't find it persuasive on reflection. As with many things in this case, they all seem possible, but the weighting of probability is a different kettle of fish in the cold, hard light of context.[27]

---

[26] Yallop makes the point, an entirely reasonable one, that if indeed the axle found under Harvey was genuinely involved, it could have come from the Tuakau tip, where the Thomas family had dumped rubbish including machinery parts since time immemorial. The tip was only about three kilometres from the spot where Crewe's body was located, and if you were looking for somewhere where you were guaranteed to find something heavy at short notice at night, a tip would be ideal. There is no way a body weighed down with an axle and dumped at Churchill Road could have made it so far down river. Additionally, we're now asking a horse to carry its rider, an additional body and a heavy car axle several kilometres across rugged terrain. Not possible.

[27] For the sake of completeness, I also considered whether Demler and his girlfriend could have been dumping evidence related to the case. Again, I have difficulty with this interpretation of the sighting. Why go to the trouble of a horse trek, and dumping evidence wrapped up in bundles, into the Waikato where they might float to the surface or be found later by police dive teams? Why not simply load the bags into your car along with other household refuse, and take it to the Whitford tip

CLOSING IN ON SUSPECT NO. 1

Another aspect touched on by both Chris Birt and Pat Booth is the possible involvement of an old gun from the Chennells estate – the farm belonging to Jeannette's late uncle which eventually became the Crewe farm. Birt makes a good case that this old hammer gun had been converted to fire .22 calibre bullets. We know the farm had a .360 calibre double-barrelled rifle, because one of these was registered to the address, having been purchased by Jeannette's grandfather Newman Chennells in 1921 from another Pukekawa farmer (remember this 1921 Pukekawa purchase – it will shortly become relevant). We know the gun wasn't on the Crewe property when the police were called, and we also know that the .360 cartridges became obsolete when manufacture ceased in 1955.

Birt quotes police documentation showing Bruce Hutton told Assistant Police Commissioner Bob Walton that police believed the gun had been modified to fire .22 bullets:

"The firearm which cannot be located is believed to be a double barrel firearm, one barrel being a shotgun and the other either of .22 or .38 calibre."

It may seem strange that shotguns were altered to fire rifle bullets, but the procedure was relatively simple: the gunsmith designed a rifle barrel capable of fitting inside the existing shotgun barrel like a sleeve. For farmers, these dual action guns were a godsend, allowing short-range shotgun blasts to scatter birds, or longer range, higher-powered shooting through the rifle modification.

So, we know the Crewe farm should have had the old Chennells gun, and we know police believed it had been modified to fire .22 calibre bullets.

Pat Booth believes this could have been the gun Jeannette used to shoot Harvey and then herself in his murder-suicide theory. Chris Birt believes this could be the gun Len Demler used to shoot Harvey and Jeannette with.

Birt, on the face of it, has good reason for his suspicions. Initially, the gun was missing. Police searched everywhere for it and couldn't find it. Then miraculously, three years later, Len Demler handed it to police just before Arthur Allan Thomas' second trial, in April 1973.

In cross examination at the second trial, Demler was asked:

Ryan: In the Chennells estate there was a rifle? [28]

– outside the district – where it will quickly blend in with the detritus of daily rubbish?
28 *Auckland Star*, 21 August 1973

Demler: Yes, the police have it now, it wasn't a rifle, it was a two barrelled shotgun, one was one...

Ryan: Was that rifle ever in your possession?

Demler: It was lying in a shed in the corner. I thought I gave it to someone and it was chucked outside in the manure shed and it was right down in the corner.

Demler claimed to have found it under some old "discs" in his implement shed – a building supposedly thoroughly searched by detectives in June and July 1970. Former Chennells farm manager Ben Hawker told Chris Birt:[29]

"I cannot believe the police missed a rifle in that manure shed, especially the way they searched his place."

Yet, as you will later see with Arthur Allan Thomas, police searched his house and missed items they were looking for which, staggeringly, Thomas then naively collected up, took to the police station and handed to Hutton with the words, "you missed these". In context then, the fact that police missed a gun in a crowded implement shed does not in itself prove beyond reasonable doubt that Demler was lying about where he found the gun.

For the sake of completeness, however, there are some discrepancies involving Demler and a gun from the Chennells estate that have emerged. For one, you'll recall police were looking for "a double barrel firearm, one barrel being a shotgun and the other either of .22 or .38 calibre."

This was in the context of the .360 hammer gun, but the hammer gun was a rifle, not a shotgun. What gives? Why were the police describing it as a shotgun? Although in his book Birt refers to the .360 as both a "double barrelled shotgun" and a "double barrelled rifle", only the latter is correct. The .360 was a rifle bullet. Indeed, the police registration details from the 1920s refer to the gun with the serial number 859 as a "double barrelled *breech loading rifle*, .360 bore". Which makes Demler's references to handing something that "wasn't a rifle, it was a two barrelled shotgun", odd.

A further clue is found in Demler's testimony to the Thomas Royal Commission hearings ten years after the murders:

"The Chennells estate had a firearm that my first wife's father brought from England," said Len Demler.

---

29 *The Final Chapter*, Birt, p148

Stop right there. "Brought from England"? If Demler is right, then this was a second gun, not the .360, because we know from official records that the .360 was purchased by Newman Chennells in 1921 from one of his Pukekawa neighbours. It appears Demler was indeed referring to a different gun, as his evidence continued:

"It was an unusual type of gun, it took a .410 cartridge and still had a rifle bore in it. I don't think there was ever any ammunition over here for it. I never saw anyone fire out of it. From the time when my brother-in-law, Mr Chennells, died onwards [ie, from 1950 on], the gun I have described was up in the old house in those days, before they built the [Crewes'] brick house. And when the old house was pulled down, I took it [the .410 gun] down home. There were not any other firearms in the Chennells estate."

I looked on the internet at around 300 pages referencing vintage .410 combination shotgun/rifles, as described by Demler. With one exception, I couldn't find any combination[30] except .410/.22, which echoes Chris Birt's results from a survey of New Zealand gun collectors. Demler says old man Chennells had a .410 shotgun/rifle combo, or "an unusual type of gun" as he called it, brought out from England, not purchased at Pukekawa. It therefore cannot have been the .360 hammer rifle found in the implement shed. Demler says he had this combo gun at his own house, yet police never found it.

Chris Birt scores a coup in his book[31] by getting Owen Priest to confirm Demler had "the Chennells estate firearm...in perfect working order...kept in a wooden box in an implement shed on the Demler farm, under a set of discs." Birt says Priest "confirmed to me on two separate occasions" that the Chennells gun was, in fact, a .410/.22 combination gun.

How did Owen Priest know? Had he seen it with his own eyes?

---

30 Some arguably murky light is shed on this by a report in the *Auckland Star* of 5 August 1971: "An old firearm from the Chennells estate (now the Crewe farm) was missing at the time of the trial. Investigations back to the makers in Britain now establish that it was an old over-and-under, .300 in one barrel and .410 in the other, last registered in Pukekawa in 1921, presumed to have been thrown away, and because of calibre, no significance." The journalist who wrote that was Robert Gilmore, who was known to get tips from police. Here's where it gets interesting. I took the trouble of importing replicas of the British gunmaker W J Jeffery's catalogues for the years 1913 through to 1920. I could not find one reference to a .300/.410 combination gun. I did, however, find a two barrelled .410 shotgun. They also supplied .360 rifles. More intriguingly, they were the British agents for American gunmaker Savage, and Savage made an over-and-under combination gun, a .410/30-30, often referred to as a .410/300. It is possible, then, that the Chennells had bought one of these rare American combination guns, from W J Jeffery & Co in London. Some of these old guns are now worth up to US$24,000 at auction today, suggesting they were quite unique.
31 *The Final Chapter*, p149

No, but he told Birt that he'd heard about the gun first-hand from Len Demler himself, after the murders, during conversations in the car on the way to court.

"I can't recall now whether it was the Lower Court [depositions hearing in November 1970] or the first Thomas trial," Priest told Birt, "but Len and I travelled together most days as we were coming from the same place. He told me that the Chennells estate weapon was a .410/.22 and that it was in excellent working order. I never saw it, but Len told me."

Objectively, you have to ask the question: if Demler was the killer, and he used the old Chennells estate gun, is he likely to then tell another police witness in the case that he just happens to have that gun in his shed, in "excellent" working order and capable of firing .22 bullets, at a time when everyone knew there was a gun missing from the Chennells estate?

That would be a mighty risk to take, on top of all the other risks. For a start, only a few months earlier, on 17 August 1970, Demler had been confronted by police about gun ownership.

"I questioned him about a .22 rifle or pistol," wrote Detective Sergeant John Hughes in his notes. "He said he had never used or owned one himself. He explained that he could not fire one because of his poor eyesight.

Question: 'What about the .22 rifle Harvey had?

Answer: 'I didn't know he had one other than the shotgun'.

"Demler said he didn't think Harvey had borrowed one or had an unregistered one. Demler said he had never borrowed a .22 firearm himself."

So that's what police had on the record. Now, we are being asked to believe that Len Demler, a man police just couldn't crack, would suddenly confess exactly the opposite to Owen Priest.

Why didn't Priest, who was sitting through the court testimony about .22 bullets and missing guns, put 2 and 2 together (no pun intended) and tip off the defence about Demler's confession? Here's what Priest would have sat through as he watched Len Demler being cross-examined in the first trial by Thomas' defence counsel Paul Temm. First of all, an admission that he had once owned a .22, despite what John Hughes had recorded in his notes:

Temm: You told us that you did at one point own a .22 rifle?

Demler: That is right.

Temm: Did the police take possession of a .22 rifle from your farm?
Demler: No, they never took any rifle from my farm.
Temm: Did you give them any particular rifle from any other place?
Demler: No.
Temm: Did you give them any .22 calibre ammunition?
Demler: No, I never had any.
Temm: So you neither owned nor possessed a .22 calibre rifle during the past year?
Demler: That is right.

If that first interchange didn't make Owen Priest prick up his ears, the next one should have:

Temm: Was there an asset in the Chennells estate which was a firearm, a rifle?
Demler: Not to my knowledge, I have never seen it.
Temm: You know a man named Harry Leech?
Demler: Yes.
Temm: Who is he?
Demler: My brother-in-law.
Temm: Did you ever talk about a firearm in the Chennells estate to him?
Demler: No.
Temm: Did you go with him to talk to another man in Pukekohe concerning that firearm?
Demler: No I did not.
Temm: At about the time of Jeannette's funeral I suggest to you? Ever seen a man in Pukekohe whom you might have lent a rifle to?
Demler: No, it didn't belong to anyone, it was out of use. It was never used.
Temm: Where is it now?
Demler: I wouldn't know.
Temm: If the records of the Chennells estate show they had a firearm in the assets would you say that is not correct?
Demler: I have not seen a firearm.
Temm: If the records show they had a firearm?
Demler: I don't think that is correct.
Temm: Have you tried to find the firearm of which you have spoken since the deaths?
Demler: No.
Temm: Have you tried to find it?

Demler: No, I have not.

Temm: Is there a rifle in existence?

Demler: A broken-down one, but it wasn't fit for use.

Now, ask yourself: which part of that testimony would have failed to ring your bell if you'd just been sitting in a car with Len Demler where he's cheerily telling you about a combination .410/.22 rifle from the Chennells estate now in his possession and in "excellent" working order? Owen Priest made no mention of this massive conflict in evidence at the time, not to defence lawyers, nor to police.

On the face of it, Demler appears to have lied through his teeth by denying the question about whether the Chennells estate had a rifle, and Demler replied not to his knowledge, he'd never seen it. He must have seen it, because three years later he would hand over the broken down and rusty .360 hammer rifle to police and tell them he'd found it in his implement shed. In that second trial he then went on the record saying the gun he'd given police was not a rifle but a two barrelled shotgun. Are we to believe that if it was the murder weapon, Demler would just hand it in to police?

But in the same way Demler only gave the police answers if they asked specific questions, he was doing the same to Temm, splitting hairs every step of the way. In the end, there was agreement that a rifle did exist, but it was broken and didn't work. Demler seven years later at the Royal Commission talked of a .410 shotgun with a rifle barrel as well, that he'd kept at his home. So was this another example of splitting hairs – denying the existence of a 'rifle' because technically it was a combination gun? Demler's testimony could be taken two ways: deliberately lying about the gun, or being deliberately obtuse to annoy his questioner. Given his personality and the lack of an obvious motive, I'm leaning towards the latter scenario.

Owen Priest, years later, thought he'd had a discussion with Demler during that court trial about the .410/.22, but distance and repeated questioning can lend enhancement to those original memories. And if the conversation happened as the late Owen Priest recalled it, doesn't it make Demler less likely to be the killer, on the grounds that the real murderer would shut up about a gun if it was relevant? People already thought Demler was a prime suspect, why would the man add to that?[32]

---

[32] Alternatively, Owen Priest may have misheard and Demler was talking about the .360, or Priest was the victim of evidence contamination through questioning about a .410/22 combo, or perhaps Priest

Even so, if Len Demler had used that gun or the officially-registered .360, why on earth didn't he leave the bodies in the house and the gun beside Harvey's chair? Let's face it, if Demler had killed the Crewes with their own gun he could have set the scene for murder-suicide beautifully. After killing the couple he could have wiped off his own prints, wiped the tip of the gun barrel in Harvey's head wound, clasped Harvey's fingers around the trigger guard and butt, and left a box of the old ammo that was used in Harvey's shed. Why go to the trouble of removing bodies? The Crewes were loners, regarded as anti-social in many ways. The financial bills were on the table with the half-eaten meal, it would have been so easy to make it appear as a tragic domestic tiff.

He could have feigned discovery of the murder-suicide the next day, removing any need to alert his new girlfriend or enlist her help in feeding Rochelle – it all would have been so much simpler if Demler had been the murderer and used a gun belonging to the Crewes to kill them.

So to me, although Demler had access to that firearm, it actually makes it even less likely he was the killer. The gun was registered to the estate now known as the Crewe farm. Demler would have known it was the Crewes' gun. His initial comments to Owen Priest when they entered the farmhouse to search were that Harvey must have snapped, and done Jeannette in. If Demler was indeed the killer, why didn't he make the crime scene look that way before he brought Priest there? Clearly the idea of murder/suicide was a scenario dancing around his head.

The Chennells gun/s, if it/they had been in working order and available, would have been the ultimate gift to a guilty Demler. Alone of all the potential suspects, Demler was uniquely placed to stage a murder suicide if he had wanted to. The fact that he made no use of the Chennells firearm/s in that way – despite their historical ties to the Crewe property – indicates again that he didn't commit the crime.

---

had this conversation with Demler years later, around the time of the Royal Commission hearing. I can't get past the issue that if Priest had really been told about Demler having an "excellent" .22 rifle in his implement shed, he would have told the defence and/or the police when he heard the issue being raised in the courtroom. He didn't raise it, therefore he can't actually have known back then what he later thought he did. The only other possibilities are either (1) that Demler was talking about two guns, the old .360 in his shed and a .410/.22 in excellent order that also existed, whereabouts unknown, and that Priest became confused in the retelling. Or (2) that Demler gave Johnston the 410 combo gun but Johnston for his own reasons decided to stick with the .360 in court.

In hindsight, then, I think the Chennells estate gun is a red herring. The real killer moved the bodies because he used his own weapon, and didn't want police tracing him through it, and couldn't leave his own gun at the scene to stage a murder suicide because clearly his gun didn't belong there, and was most likely a registered firearm with a name attached to its serial number. Moving the bodies is unusual in a murder. In most cases, disposal of the weapon is all that's required to prevent police connecting the fatal bullets with a particular gun. The only reason for shifting the Crewes that makes sense to me is that the real killer knew there was a possibility he could be questioned at some point, and that police would expect him to be able to show them his registered weapon. He had no option but to get rid of the Crewes instead, because he couldn't get rid of his registered gun. There is one other reason for shifting the bodies: a sexual crime involving body fluids. There's no suggestion Demler was that way inclined to his daughter, so that option isn't open to us.

Demler did not have a .22 registered to him, which meant he would not have needed to move the bodies because the bullets couldn't be traced to him anyway. And if he'd had the Chennells gun, he could have left it with the bodies as an apparent murder suicide. Yet more circumstantial detail, then, in a growing list that indicates Demler didn't do it.

For his part, Birt speculates that perhaps the .360 presented in court as Exhibit 12 in the second Thomas trial, April 1973, had been switched with another gun, or alternatively that police had faked the registration document. That registration document, however, was dug up in August 1970 at a time when police were still hoping they could pin the murders on Demler. The gun's serial number was mentioned in dispatches, and the gun produced in court in 1973 had the same serial number. If the registration was a fake, then miraculously they found a gun three years later to match the fake serial number from 1970!

The cop who presented the evidence to court was one of Bruce Hutton's most trusted officers – Detective Sergeant Lenrick Johnston. As you will see later in the book, Johnston was as crooked as a dog's hind leg and then some, so the idea that Johnston may have presented a different .360 in court and simply bluffed about the matching serial number has some tempting appeal as a theory.

However, in my experience as a court reporter, defence lawyers check Crown exhibits for precisely that kind of tomfoolery, in advance of the hearing[33]. I'm sure Arthur Allan Thomas' lawyer Kevin Ryan checked this mysterious new gun that had been missing in the first trial, and I'm equally sure he would have seen enough of the serial number to be confident it matched. In the absence of evidence to the contrary, we should accept this as a given.

There is one odd thing I'll concede, however, and it comes from the police. On 5 August 1971, an *Auckland Star* reporter known to have police contacts published a story saying police had traced the old Chennells estate gun, a .410/.300 combo, and it wasn't relevant to the inquiry. (see footnote 30). However, at the second trial of Arthur Thomas in 1973 – two years later – Demler gave evidence on oath that he'd just found the missing Chennells estate gun:

"It was lying in a shed in the corner," Demler told the court. "I thought I gave it away to someone and it was chucked outside the manure shed and it was right down in the corner. I found it when I was shifting the other day and I gave it to Mr Hutton."[34]

That gun was the .360 hammer gun, as we now know. It matched a 1921 and 1924 gun registration record. But if Demler had found it only a couple of days earlier, what on earth was the gun police claimed to have traced back to the manufacturers in 1971, a .410/.300 combo of some kind? It has never been presented to the court. We know Hutton had rung the *Star* journalist who wrote about it on a different occasion, was Hutton the source of this misleading news tip as well? I've got the police documentation. I know police had a gun registration for the .360. It's nothing like a .410/.300.

After finding out that a .410/30-30 combination gun was made by the Savage company in the US in the late 1800s, and sold by W J Jeffery and Co in England, I spoke to US gun expert David Powell about the Thomas case. "The .410/30-30 was definitely an over-and-under gun," he said. "I've handled one." He told me there were two common methods of altering big guns to fire .22 bullets.[35]

"In one method, there are tiny sleeves, literally only an inch or less, that fit right in the base of, say, a shotgun barrel. They're made to

---

33 And indeed, in the case of the cartridge cases used to convict Thomas, defence counsel and forensic scientist Jim Sprott did precisely that.
34 Although Demler swore he'd given the gun to Hutton, Detective Len Johnston swore that he was the police officer who had taken possession, not Hutton.
35 David Powell runs the collector's website, gunsinternational.com and has been a consultant for Court TV and other networks in the US.

fit the particular gauge and they hold the .22 in place so the firing pin hits it properly to fire the bullet."

The closest analogy I can think of is if you imagine the cardboard tube left over from a roll of tinfoil is the gun barrel, and you shove a cotton reel in one end. The cotton reel is the sleeve, and the hole in the middle of the cotton reel holds the bullet. The sleeve is sized so the lead nose of the bullet pokes out the end, unobstructed.

"Once the bullet is fired from one of these sleeves, there are no rifling marks because the bullet is far too small to touch the sides of the larger barrel it's travelling through. So if your murderer used one of these sleeves on, say, the .360, there would be no rifling landing marks on the bullets they found in the bodies."

Except we know there were rifling marks, so the killer cannot have used one of these mini-sleeves, even though they sound ideal for creating almost untraceable bullets.

Option two was a long form sleeve, either nine or 14 inches long, which contained its own rifling pattern. As a rule, these proper sleeves provided more accuracy and power in the gunshot and, because they had rifling, they left marks on a bullet. Sleeves were available to retrofit both .410s or .360s or 30-30s if required. Alternatively, the killer may have used an original .22 weapon of some kind.

It's worth noting that forensic tests by the British Home Office on the Crewe bullets found a very high likelihood that the bullets were in fact fired by a pistol, not a rifle. Of 15 matches they achieved in their own weapons tests, 11 of the matching weapons were .22 handguns, only four were rifles.[36]

So, for one thing, Chris Birt's theories nailing Demler are elegant, but they don't cover all bases and it appears a .410 combo gun did come in a 30-30 variant sold via the English gunmaker the Chennells family may have dealt with.

We know that the Crewes' haybarn was torched on June 17, 1969, exactly one year to the day before they were murdered on June 17, 1970. Are we to believe that Len Demler was angry with his daughter and son-in-law at that point, months before Jeannette's mother Maisie had changed her will? What was the motive for Demler's anger in June 1969? Why pick the anniversary of that haybarn fire as the date to murder them both?

---

36 *Auckland Star*, 13 November 1978

What was his motive for setting fire to his daughter's house using his infant granddaughter's own baby clothes as fuel, just a week after she was born in 1968? It can't have been the will – it didn't exist.

Someone carried out these crimes, and they seem a touch personal. If it was a house in a crowded street in a bad area of a large town I'd probably venture "coincidence", but this was a remote farmhouse, 60 metres off the road requiring someone to make a conscious effort to target it.

Frederick Hoskins, whose farm adjoined the back of the Crewe property, told police these earlier crimes were highly strange.

"[Hoskins] did mention that all the burglaries and the thefts at the house were most unusual – not in any other part of the district," Detective Metcalfe told a police briefing early on in the case. In other words, the break-ins at the Crewe house prior to the murders were not common events in the area. They were rare enough to be considered unique.

There's an element of farce in the police transcripts, incidentally. Detective Inspector Bruce Hutton's suspicions of Demler were aroused because Demler used the 'k' word:

"One thing I felt was a slip during the interview, if this man is in any way a suspect," said Hutton, probably leaning forward and jabbing his finger in the air to make the point, "I let him have a look at a photo – did he see them, etc? At that stage he was off guard and he said 'I can't see how she could have been *killed*'. This is the only time during the interview that he may have known she was dead. At no time did I mention she was dead," continued Bruce Hutton, probably glancing around the faces of his subordinates as their heads nodded in knowing agreement. "He is either a good liar, or a real psycho type."

Yes, I can see how speculating aloud about murder, after you find your daughter's home bloodspattered where a body has clearly been dragged, and empty with a baby left alone in the cot, makes you a suspect for daring to state the obvious. Half of New Zealand suspected the Crewes were dead. So did the police. That's why they were there. To react with false shock when a civilian draws the same conclusion is, to be frank, laughable.

This feigned shock by police, however, came in the same interview where Bruce Hutton had directly accused Demler of moving the bodies. Then there's the problem of no blood being found. Supposedly, Demler had to man-handle two bodies, one mutilated, yet forensic experts found no unusual fibres on any of his clothes, nor any blood from the deceased.

"He must surely have had some blood stains or brain tissue on him, on his hands or clothing?" probed Crown Prosecutor David Morris at one point in the special strategy session. Hutton's response was that Demler was a cleanliness "fanatic" who'd had five days to clean up. But David Morris wasn't buying it.

"This is worrying me," he frowned. "No blood on him at all."[37]

Morris, a brusque 35 year old with a mop of ginger hair and a strong Scottish brogue despite 20 years' living in New Zealand, would become a driving force on the Crewe murders prosecution. But he also undoubtedly knew of the holes in the case. One of Morris' staff solicitors, now Governor-General, Anand Satyanand, later described his former boss as someone who could instantly detect problems in a police investigation, saying he had "an instinct for discerning quickly and accurately the strong or weak points of a case without necessarily letting that be known more widely than necessary."[38]

Why, Morris wondered, if Demler was such a "fanatic", had he failed to wipe away a four inch long blood stain smack bang in the front seat of his Cortina? Surely if he'd carried the bodies in the front seat, and he was a fastidious cleaner, that would have been the first bloodstain to be washed away?

"Always mistakes made," Hutton countered, with a shrug of the shoulders. The blood matched Jeannette's blood group, but Demler claimed she'd cut her hand months earlier while using the car. It seems beyond belief that Demler would not have tackled that bloodstain if he had been the killer on a clean-up mission.

There's no discussion, in the police documents released so far, of the improbability that Len Demler would stave his own daughter's face in. Another who has problems with that accusation is Arthur Allan Thomas' youngest brother, Des.

"Jeannette had six teeth smashed out of her jaw, and I can't believe Len Demler would have done that," agrees Des Thomas.

---

[37] Demler did, in fact, have a scratch on his shoulder blade which Hutton suspected could have been caused in a struggle with Jeannette. Demler said he'd scraped it while working in the bush. The only problem with Hutton's theory, and probably why he didn't pursue it, was that a scratch in that area couldn't be made by a human hand through clothing.

[38] "Farewelling the ultimate prosecutor – the Honourable David Stewart Morris" by Simon Moore, Crown prosecutor, Meredith Connell solrs

So, to recap on the police case against Len Demler:
1. The motive was non-existent. He was not financially hurt by Jeannette Crewe's inheritance, and police eventually conceded this
2. If Demler slaughtered his own daughter, he had to convince another woman – knowing this – to help him clean up, feed Rochelle and move the bodies
3. There was no forensic evidence linking him to the crime
4. The murders happened on the precise anniversary of an arson attack on the Crewe farm, itself staged on the eve of their wedding anniversary. Demler had an alibi for at least one of the previous incidents on the Crewe property
5. Demler was shadowing police all the time as they searched his farm, yet the real killer knew the bodies were miles away in the Waikato river

To prove Demler *did* commit the murders, we also have to explain:
1. Why he would go to the trouble of hiding the murder weapon, then tell a suspicious neighbour that he secretly had it in his possession and how "excellent" it was. (I mean, *really??*)
2. Why, having carried out double murders and leaving absolutely no forensic trace at the scene, disposing of the bodies without being seen, he would have absolutely no coherent plan as to how the crime should be discovered?
3. What, on earth, was the motive, and why would he smash his child's face in?

There is some speculation about financial or social links between Bruce Hutton and Len Demler. Lawyer Gerald Ryan told me he'd discovered Hutton had borrowed money from Demler at one point to finance a property in the Helensville district.

"Not a lot of people know that. He got tipped off that I was researching it, and the next thing I know I got a warning from police, telling me it was 'highly inappropriate' for me to be making such enquiries."

It seemed like a promising lead, except for the timing. According to Ryan, the deal didn't go down until after the first trial. "It was just after Arthur was found guilty". There was no evidence of a prior relationship. Nor is there any hint in the police documents that Hutton had anything less than a total desire to nail Demler if possible in the first part of the police inquiry.

When push comes to shove, however, I still struggle with Len

Demler as the man who savagely destroyed his daughter's face before callously holding the rifle barrel to the skin on the side of her head and blowing her brains out.

I struggle even more with Demler's new girlfriend being cast in the role of willing participant in the clean-up, for reasons you are about to discover.

CHAPTER 5

Did Norma Demler Feed The Baby?

If you've read the *North & South* article on the Crewe murders this year, watched television or seen numerous newspaper stories, you'll know there have been extensive but coy references to a "mystery woman" still living in Auckland who's believed to have fed Rochelle Crewe during the five days between the murders and apparent discovery.

Everyone has been too scared to name the woman for legal reasons. I'm not. She is Norma Demler, the now 90 year old second wife of Len Demler, born Norma Thomas (no relation to Arthur Allan Thomas). Officially, she appeared on the scene *after* the deaths of Harvey and Jeannette, but unofficially she must have been involved in some way with Len Demler earlier than that, because author Chris Birt gave police a dossier three years ago saying he has "evidence which puts her in the district a year before the murders".

Additionally, Norma Demler herself appeared to concede the point in a *Sunday Star-Times* interview with the "mystery woman" when she admitted she "sort of" knew the Crewes, and described them as "a lovely couple". She couldn't have formed such opinions without having been involved in some way with Len Demler, perhaps even prior to the February 1970 death of Len's first wife, Maisie.

"It was the most dreadful, dreadful thing," Norma Demler told the newspaper when they asked about the murders. "Who the heck did it? I don't know. I had nothing whatsoever to do with it," Norma Demler said. "I have a clear conscience. I can put my head on the pillow every night and go to sleep."

For the record, I believe her. You'll find out why shortly.

But first, let's return to the original sightings of the mystery woman.

The key witness in this regard is Bruce Roddick, whose first statement to police was given on June 23, 1970, after remarking to his parents that Jeannette Crewe can't have been killed on 17 June, because he'd seen her at the house on the morning of the 19th. When police came to see him it quickly became apparent he'd never actually met Jeannette and therefore had merely assumed that the woman he saw was her. He detailed exactly what he saw in this more comprehensive statement to police two days later, six days after the sighting.

"Last Friday morning [June 19, 1970] at about 7:30 am, I was at home when Mr Chitty telephoned me. He asked me if I could come up and help him to feed out hay. He was going to be busy at 10 am with some buyers from Gisborne. I said, 'all right. I could work for a couple of hours in the morning'. I left home at about 8:15 am so it would have been around 8:30 am when I passed the Crewe house. I did not notice anything.

"Later I was feeding out hay just behind Ron Chitty's old cottage where the police are now. This would be just after 9 am. The car was just parked on the grass outside the small front gate. I have seen the car before, it is a green Hillman, the modern shape, bigger than the Imp. It was facing north.

"There was a woman standing just inside the fence from the gateway. She seemed to be looking in my direction. She would be in her 30s, and about 5'10" to 5'11". I am 5'10" and she looked very tall to me. Her hair was not blonde, but light brown, her hair was cut short but curled up at the bottom.

"I was about 75 yards away, and she looked quite good looking to me. She was wearing dark slacks but I don't know about the rest. It was a dull day, no sunshine at all. I was there for about two or three minutes and I did not see anybody else. I don't know Mrs Crewe and I have never worked for them. I don't know whether the woman I saw was Mrs Crewe or not. If I saw this woman again I think I could recognise her. I have just remembered she would be about medium build, I would not say she was slim."

A dark green Hillman car (a Hillman Hunter, for the record) belonged to the Crewes, and its placement in the open suggests it may have been the vehicle used to dispose of the bodies, because the car was found parked in its garage by detectives called to the murder scene the following Monday.

However, there are a couple of other details to consider here. It remains possible the mystery woman's own vehicle was a green Hillman as well: as you'll see from the bonus chapter on the Jennifer Beard murder case, there were really only a few models of car to choose from in NZ in 1970, and green was a highly popular colour!

The second detail in Roddick's statement worth noting is the phrase "she seemed to be looking in my direction". It's not a definite. It was a dull day, with no glare, but Roddick couldn't tell for sure from 75 metres away whether in fact the woman was looking directly at him. This gives a clue as to how later claims to certainty in terms of recognition are probably wrong.

In Pat Booth's theory, Jeannette Crewe stayed alive for several days and was the woman seen by Roddick. But again this is unlikely, because Roddick described the woman as "quite good looking to me" – something you wouldn't normally say about a woman whose lips have been shredded, front teeth smashed off and nose broken. The bone surrounding her right eye socket had been smashed as well, and her skull cracked right around. Not a beauty queen, and not someone likely to be frolicking by the farm gate with those kinds of injuries. Jeannette Crewe, incidentally, was dark-haired, not fair.

In addition to Roddick, a woman named Queenie McConachie had also seen activity in the front yard of the Crewe house, this time the following day, Saturday afternoon around 1.30, June 20, 1970. While driving past she noticed a young toddler playing in the front yard and a light-coloured car. The child in McConachie's description was wearing overalls that turned out to match an outfit seen on baby Rochelle the previous Wednesday, the day of the murders. Queenie McConachie was expecting her own child at the time, so was more keenly observant of matters maternal than other passers-by might have been.

Journalist Pat Booth records that "a brown International truck was seen close to the Crewe woolshed on the Sunday", a fact that appears to have been overlooked by David Yallop and subsequent books on the case. A truck implies someone with commercial ties.[39]

What does all this tell us? Firstly, that the killer – or possibly just his accomplice – had returned to the scene of the crime sometime early Friday morning, and again on the Saturday. It is possible

---

39 *Trial by Ambush*, by Pat Booth, South Pacific Press, 1975, p33

the killer merely dropped the woman off before sunrise (around 7.20am) with instructions to hide if anyone turned up, and/or that the killer was using the Crewes' car. This may seem strange but if people saw the vehicle around they might assume the Crewes were out and about, rather than dead. However, the Crewes' car was that dark Hillman green, whereas McConachie had seen a "light coloured" car.

Interestingly, Chris Birt reports a statement by Arthur Thomas' brother Richard, which suggests that Roddick had in fact seen the mystery woman driving the Crewes' dark green Hillman on June 18, the morning *after* the murders but the day *before* he saw the woman he talked of in his first statement to police.

"In May 1972," Richard Thomas writes[40], "I went to see Bruce about his sighting of the mystery woman and he said he was also interested in finding out who she was. He agreed to accompany me to a local property.

"While driving there that day, which I now know to be 15 May 1972, Bruce told me that he had seen the same woman driving the Crewe car towards the Pukekawa store early the morning before the day he saw her in the front yard of the Crewe house. He said she waved to him. I believe that this was the first time Bruce had mentioned to anyone the sighting of the woman the morning after the Crewes were murdered.

"This was a major revelation to me and I remember the conversation very clearly, including the fact that he had seen the woman driving the car the day before his sighting of her in the front yard," Richard Thomas stated.

Unfortunately, it is not clear that this evidence was ever given directly by Roddick himself on oath, and we are left only with Richard Thomas' hearsay statement because Bruce Roddick is now dead and can't tell us whether Thomas has quoted him accurately.[41]

---

40 *The Final Chapter*, Chris Birt, page 194
41 Norma Demler was, in fact partially named in relation to the case in Pat Booth's 1975 book *Trial by Ambush*, at page 35: "The police did not reveal either, although a signed statement from Bruce Roddick makes it plain, that as well as taking Vivien Thomas to an identity parade, they also arranged for Roddick to go to the Demler farm between trials, in June 1972, to see if the second Mrs Demler was the light haired woman in slacks he had seen at the Crewe farm that Friday. Roddick said she wasn't." That last sentence is interesting in light of what you have just read in this chapter, and also given Booth's close involvement with the Retrial Committee. It appears this early public identification of Norma Demler as a possible 'mystery woman' was forgotten, partly because Pat's book had no index and partly because his book has been out of print for three decades. Pat, who had such a strong involvement with the case back then, evidently didn't believe Norma Demler was the mystery woman either, despite early excitement among Committee members.

What we do know, on the record, is that Roddick testified to the Royal Commission on 26 July 1980 – ten years after the events in question – to say that he recalled seeing the mystery woman driving towards Pukekawa, either *a week or two weeks before* the murders.[42]

If Roddick was adamant in 1972 that the sighting had been the day after the murders, that certainty had been lost by the time of the Commission hearings.

Robert Adams-Smith, QC, who investigated the case for Prime Minister Robert Muldoon, wrote in his report after interviewing Bruce Roddick directly, that the distance between them on the Friday fenceline sighting, of 75 metres, prevented Roddick from getting a precise facial recognition, and he added that:

"He was sufficiently close to be able to distinguish a person of dark colouring as opposed to light colouring, and would have been able to make a reasonably accurate assessment as to the build of a person.

"But while Roddick was sufficiently close to tell that a woman was not elderly, I cannot accept that he could distinguish between a woman of athletic build in her 30s and a woman of athletic build in her 50s."

Roddick himself acknowledged he didn't see the woman well enough to accurately recall her face,[43] and he couldn't even be sure whether she was looking in his direction or not. But like young kids in sexual abuse cases being subjected to leading questions by over-enthusiastic investigators, Roddick's memory of the sightings was quite possibly damaged by a chain of events that followed the murders.

As speculation grew that Len Demler might have slain his daughter and her husband, locals noticed that the new woman in 61 year old Demler's life, 49 year old Norma Thomas, was blonde. Norma was an observer at the depositions hearing against Arthur Allan Thomas at the Otahuhu magistrates court in December 1970.

It was there that Bruce Roddick noticed Norma Demler in the crowd, although he didn't know who she was. By his own admission he made no mental connection at that point between the court

---

42 See *The Final Chapter*, p193
43 David Yallop, in *Beyond Reasonable Doubt* (page 260), did a distance reconstruction at the scene, and reckons Roddick would have known who the woman was if he'd seen her before, from 75 metres away. If so, this would actually lend weight to the argument that the woman who waved at him either a day or two weeks earlier, would not have been the same person. Roddick remembered the blonde woman driving past him, looking at him and waving. If they were the same people, with the same car, why didn't he make that instant reflex connection in his first police statements just days after the sightings in question or through the court hearings? The reality is, he didn't; and I submit that's because they were two different women, driving similar but not necessarily matching cars, and probably there was a two week gap, rather than one day, between the sightings.

sighting and the woman outside the farmhouse. It wasn't until he saw her again the following year at the first Supreme Court trial that he realised he recognised her, but even then, according to the Adams-Smith report, he didn't recognise her as the woman from the farm gate.

"On a closer analysis of what he had to say about that, it would seem that even then there was no sudden flash of recognition. What he said was that when he had finished giving evidence, he noticed this woman, apparently having come down the stairs from the gallery. He felt that she had turned her head so as to discourage him from seeing her face. His later thought was that he wondered what she was doing back there, but he did recognise her from the Otahuhu Court.

"His thought process," notes Adams-Smith, "was not that he had recognised her from the Friday morning at the Crewes', but that he had seen the woman before at the Otahuhu Court, wondered what she was doing back again, and wondered if she was just listening to his evidence or was it that she was the woman he saw at the Crewe farm."

You can see the mental processes that must have been ticking over in Roddick. A blonde, mature woman mysteriously turning up at court hearings, trying to hide her face on this occasion. If he'd known she was Len Demler's new woman, that might have set his mind at rest as to why she was at court. Instead, he was left in the dark and his mind began filling the gaps on its own accord. Subconsciously, Roddick's entire *raison d'etre* in this case was centred around his sighting of an unidentified fair haired woman. His brain would quietly register every blonde he saw and test her against that matrix. Most, of course, would be out of context and subconsciously dismissed as non-starters, but any blonde woman in the Pukekawa district or hanging around the court case would trigger contextual alerts in his thoughts creating an elevated sense of expectation. That's how the mind works.

It's worth bearing in mind, however: he'd now seen Norma Demler twice close up, yet had not made a lightning bolt, 'she's the one' connection. If Norma Demler had really been the one feeding Rochelle, knowing the community was buzzing about the mysterious blonde woman who'd been seen by Bruce Roddick, do you think she'd for a moment sit in the public gallery of the majestic Supreme Court and run the risk of Roddick suddenly pointing at her, mid-testimony, with the words, "And I tell you, your Honour, that woman is here in this very courtroom, today!"?[44]

What I think happened is that Roddick confused himself over the years, with the help of others, and his evidence became contaminated.[45] If you go back to that 15th of May 1972 encounter when Richard Thomas invited Bruce Roddick to come and see something at a local property, you'll see that while they were in the car they were clearly discussing the mystery woman, and that's how the subject of Roddick seeing her driving the day after the murders apparently came up. We've dealt with that angle, but now it's time for the rest of that story because it shows, I think, the power of suggestion; what Robert Adams-Smith QC once called "unwitting embellishment".

Richard Thomas already thought he knew who Roddick's mystery woman was: Norma Demler. He didn't tell Roddick her name, but he was taking Roddick to a point overlooking the Demler farm, where he invited Roddick to peer through binoculars at a distant farmhouse:

"After a short time," says Thomas in his statement, "a woman emerged from the house and Bruce's hands began to shake. He stared through the binoculars for a long time and then told me adamantly that the woman he was looking at was the same woman he had seen driving the Crewe car and the same woman he had

---

44 According to Roddick's surviving family, Bruce *did* make a connection in the initial sighting outside the Otahuhu Magistrates Court. Brother Graham, now 69, told *North & South* magazine (July 2010) that Bruce had mentioned seeing "the woman from the Crewes and had told a police officer, but had been rebuffed. The cop didn't want to know." There's no question Graham Roddick is sincere in his recollection 40 years later, but Bruce was quizzed on this very point by Robert Adams-Smith QC much closer to the events in question, who determined Bruce had *not* made the connection that early (see quote above). I suspect Bruce Roddick's comments to his brother dated from later, and the timing has been compressed in the recollection. Chris Birt writes in *North & South* that Roddick "later, to his family...disclosed she was the girlfriend of a local farmer". It is an agreed matter of record however that Roddick did *not* know the identity of the woman he saw in 1970 at the courts until the May 1972 stakeout of Demler's place with Richard Thomas, two years after the murders, not six months.

45 Just as this book was going to press, new research from the University of Sydney was released on precisely this point: "Memories can't be trusted and become contaminated when people discuss their memories of an event with others, according to a University of Sydney study. Lead researcher, Dr Helen Paterson said sharing memories can contaminate people's recollections and create false memories.

" 'A false memory is the recollection of an event, or details of an event, that did not actually occur,' she said. 'My research focuses on how people can contaminate each other's memories for an event by discussing it with one another.' Dr Paterson said a key finding of the research was that misleading information presented through discussion with another person who observed the event can also lead to memory distortion. 'That is, witnesses who discuss an event with a co-witness are very likely to incorporate misinformation presented by the co-witness into their own memory for the event,' she said. 'Once their memory has been contaminated in this way, the witness is often unable to distinguish between the accurate and inaccurate memories'."

See "Sydney study finds false memories are common", University of Sydney news release, 9 August 2010

seen in the front yard. It was apparent to us both that the woman was staying at the house."

The woman, of course, was Norma Demler.

All the hype, all the suspicion and paranoia, and Richard Thomas leading Roddick by the hand implying he'd found something important and related to Roddick's sightings – all of that built up Roddick's subconscious expectations.

His clean, fresh statement given to police two years earlier, which made no connection whatsoever between the woman in the Crewes' front yard and a woman seen driving a car either a day or two weeks earlier, had now been contaminated by seeds planted by Richard Thomas, and by Roddick's own less-than-lightning-flash encounters with Norma Demler at two court appearances – where according to Muldoon's special investigator he'd still failed to make a definitive connection between her and the mystery woman.

But now, and forever more, the well-meaning Richard Thomas had contaminated Roddick's memory of events. The upshot of this "dramatic" new development was that they raced off to lawyer Kevin Ryan with Roddick's positive identification of the mystery woman. The news was leaked to the *Sunday News*:[46]

"Pukekawa farmhand Bruce Roddick has identified the mystery woman in Crewe murder case. The sensational development in the fight to gain a new trial for Arthur Allan Thomas, was confirmed by *Sunday News* last night. The mystery woman's identity was a key issue during the trial in which farmer Thomas was convicted of the murders of Harvey and Jeannette Crewe. ... her identity has been in doubt until Mr. Roddick was able to identify her this month.

"A retrial committee spokesman said last night that the matter was 'in hand' and that 'very close checks' were being made. The mystery woman's identity is a closely guarded secret. Her name is known to only a few and they are tight-lipped."

That was 1972. She's been named for the first time in this book. It's now 2010.

Whoever leaked details of the identification made sure all the newspapers had a bite at it:[47]

"A prominent resident told the *Sunday Herald*: 'a woman has definitely been identified. All I can say at the moment is she is in

---

46 "Crewe murder woman named", *Sunday News*, front page, 28 May 1972
47 "Crewe case mystery woman is identified", *Sunday Herald*, 28 May 1972

no way connected with Arthur Thomas.' A retrial committee chairman, Mr. Pat Vesey said 'this is a very important matter and I am afraid we have to put a blanket *no comment* on it'."

One who thought her nightmare was perhaps over was dark-haired Vivien Thomas, who'd been accused herself of being the mystery blonde: "Fabulous. Absolutely fabulous. This could be just what we have been waiting for."

Except, it wasn't to be.

For nearly 40 years, Vivien too has believed the woman to be Norma Demler, just as she told *North & South* magazine this past July.[48] "It's now very clear who that woman was. Bruce Roddick reported seeing this woman at the Crewes' house two days after they were killed. He saw her on four subsequent occasions.

"Bruce was reluctant to actually name the woman, but I know now that he was doing so in the close confines of his family, almost from the outset. The pieces of the jigsaw have been put together and the puzzle is complete. The question is why the police are not forcing her to say where she was during those crucial five days."

The heavy reliance of Vivien Harrison and the Thomas family on the identification of Norma Demler as the mystery woman is based, ultimately, on a sighting made from 75 metres away where Roddick could not even be sure the woman was looking at him and – if it was Norma Demler – he underestimated her age by 15 years. To put that sighting in perspective, 75 metres is the distance across the paddock at Eden Park, or one and a half times longer than an Olympic-size swimming pool. If the death sentence still existed, would you vouch for Roddick's ability to recognise someone he'd never seen before from that distance, and know her for certain six months, a year, later? I want you to remember that guy who yelled out across the rugby field at that match you went to six months ago. Now I want you to positively identify him – because that's the demand all of us, including Roddick himself, are making of him. No one is questioning Bruce Roddick's sincerity or the importance of his evidence in regard to the initial sighting, but to me his mind has merged definite later close-up sightings of Norma Demler hanging around the court case, with the fleeting distance view of a blondish or light brown-haired woman at the time of the crime.

---

48 "A Life Sentence", Chris Birt, *North & South*, July 2010

Significantly, despite being told the mystery woman's identity, Arthur Allan Thomas' lawyers chose not to raise the issue at his second trial. Admittedly, as a police witness Bruce Roddick would be called at the Crown's discretion, but three days before the second trial in 1973 police advised Ryan that Roddick was released as a Crown witness and could appear for the defence. Norma Demler could have been named in court. She wasn't.

Lawyer Gerald Ryan, who assisted his brother Kevin in that second Thomas trial, told me why they never asked Roddick *that* question and it is just as I suspected: "At that time, Bruce Roddick wasn't certain it was Norma Demler. We weighed up asking him on the stand, but there was always a danger that under cross-examination he would have to admit what he told us – that he could not be certain it was Norma that he saw. It was too much of a risk."

The veiled assertions this year in *North & South* and *Close-Up* that Norma Demler is the mystery woman suffer a further body blow at the hands of the late Bruce Roddick himself. In late 1978, he was visited by the *Auckland Star's* Deputy Editor, Pat Booth, in Melbourne, and asked to pick the mystery woman from a set of photographs provided by David Yallop.[49]

"He unhesitatingly picked the photo of one woman from a set of similar photographs I showed him," reported Booth. "I know the woman he picked from the set was the woman Mr Yallop has named [to Prime Minister Muldoon] as the mystery woman. But Mr Roddick told me he could go no further than saying 'She is similar to the woman I saw'."

Here's the kicker then: the woman who David Yallop named was *not* Norma Demler. The woman Roddick picked out of the lineup of photos was *not* Norma Demler. And the best he could do was to say Yallop's woman was merely "similar" to the woman he'd seen eight years earlier.

"He was...adamant," wrote Pat Booth, "that if submissions to the Prime Minister suggested he could positively identify the woman, then that took the matter too far." Which is exactly what I have just been arguing.

For the record, the woman Yallop named and who Roddick picked as "similar" from the lineup was Jeannette Crewe's sister

---

49 *Auckland Star,* 24 November 1978

Heather Souter. She was not involved. Customs and immigration data proved she was out of the country at the time of the killings and the Royal Commission absolutely rejected her involvement. For our purposes, though, Pat Booth's story shows Roddick failed to pick Norma Demler out of a photo lineup in 1978, and instead picked someone else.

The investigator appointed by Prime Minister Muldoon, Robert Adams-Smith QC, also questioned Roddick about other sightings of the mystery woman supposedly driving the Crewe car a few days or a week before the murders.[50]

"He could not and he does not say that she was the same woman as he had seen on the Friday morning, or even had similar characteristics as that woman," the QC reported. In other words, the endless claims you've heard in the media for nearly 40 years that the mystery woman who fed Rochelle Crewe has been identified are clearly wrong.

So why do I think Norma Demler is innocent? Let's look at the key points of evidence. The earliest statements to police put the mystery woman in her 30s. Demler was only a smidgen south of 50.

The mystery woman must have been the person who helped shift the bodies, including that of a battered Jeannette Crewe, daughter of Len Demler, unless we are arguing there were two men *and* the mystery woman involved. For a crime of passion, that seems just a touch excessive.

Now, suppose you are a 49 year old woman, hooking up with a widower farmer, who suddenly confesses to you that he's shot dead his eldest daughter and her husband and, curses, the baby needs feeding. You get to the scene, and find Jeannette's eyes staring up at you, cold and glazed (well, one of them – her right eye socket was damaged), a drizzle of dried blood pooled underneath her head on the carpet, her mouth locked in a death rictus of jagged and missing teeth, smashed jaw and pulverised lips, where the rifle butt has been pounded into her face hard enough to crack her skull right around.

You slowly raise your horrified gaze up from the carnage in front of you and into the eyes of your new lover, and your instant reaction is, what, "Love your work, let's get married!"?

I don't think so. You might go along with the clean-up to avoid being

---

50 *The Dominion*, 27 January 1979

shot yourself by the monster across the living room, but at the first opportunity you'd be ringing the police and fleeing to safe quarters.

Let's assume, for argument's sake, that Len doesn't confess to the murders but instead tells you Harvey has beaten Jeannette and she, in self defence, has shot him then killed herself. You instantly suggest calling the police, but your new lover says no, let's hide the bodies and pretend it never happened.

Do you,
    a) Look at him as if he's barking mad
    b) Think, 'Yeah, that's a great idea'
    c) Quietly make a mental note to stop dating the wrong men, escape at the first opportunity and later sell your story to Oprah

I mean, *seriously*. To believe Norma Demler is the mystery woman requires a suspension of logic and human nature on an epic scale. People have only gotten away with this speculation because they haven't named her. If they'd named her, the public would quickly have worked out the theory was a lemon.

Len Demler has been dead 18 years. At any point in that time Norma could have come forward and confessed that Len did it and forced her to help clean up. She hasn't. And all this is assuming we first accept that Len Demler is the killer. For reasons already outlined, I honestly don't think he was, which reduces the probability of Norma being the mystery woman to zero.

Yes, if Demler was the killer, then Norma had opportunity to be there. Do I believe, like Chris Birt, that Norma knew Demler before the murders? Yes. Do I believe she had visited the area despite her denials? Yes. Do I believe that makes her a liar? On that construction, yes. Do I believe she helped Len fling a dead 16 stone Harvey across the back of a horse, ride down to the river and throw both him and the body of Len Demler's viciously beaten daughter into the Waikato River while calmly chatting to a whitebaiter, and then went on to marry the rogue Demler? No.

What's the upside for Norma in helping cover up a double murder or murder/suicide? *She has no motive.* Len Demler gained nothing financially from the killings as the farm was inherited by Rochelle, meaning Norma gained nothing. She was already a woman of independent means, with her own property in Howick at the time. By hanging around, and in fact marrying Len, she was making herself a target of the whispering campaign surrounding the Demler name.

Where's the payoff? I see none, just a massive downside, let alone the fear that one day the man sleeping beside you might kill you in the night as well.

If Norma was the mystery woman, and she and Len had dumped the bodies on horseback, then why on earth was she driving the Crewes' Hillman Hunter? Access to feed Rochelle could have been easily and surreptitiously gained just by riding a horse across the paddock from Demler's place to the Crewes after dark; no need to turn up at 9 in the morning in their car. Heck, it was only 700 metres, she could even have walked! My driveway is that long.

There's one thing that might assist a fresh police investigation into the killings. The rear-view mirror of Harvey Crewe's car carried a fingerprint that didn't come from either Harvey or Jeannette. That fingerprint should still be on the police file. To date, police have never revealed whose fingerprint it was, but it's a fair bet that if it was Demler's it would appear in the case notes as part of the evidence against him.

It would be a simple matter to fingerprint Norma Demler to exclude her, or anyone else who might pop up later in this book.

So here we are – we've reached a point where we've cleared the man long believed to have committed the murders, Len Demler, and we've named and cleared his alleged accomplice, second wife Norma Demler.

Forty years ago, when he too reached the decision that Demler wasn't his target, Detective Inspector Bruce Hutton and his team – desperate to close the case – quickly found someone else to pin all their hopes on.

Arthur Allan Thomas, a 32 year old farmer who lived 20 minutes away, was about to be sliced up, diced up and served up in the most well-documented case of police corruption in the past four decades.

CHAPTER 6

Murder Suspect No. 2

The first inkling Arthur Allan Thomas had of trouble in sleepy Pukekawa was some news on the bush telegraph on the afternoon of June 17, 1970. "I think a stock agent said that four miles from Tuakau Bridge, there's a bloodstained farm or something. I was trying to work out where this particular place was, the bloodstained farm, and that's before the news came out. Then later, maybe it was the next day, we heard Jeannette and Harvey Crewe were missing."

I ask Thomas what went through his mind when he found out Jeannette, a girl he'd tried to "court", had disappeared. He looks down for a moment, remembering. "S*** a brick, you know, it's Jeannette! I used to chase her along a bit in school. And the bloodstains, see? There's nothing missing, just bloodstains there. Something's wrong, it told me."

Thomas was rapt, he says, that police and members of the community had initiated big searches to find Jeannette and Harvey. "I couldn't search myself," he explains, answering a question that's often been raised, "because I had the farm and no workers to help me." He and Vivien were also dealing with a very sick cow that later became crucial to his case. Nonetheless, Vivien did help out where she could. "The ex did make up some scones to give the searchers, to help support them. I was rapt to see the police with the big search, people, everyone, go and look over the whole farm and checking dams and creeks and water tanks and everything they can think where they might be – even the hay bales had been shifted. Everything – everything was well checked out and I was rapt about the fact they're on to it."

The big issue on everyone's mind, he remembers, was "what the hell's happened up there? I told Vivien I went to school with her, and I chased her along a bit."

Vivien remembers that conversation. "When it first came out that the Crewes were missing, I think Arthur may have said that while he was at Maramarua working in forestry, he'd tried to take Jeannette out. But he only said that in passing.[51] We wondered what had happened and what a terrible thing it was. Arthur would say that Jeannette was a lovely girl and too nice to have something like that happen to her."

Before going any further, it is probably worth briefly highlighting what would become the foundation stones of the police case against Arthur Thomas, so you can keep them in mind as we move forward. With absolutely no forensic evidence (fingerprints, hair samples etc) linking Thomas to the scene of the crime, the actual police case against the Pukekawa farmer hinged on a handful of main allegations which I'll itemise here for simplicity:

1. **BULLET FRAGMENTS COULD HAVE BEEN FIRED BY THOMAS RIFLE**
2. **CARTRIDGE CASE DEFINITELY FIRED BY THOMAS RIFLE**
3. **AXLE UNDER HARVEY CAME FROM THOMAS FARM**
4. **WIRE ON BODIES MATCHED WIRE ON THOMAS FARM**
5. **THOMAS LIED ABOUT MEETING HARVEY CREWE**
6. **WATCH STOLEN FROM HARVEY TAKEN BY THOMAS TO LOCAL JEWELLER**
7. **MOTIVE & OPPORTUNITY**
8. **MYSTERY WOMAN WAS REALLY VIVIEN**

We'll return to these as a group in the Trial chapters, but for now, simply keep them in mind while the evidence you are about to read follows the chronology of the case as police wove their web.

For the first two weeks after Jeannette and Harvey's disappearance, it had been a relatively distant – albeit disturbing – community event. But Arthur Thomas' world was about to endure a seismic shift. On July 2, 1970, he received a visit from Detective Sergeant John Hughes making a "routine inquiry". It was a hair-raising experience.

"Hughes came to question me. I was just coming back from my

---
51 "A life sentence", *North & South*, July 2010

tractor, feeding out, and Hughes was there. He got caught in the electric fence – he swung open his car door and caught the electric fence and got a bit of a shock, but anyhow, he just wanted to question me about where I was on the night of the 17th, and I said, 'Yeah, I was home that night'. That went on about half an hour I suppose. I told him all the bits and pieces between me and Jeannette, went to school with her and all this, and he went 'Oh yeah, yeah, yeah' and all the stuff and then he went off."

Arthur was one of those people who volunteered everything to police, so he explained how he'd corresponded with the missing woman back in the early 60s, and how it was a terrible thing that had happened down there at the Pukekawa farm, and how he'd even worked there once or twice topdressing, long before Harvey and Jeannette took over, back when it was run by a manager, John Handcock. Hughes, to his discredit, would later falsify his notes to tell the court Arthur had admitted meeting Harvey Crewe "there" at the farm. It wasn't possible. Barr Brothers Aviation records confirmed Thomas' last job with them was early 1965, more than a year before Harvey Crewe came up to Pukekawa from Wanganui.

"He was not able to give me anything specific," John Hughes noted about Thomas' movements between the 17th and 22nd of June, "and I asked him to think back to the night of 17 June. He said that he would have been home with his wife. He said he couldn't say why he was certain of this, but knew he had been."

Hughes climbed back in his car, careful to avoid the electric fence this time, and disappeared down the dusty country road. For the Det. Sgt., this was just intelligence gathering. As far as the police officer was concerned, Len Demler was still the guilty one and a few days later he would tell Len exactly that "in no uncertain terms", according to his police file notes. We can only speculate, when Demler was bemoaning how somebody had electrified his front gate, whether John Hughes patted him sympathetically on the shoulder and said, "been there, done that".

The police didn't return to Arthur Thomas until a month later, August 12, 1970. During their search of the Crewe house, police had found an old Christmas gift from 1962, a brush and comb set, apparently still wrapped up, stored in a spare room. The card read, "To Jeannette, best wishes for a Happy New Year. From Arthur." Detective Bruce Parkes was assigned the job of visiting Thomas to confirm it was his writing, and later admitted at the second trial he told Thomas about the wrapped up present.

"One of the police came around with a Christmas card," says Arthur, taking a sip of steaming coffee. "He made sure I didn't touch it though – fingerprints! I just told him, 'Yeah, that's my card', and he said 'alright' and walked away."

Police still had no real leads. Demler remained the main suspect, but by early August police still had no forensic evidence to nail the old farmer with and, more to the point, no motive – not even one they could massage across the finish line. They'd called off the search for the bodies of Jeannette and Harvey the previous week – after nearly eight weeks of sifting through bush, pasture, river and reeds to no avail. Suddenly, on August 16, all that changed.

Two men, Joseph Adams and John Gerbowitz, whitebaiting in an area known as "The Devil's Elbow" – where the Waikato river gathers its skirts for a final dash to the sea out towards Port Waikato – had come across what appeared to be a body wrapped in bedclothes, tied with wire. Det. Inspector Hutton arranged for Len Demler to be brought to the riverbank for the unveiling of the face – formal identification.

"I just took Demler down and showed him her body when we brought it out of the water," Hutton later told David Yallop, "and I was watching him like a damn hawk, looking for any glimmer of reaction."

Clearly, Jeannette had been shot in the head. Her face was also badly injured and the body bore the ravages of two months in the water. A post-mortem that evening confirmed the deceased was Jeannette Crewe, and that she'd died from a bullet delivered by a .22 calibre firearm held to her right temple while she lay on the ground with the left side of her head on the carpet.

Pathologist Frank Cairns, who'd earlier told police guns were not involved, provided a report to the initial depositions hearing. "The line of fire of the bullet was from right to left and slightly forwards...I think it...likely that the weapon was fired when she was lying on the floor with the left side of her face to the floor. From the reconstruction of the bloodstains and from the other injuries she showed, that is to say, the injury to the tissue about the right eye, the injury to the nose and the fracture to the nose, these all suggested to me that she had received a blow to the face with a blunt weapon and that this had knocked her to the ground and while on the ground the shot had been fired. The bloodstain on the carpet suggested that she had been bleeding on the floor, there was a clear area in front of the fire where there were no bloodstains and this suggested that she had been lying partly on a mat which could have been in front of the fire."

For the record, Dr Cairns' initial examination found an exit wound in Jeannette's left temple, although police had found no bullet fragments or bullet holes in the house itself, and the fatal shot appeared to have been a contact wound. "There was blackening around the edge of the skin wound and in the entrance wound in the skull. These appearances would suggest a firearm fired at close range."

Knowing they were dealing with a shooting, Hutton's men fanned out to seize .22 rifles or pistols from anyone living within a five mile (eight kilometre) radius of the Crewe farm. Why five miles? It appears to have been an arbitrary, doodle-on-the-back-of-an-envelope punt by Hutton that had no basis in logic. The killer could have been anyone in the wider Pukekawa district or even from outside it, but limiting the search to a five mile radius meant ruling out potential suspects. In contrast, Det. Inspector Emmett Mitten's hunt for the December 31st 1969 killer of hitchhiker Jennifer Beard was also still underway at time of the Crewe murders, and virtually every green mid-50s Vauxhall Velox car in the whole of New Zealand (29,000 of them) was traced (see Appendix chapter on new leads in Beard case). Mitten told me nearly 50,000 people were interviewed in relation to the Beard murder.

Although Arthur Thomas lived outside the five mile radius, police came to seize his Browning pump action rifle because of his previous acquaintance of Jeannette Crewe. "They told me they wanted to take my gun for testing. I said 'not a worry, that's not a worry at all'. So they grabbed my .22." These days, he says, he'd tell police to go away and get a warrant, but back then Thomas says he was a huge fan of police.

"When that policeman came to collect the rifle," Vivien Harrison told *North & South*, "Arthur told me not to worry about it. He said they were doing an investigation and we had to do everything we could to help."

Arthur's rifle was one of only 64 taken away to the DSIR for forensic analysis; there were some 2,000 similar rifles in the Pukekawa farming district. Test firing, with the bullets then compared to the one removed from the body of Jeannette Crewe, showed 62 of the 64 seized rifles could not have fired the fatal shot. Guns, like fingers, leave individual prints on the bullets as they travel down the barrel being spun by the rifling groove that gives that type of gun its name. According to the DSIR, the Thomas rifle, and another in the possession of local resident Mickey Eyre[52], could not be ruled out at this stage, based on the partial bullet fragments police had recovered. The problem is, if two guns out of 64 couldn't be ruled out, how many more guns might have been listed as potential murder weapons if the 80,000 or so .22 rifles in the greater Auckland area had been tested?

But which of the two remaining rifles was closest in match to the bullet fragments?

"On two of these rifles," the DSIR's Donald Nelson discovered, "the width of the land markings [rifling marks] was identical."[53] Not just close – identical. One of these was the Thomas rifle, the other, of course, was Mickey Eyre's. The fact that two different guns could have "identical" marks to one bullet clearly shows a problem. Either gun could have fired the fatal shots, but obviously so could another gun entirely.

Remember, police did not have a perfect full bullet so they could never get a perfect match. There was always going to be a certain ratio of guns which matched at least the parts of the bullets recovered. If the margin of error was 3% (two out of 64), then 3% of 80,000 guns would leave more than two thousand four hundred .22 rifles that couldn't be ruled out, based on the law of averages.[54]

Still holding his gun, police called Arthur Thomas into the station

---

52 The gun itself belonged to Jack Brewster, a friend of the Eyres.
53 Testimony to first trial, 1971
54 In my opinion, Bruce Hutton's investigation of the Crewe murders was one of the most third-rate police investigations it has ever been my misfortune to witness. The failure to test a wider range of guns bordered on criminal negligence, and in stark contrast to police efforts on the Jennifer Beard murder where nearly every Vauxhall in NZ was checked. The Thomas files disclose comparisons to a 1948 British case, where a three year old girl named June Anne Devaney was snatched from a hospital ward, raped in a nearby park and then her little body dashed against a wall to kill her in the city of Blackburn. Police knew they had the fingerprints of the killer, but they had no leads on who the killer was. If Hutton had been in charge I'm confident the killer would never have been found, but luckily he wasn't. Blackburn Police made the tough call that they would fingerprint *every man living in the city* in their hunt for the murdering rapist who tortured and slew the three year old. After checking 45,000 fingerprints, they found their man, a 22 year old soldier who subsequently admitted his guilt and was hanged. You can Google her name for details of the case if desired. Now, that's a real investigation. Hutton's was a screw-up from beginning to end.

on 7 September 1970 for an interrogation. "Arthur," began Detective Bruce Parkes, "it was your rifle that was used to kill the Crewes. What do you say to that?"

Thomas' eyes went as round as saucers. This was a development he hadn't expected. "If you say it was my gun, it must have been, but I didn't do it," he stammered. Looking back on it now, Thomas accepts he was far too trusting of the boys in blue.

"Me, yep, 100%. Police A1 – A1 in my day. Yes, we were taught that. And when the Crewes were found to be murdered, the bodies were found, let's find out who done this, you know. That's why I was very forward in telling the police where I was, call it my alibi – it's my whereabouts on the night of the crime. *Very* important where I was – with my cousin Peter and my wife. Not nine miles away [at the Crewe house]."

Thomas kept on hammering the point home to the detectives, it was all he had: "I wasn't out on the night of the 17th of June. We had a sick cow, Vivien and me had been to the dentist that day. We told him about the sick cow and that it was about to calf. There was a ratepayers meeting at the hall on that night we were supposed to go to but we couldn't. My cousin Peter Thomas was with us, so we just had a night in."

Arthur pauses in the interview, clearly reminiscing in his memory. I wanted to know if he'd ever doubted himself. "Did you ever," I ask, "I mean some of the things that sometimes happen to people when they're interrogated and harassed by police, after a while they sometimes even half begin to suspect maybe what if I did do it and I've just forgotten. Did you ever go through a dark moment like that and wonder if you'd blacked out or done something silly?"

"No. No. Never done. No," Thomas replies emphatically. "You've got to remember, it wasn't just me that would have had to forget, it was Vivien and Peter who had to forget hearing me, and everyone along the road who had to forget hearing me car, and me dogs blacking out and forgetting to bark when I came home again. I knew I was at home. I always knew. So did the ex.

"They gave me a very hard questioning in Tuakau Police Station. Phil Seaman – he's just died too – he's from Rotorua I think he is – was. And he really give me a big grilling one part. Very severe. Not hitting round the head or anything like that, but really got stuck into me."

Police, playing a traditional good cop/bad cop routine, threatened to book Arthur for the double murders on the spot, but he kept on denying any involvement in the crime. Relenting, they took him home, and the next morning Det. Sgt. Mike Charles called around to return Arthur's gun.

"The gun's been tested," Thomas recalls him saying, "and it's not the gun we're looking for."

"Well, I knew that!" Thomas snorts as he relives it. He presumed that was the end of it. As we all know, it wasn't. The following week, September 16, the body of Harvey Crewe was found – this time by local Tuakau policeman Constable Gerald Wylie – the man who was first on the scene when the Crewes were reported missing. According to David Yallop, Bruce Hutton had "dreamed" the previous night that he was about to find Harvey, although Hutton wisely didn't mention this in his depositions evidence, where he described the find:

"On pulling my own boat closer in, I was able to observe a thin wire around the body, firstly travelling under the left armpit, across the back and over the right shoulder. A further piece of wire could be seen around the stomach of the body."

While police divers tried to slip a body-cradle underneath the decomposing corpse, Hutton says he "reached over and placed one hand under the shoulder of the body nearest to me in an attempt to free the body as at that stage we either thought it was weighted or deeply entrenched on numerous snags that were present.

"At that precise moment, I felt an object under the body and close to it...The object I felt," said Hutton, "felt to me like iron or something very solid but the weight was such that I had no chance to pull it towards me." That object, allegedly, was a car axle, later retrieved by the police dive team. The following day the axle was taken to Peter Garratt, a workshop owner in Pukekawa, later appointed a Justice of the Peace. Police wanted to find out if Garratt was responsible for repair work on the axle, and if so whether he knew who owned it.

"Within a day of taking the axle out of the river," Garratt has said, "they brought it to me at the garage in Pukekawa...The axle had obviously had some welding work done on it at some time."[55]

So far, so good, but Garratt was surprised, in 1978, when shown

---

55 *Beyond Reasonable Doubt*, page 54

photos of the axle and then the axle itself, to discover the axle presented as evidence in Arthur Allan Thomas' trial did not appear to be the same axle police had brought to him from the river in 1970.

"The axle I have recently seen at Dr Sprott's was not the same axle. I can't swear to it, but I'm pretty sure that was not the one that the police brought to me after they had recovered the body of Harvey Crewe from the river," said Garratt. "The one I saw at the laboratory has got one stub on and the other missing. The axle they showed me that afternoon at Pukekawa either had two stubs or none at all. In either event, the ends were uniform."

For David Yallop, this testimony formed the basis of a 'switcheroo-theory' – that perhaps police had swapped the original axle hauled from the water with one more evidentially favourable to their case against Thomas. It's possible, but I'm not convinced. There's a photo of Harvey Crewe's body in the water, and Det. Insp. Hutton holding the axle right above it. In that first photo, there are no stub axles (the part that the wheel is bolted to) attached to the main shaft – both ends are uniform.[56]

However if police had found Harvey Crewe's body in six feet of water in the Waikato – not because of an observant constable who just happened to be in the right obscure spot at the right time, but because someone had tipped them off, then a range of possibilities as to the framing of Arthur Thomas suddenly emerge. Supposedly, Harvey's body had been weighed down with a cast iron car axle. If so, that meant it was likely to have been found in the place where it was dumped – it had to have been because Hutton claims the axle appeared to be attached to the body until he shifted it.

Except, if a rogue cop such as Hutton's offside Detective Len Johnston knew the identity of the real killer and was protecting him, then he could also have known where the body was.

Johnston, you see, was about to become a key player in the Crewe murders – with a role in procuring virtually every single piece of evidence against Arthur Thomas. And if Johnston knew where the body was, then he could also arrange for it to be found with important evidence. I simply flag this for now. Keep it in mind – later in the book it will become much more relevant.

---

56 There is however the strange matter of an Auckland car restorer who in 1979 confirmed police had taken a Nash car axle away from a vehicle he was restoring, and had not returned it for a long time. Yet police denied taking his axle when questioned by the media.

It was Len Johnston who went to knock on Arthur Thomas' door with a list of questions about the axle. Johnston had just happened to have taken a phone call from a man who remembered selling a trailer based on the axle of a 1929 Nash car, to someone in 1958. As police checked the records, they found that trailer was eventually purchased in 1959 by one Allan Thomas, father of Arthur. That knock on the door, October 13, 1970, was the first time Arthur Thomas had met Len Johnston.

"Yeah, he came on the axle business, questioned me about the axle and all this stuff. 'There's no bloody axle,' I told him. 'I don't know anything about axles on this farm'." Arthur remembers steering them in the direction of his father, then living at Matakana near Warkworth, for further information. Johnston left, but only after taking some wire samples and all of Arthur Thomas' .22 ammunition he could find. "They grabbed my bullets, a whole packet of bullets," Thomas recalls. They turned out to be crucial bullets in the case against Thomas.

There was one other thing Len Johnston reported about his conversation with Thomas that day. He quizzed him about the brush and comb set he'd given Jeannette back in 1962, and whether Arthur knew what had happened to it. "It could still be wrapped up for all I know," Arthur allegedly said according to Johnston's notes, probably recalling what Detective Bruce Parkes had told him on the previous visit to verify the card.

That night Johnston was back at the Crewe farm, firing a gun in the company of Hutton and DSIR scientist Donald Nelson. He'd come up with the idea that Harvey Crewe had been shot by a killer crouched on the kitchen window ledge, firing through open, curtainless louvre windows. He reached this conclusion after realising the louvres had been found in the open position when police turned up.

"It was quite possible, in fact relatively easy, to shoot accurately… from the position I was in," Dr Nelson told jurors at Thomas' first trial. It may well have been easy, but it was highly unlikely that the Crewes had left their windows open, or that the killer had opened them to take a shot.

There may have been a couple of reasons for those windows being found open which had nothing to do with gunshots whatsoever. Firstly, baby Rochelle's dirty nappies had been left atop the fridge by whoever had looked after her, and additionally the nappy she was found in was a stinker – by the agreement of all who ventured on the scene. So it's possible the killer or his accomplice had opened the windows to freshen the air. The second, and even more likely theory is that the killer opened the windows after the Crewes had died, while he was burning a cushion and some other evidence in the fireplace. Quite probably, it got far too smoky inside and the room needed to be aired out, not just so the killer could breathe but for that matter baby Rochelle.[57]

What I don't subscribe to for a second is rogue cop Len Johnston and Hutton's claim that Arthur Allan Thomas perched precariously on a window ledge in darkness, in the middle of a winter storm, and opened the louvre windows just three metres away from Harvey Crewe, seated in his armchair, in order to take a shot. That's the police fabrication, and it simply doesn't work. We know from the bullet trajectory that Crewe was shot from behind and to the side. If your kitchen windows (they were louvres so when open they created a gap about 60cm square) suddenly opened in the middle of a winter storm metres from where you sat, you'd turn around, yes? Additionally, they make a grating noise as they open, over and above the wind and rain rushing in.

Journalist Pat Booth checked the weather records for the day in question and found winds reached speeds of around 30 knots that evening – officially regarded as "moderate gale force". There had been nearly an inch of rain that day. The vision I get in my head of the killer perched on the windowsill in such circumstances has more in common with a hapless *Pink Panther* cartoon than real life. The windows had no curtains, and the killer could easily have been seen. With a decent gust of wind the killer could have been blown into the kitchen!

And is it likely, as the Crown argued, that the Crewes had a fire on, on the one hand, and yet they had deliberately left their kitchen windows open at the same time in a winter storm? No. The killer could not possibly have surprised the Crewes in this way, yet regardless of that inconvenient fact two juries bought this lie.

---

57 We know something was burnt in the fire because forensic experts found the remains of a kapok cushion there. We know that burning took place at around 7.30pm on the evening of Friday 19 June, because farmer Ross Fleming and his eight year old son Robert drove past the Crewe house and noticed sparks coming out the chimney, and Fleming told police this on Tuesday June 23. We also know it cannot have been Arthur and Vivien Thomas burning anything at the house, because they have a cast-iron alibi: at 7.30pm that Friday they were both attending a 21st party for Arthur's sister Margaret Stuckey in Pukekohe, where they remained until close to midnight. All of which the police knew, long before they charged Thomas.

Having tested his windowsill gunshot theory at the Crewe house, and then been to see Arthur's father for more information on where old trailer parts could be located on the Pukekawa property, on 15 October Len Johnston returned to the Thomas farm at Pukekawa to put his newly acquired data into action.

He was just an obliging sort of a guy," Thomas recalls, "had cups of tea with us, when he was looking on the farm for axles and needing part of the axles at the start. I remember him grabbing some banana passionfruit and he had a little scoff there when I was talking to him." Johnston certainly knew how to ingratiate himself.

Ever the accommodating host, Arthur Thomas even helped Johnston search the three dumps on his farm for any parts relevant to the axle. Johnston and one of his colleagues were crawling through the dumps, occasionally joined by Thomas. "Len Johnston and I were scraping all the bits and pieces through, and I threw some stuff, trailer parts, onto the top of the grass for them."

Try as they might, however, they found nothing in the Thomas farm dumps on October 15 that was relevant to the axle. Detective Len Johnston was to enjoy stunning good fortune on October 20, however, when he returned to the Thomas farm yet again with Detective Bruce Parkes. He asked for more wire samples. "Sure thing," ventured Arthur. Then Parkes asked if he could have Arthur's rifle again.

"Sorry Arthur, we'd like your gun back to do some re-testing."

"But the gun's been tested!" Arthur remembers protesting, "and it wasn't the one." Vivien, too, queried why the gun would be needed again, but nonetheless fetched it from the laundry. Police had already taken and test-fired the Thomas gun a month earlier, so the couple knew that can't have been the real reason. Johnston had another request up his sleeve: he wanted to search the dumps on the property again. "You don't have a spade I could borrow, do you?" he asked genially.

"Go for it," said Arthur, not expecting what happened next. The only thing that could have topped it was if Johnston had forced Thomas to do the digging and told him 'it's your grave, son'. The police had only been gone a minute or two when Johnston came back, carrying the spade and a barely disguised grin. The two stub axles he'd found had been put straight into the police car – Johnston didn't tell the Thomases what he'd discovered and taken. Forty years after the event, Arthur Thomas now realises he was done like a dinner by Johnston.

"Oh, they planted them alright, the cops planted them. I'll tell you why. Johnston and myself looked over the whole area [during the search on the 15th] and then we started pulling bits and pieces off. First we checked the area, then looked around at the dump, it was a big steep sort of a cliff thing. And we walked the whole blinkin' area and then we started to rake stuff out. Any part of an axle or any part of a trailer, I had to throw up on top of the bank and no doubt, in his mind and in my mind, because there's no bloody stubs there at the surface; yet a couple of days later this particular cop hopped in there – 'oh, they're there!' – you know damn well … that was a set up."

The Royal Commission came to pretty much the same conclusion:

"Inspector Parkes gave evidence that they collected their wire samples and that Detective Johnston then borrowed a spade and began foraging around on the tip. He said that, of three tips on the farm, Detective Johnston was concerned to search only one. After only a few minutes, to use Inspector Parkes' words, 'Detective Johnston located two stub axles. One was probably partly uncovered, but the other was buried.'

"Inspector Parkes said that Mr Johnston knew what they were, and seemed quite excited by his find. He did not search the tip any further that day. Inspector Parkes very fairly agreed that it was an extraordinary piece of luck that the two stub axles, which were to become such significant exhibits, just fell into Detective Johnston's hands. We can only agree, particularly having regard to the fact that he had already searched the tip 5 days before. We find the circumstances in which the stub axles were located peculiar in the extreme."

It's a matter of public record that of three dumps on the farm, Johnston made a beeline for one only (and it had been previously searched without anything being found) and located two stub axles, one buried, within minutes. In my experience as an investigative journalist, particularly in criminal matters, I've found the concept of "coincidence theory" is vastly overrated: when there's a lot at stake in something, coincidence rarely gets a nose in.

What was taking place was the stuff of legend: police were attempting to frame an innocent man for the murder of Harvey and Jeannette Crewe. You'll recall how Len Johnston had seized a box of

Thomas' .22 ammunition back on October 13. Significantly, Johnston entered no record of precisely how many bullets he had taken from Thomas. Then, that very evening of October 13, police had test-fired a gun at the scene of the crime.

Clearly Johnston had a plan, and with the seizure of Thomas' gun for a second time it was about to play out. Johnston didn't need the gun for ballistics testing – he and Hutton needed it to fabricate evidence against Thomas.

Julie and Owen Priest, farmers who lived across the road from the Crewes, were surprised to hear gunshots coming from the Crewe house one afternoon in the latter half of October.

"They were standing near the roadway on their property when they heard two shots from the direction of the Crewe home," the Thomas Royal Commission later found. "They looked in that direction and saw two men near the back door. A short time later, while they were walking along the road, Mr Hutton and Mr Johnston came along in a car. A conversation followed. We accept the evidence of Mr and Mrs Priest that Mr Priest asserted the two policemen had just fired two shots at the Crewe farm. Far from denying this, Mr Johnston said 'How do you know?' To which Mr Priest replied 'We heard you'. Giving evidence before us, Mr Hutton denied firing the shots, but we do not believe him. We find that Mr Hutton and Mr Johnston fired two shots at the Crewe home that day," said the Royal Commission report.

It is now certain, based on what the Royal Commission discovered, that police fired Arthur Allan Thomas' gun, using Arthur Allan Thomas' bullets they'd seized (conveniently uncounted by Len Johnston so lawyers could never pin police down on whether bullets were missing), and had planted one of the spent cartridge cases in the garden. This faking of the evidence was crucial to the police case, but it necessitated a complex and utterly unbelievable "just so" story of how the Crewes died. It was well known police had found no cartridge cases inside the house, therefore they could not suddenly now "find" a case in the middle of the lounge floor. But if they could plant a shell *outside* the house, they could get away with saying it had been missed in the initial search. However, an outside shell required an outside shooting, and that's why Johnston and Hutton ran a series of tests at the house to see if they could create an outside shot through the louvre windows to hit Harvey.

When they found they could, they went back to get Thomas' gun, so they could create a shell to match their chosen murder weapon and snap the trap shut. All this, at the same time as they fitted Thomas up over the axle.

The "discovery" of that planted cartridge would not happen for a few days yet, however. Instead, on October 21, the day after the stub axles had been "found" in the Thomas farm dump, detectives executed an 8am search warrant on the property. They scoured the dumps again, they pored over the Thomas car, they searched inside and outside the house. Among the items they took away were letters from old girlfriends, which then became "unavailable" to defence lawyers who needed to show that Arthur's attention to Jeannette was nothing special.

Among the items seized that day was a single .22 bullet, "found" in an old apple box full of nuts and bolts. Detective Stan Keith, who rose to the rank of Detective Inspector by the time of his retirement in the early 1990s, was the man who found what became the smoking bullet, later referred to as Exhibit 343. That single bullet just happened to be an exact match of the type of bullet, known as a 'number 8' because of the numeral imprinted on the base of the lead, found in the heads of Harvey and Jeannette Crewe.

There's no suggestion Keith planted the bullet himself, because it's certain – given the other fabrication going on – that Len Johnston planted it in the shed during his visit the day before, where he knew one of his colleagues, who'd been properly briefed on what kind of things to thoroughly search, was bound to find it.

While snooping around in the shed, Stan Keith looked through a crack in the wall and says he saw Arthur and Vivien Thomas discussing something in the garden. He claims to have overheard the softly-spoken Arthur say, "If they think I am guilty, I am and that's that". Keith says he couldn't hear anything the sharper-voiced Vivien said.

The words would later assume great significance at Thomas' trials, but it was pretty obvious to a fair and objective observer that they were taken out of context. If Arthur Thomas had uttered them, they turned out to be highly prophetic, because police did indeed do everything they could to make the crime fit him. Thomas, however, maintains he didn't say it.

"What happened there?" I asked him at his home.

Arthur: I was working at a rotary hoe. I did talk with the ex but his words were that, "Oh, if they think I'm guilty, I am and that's that." I think that's the words he used. I did talk to the ex and whether he changed some wordings around to suit himself; I don't know. But I say, I can't remember saying that.
Jenny: That would be a typical reaction of you though.
Arthur: A typical reaction of the police, 'oh let's duddy this up.'
Jenny: Cos you're like that; that would be a typical...
Arthur: Yeah.
Jenny: I can see you saying that.
Arthur: Oh stuff them, you know, but.
Jenny: He's obstinate at times; he's...
Arthur: Yeah, but to use those words; no, that's...as I said to Hutton, no I can't remember. I can remember the conversation and the rotary hoe, yeah. but he listened through a wall, a wall in the car garage. I was outside with the rotary hoe going. And either himself, changing some words around or whatever to suit – dud it up a wee bit – that's common for the police to do.

And indeed, that's precisely what Det. Sgt. John Hughes would end up doing later in court in regard to one of his own conversations with him. It wasn't difficult for police to latch onto Arthur's unique verbal style, and doctor up a phrase that sounded like something Arthur would say. You could almost turn it into a parlour game creating new Arthurisms: "If the police say I'm a ten-foot tall bunny with big floppy ears and yellow spots, well I must be, but I can't see it myself." Arthur Thomas has an instinctive deference to authority – if an official says something he accepts them at their word even if he disagrees with it. It's not stupidity – Thomas is a smart man – it's being too polite for his own good.

The effectiveness of Stan Keith's version was proven in that even Arthur's wife Jenny, his partner of thirty years, recognised the Arthurism. Yet as Arthur points out, Detective Stan Keith claimed he heard this over the sound of a rotary hoe and strong wind.

"This conversation, as stated, never took place," Vivien told *North & South* magazine in July 2010. "There was certainly a conversation that day. I'd just cleaned the house and I was pretty upset [about police searchers trashing it, walking mud through the house]. What's really strange is that Keith claims he heard me say something to Arthur that he did not hear. But he heard Arthur's reply. I find this baffling because my voice is far more penetrating than Arthur's."

The phrase, although in Arthur's style, was out of character. This was a man who had repeatedly told the police it wasn't him, he had an alibi supported by two witnesses. He spent nine years protesting his innocence from behind bars. The actual words Keith claims to have heard reek of utter resignation to his fate – one thing that Arthur Thomas could never be accused of. For that reason, above all others, I think police made it up or utterly misheard or misrepresented what was actually said.

So these were the events of October 21, 1970. On October 22, Bruce Hutton came to meet the man he was framing for murder. It was just a brief visit, on the pretence of seeking Arthur Thomas' permission to uplift records from his solicitor. They would meet again on Sunday 25 October. The Thomases had been to a fancy dress fundraiser at the Onewhero Football Club on the Saturday night, October 24th; they didn't know it but it was one of their last social functions together as a married couple and it was marked by the now famous "pyjama photo". Knowing they'd been out late, Hutton decided to wake them up bright and early on Sunday morning and take Arthur and Vivien all the way to Otahuhu Police Station, 40 km away, for questioning.

Vivien was escorted to an interview room by Detective Len Johnston, while Arthur Thomas remembers getting a guided tour of the evidence police had assembled against him from Bruce Hutton.[58]

"Hutton showed me in his room, my rifle in the corner with a packet of bullets tied to the trigger, that's the last time I saw me gun. Well, it looked similar to my gun – it was supposed to be locked up but I did see a gun similar to mine in the corner of his office. Beside the rifle was the Christmas present and copper and galvanised wire. We went into the next room and he showed me the axle with the stubs on each side."

"What have you got to say in response to that?" Hutton asked.

Thomas cocked his head, looking at the neat fit of the stub axles to the main shaft. "They obviously go together," he answered after a moment. They walked back into Hutton's office.

"Arthur, did you go for a quiet drive up the road, I mean there is no harm in going for a drive".

---

[58] Based both on my interviews with Thomas, and the original handwritten notes of Thomas, republished by Pat Booth in *Trial by Ambush*, p117

"No, Mr Hutton, I never left the farm".

The Inspector wondered whether some of the famous Thomas moonshine – homemade wine – might have fuelled his prey on the night of the murders. "Sure you didn't get stuck into that and go for a drive?"

"I never touch the drink," Thomas replied, although his later experiences in prison would change all that. "Supposing I did," he ventured after a moment, "I'd need to get pretty rotten to do a thing like this. How am I going to get there with all the power poles and corners on the road. Supposing I was lucky and got there and did the job what was I going to do?"

The thought evidently occurred to Hutton as well, because he didn't bother answering and the idea of a drunken Thomas nevertheless committing the perfect murders never surfaced at trial. Instead, Hutton changed tack. "Well Arthur, the rifle, bullets, wire and axle all came off your farm, what do you say about that?"

Thomas, who was standing behind Hutton's desk, began to pace as the implications hit him. "Someone has obviously come on me farm during the night or the weekend, planning the murders, and they've taken what they needed so if it all blows up there's only one man to blame."

"Are you saying you've been framed?," challenged Hutton.

"Well, if that's the word you use then yes, that's what I mean, I have been framed," replied the farmer. Thomas remembers Hutton saying one other thing in particular, and it stuck with him through the trials and through the last four decades.

"Arthur, I have one other piece of evidence up my sleeve. I'm not going to tell anyone. I've a good mind to lock you up but, Arthur, I'm going to give you a chance".

Hutton has always denied saying he had another piece of evidence up his sleeve, but the way Arthur tells it he came away thinking Hutton was the good cop, his mate, while Johnston was the bad cop.

"Johnston did say to the ex about this evidence they had that points to me, and Hutton told me he had something up his sleeve, not telling me or anyone, and Johnston did say to the ex , 'We've got evidence that proved Thomas did it. Your husband did it'."

When Bruce Hutton offered Arthur the chance to sign a statement police had prepared, Arthur thought he was doing the right thing by the police inquiry:

I am a married man 32 years of age. I reside with my wife Vivien Thomas on my father's farm at Mercer Ferry Road, Pukekawa. The phone number is Pukekawa 838. I lease the farm from my father Allen Thomas who is living at Pt Wells, Matakana.

I am being spoken to by Detective Inspector Hutton about the deaths of Jeannette and Harvey Crewe in June of this year. I have been warned that I am not obliged to say anything more about this matter or to answer any further questions unless I wish to do so and that anything that I might say will be taken down and may be used in evidence.

I was brought up on the farm that I am now leasing from my father. In 1966 my father agreed to lease the farm to me for $2000 a year. I have been on the farm ever since. My marriage is quite a happy one. We do not have children but that is my fault.

I remember going to Pukekawa Primary School with Jeannette Crewe. We were both in the same class right through primary school. On second thoughts I was a class ahead of her until she caught up when I failed a year in standard one. I had quite a schoolboy crush on Jeannette at school. When I finished primary school I went and started work on the farm with my father. Jeannette carried on her education by going to St Cuthbert's. After this she became a schoolteacher at Maramarua. At this time I was working in the Forestry at Maramarua.

I met Heather Demler one night at a dance at Pukekawa and she mentioned that Jeannette was a schoolteacher at Maramarua. She told me that I should look Jeannette up. On my return to Maramarua I went and looked Jeannette up. I actually visited her a couple of times but I never took her out. Not very long later I heard Jeannette had gone overseas to England. I went round and saw Len Demler and asked him for Jeannette's address so I could write to her. I think I wrote to her twice whilst she was away. She was away for about two years. She replied to my letters. I now hand one of the letters from her to the police. Later when Jeannette returned I took her round a Christmas present. The brush and comb set I have just looked at is the one I gave her. The card has my handwriting on it. I did not take Jeannette out.

She did mention at the time I gave her the present that she had a boyfriend.

I have been asked about my movements on the night of the ratepayers' meeting of 17 June 1970. I remember soon after Jeannette and Harvey were missing Vivien and I discussed what we were doing that night. I recall remembering that we were home attending a sick cow. Peter

Thomas was home also. The cow had been sick for some time and I think Peter helped me the previous night but I am not sure. This cow was in a sling in the tractor shed and was sick for some time. I finally had to shoot this cow with my .22 rifle. I also remember that day as I think both Vivien and I went to our dentist in Pukekohe. We arrived back home at about 4 p.m. We attended to the cow between 5 p.m. and 6 p.m. I think I intended going to the ratepayers' meeting but by the time we had tea it was too late to go.

I have been shown the axle which was found with Harvey Crewe's body together with the two stub axles found by the police on my farm tip. After looking closely at these and also some photographs I agree that the axle and stub axles belong together. I cannot recall any of these articles being on my farm. I cannot explain how the axle got with Harvey Crewe's body. After looking at the axles I think they must belong to the old trailer.

I faintly recall the old trailer and the fact that there was some blue on it. I do not know what happened to that old trailer. Seems like the axle must have been on my farm but I cannot help any further.

I have been asked about my .22 rifle and where it was on the night of 17 June 1970. I am almost certain that this rifle could not have been taken out of my house without me knowing. I certainly did not lend it to anyone round that time. I remember using this rifle to shoot the sick cow I have mentioned, about two weeks after Jeannette and Harvey went missing. That dead cow is now on the tip on the farm where the stub axles were found. I also used the same rifle about a month ago to shoot a blind dog. I also put the carcass of this dog down at the farm dump. I also used to use this rifle to shoot rabbits with. Vivien does not shoot and Peter Thomas has never used this rifle to my knowledge.

I have been told that samples of wire found on my farm are similar to wire found on Harvey Crewe's body. I can only say that someone must have come on to my farm and taken the wire and axle. I have been told that the .22 bullets in Harvey and Jeannette's body had the figure 8 stamped on them and that similar ammunition with this number has been found at my farm. I cannot explain this. I was aware however that ammunition does have numbers stamped on the bullet.

I have viewed the brush and comb set I gave to Jeannette. I think this present cost me about four or five pounds. This was in 1962. I know Len Demler quite well but he has never been to visit me at my farm.

I have been told that a detective overhead me say to Vivien when I *was planting seeds on Friday something to the effect that if the police thought I was guilty then I must be guilty. I cannot remember saying anything like this to Vivien.*

I have been told about a pair of overalls found in the boot of my car having blood on them. I do not remember any blood getting on these. I use these overalls to fix a puncture or other repairs to the car when I am in good clothes.

The rubbish tip on my farm is used by me when necessary. I use it regularly and take all sorts of things to it. I remember a few weeks ago taking some stuff out of the horse stable to the farm dump. I also remember some time ago cleaning stuff out of a stable to put the Dodge truck inside. This was about two years ago. I remember seeing one of the wheel rims found by the police on my farm dump but I have not seen the axles there.

I did not help the police and local farmers with the search for Jeannette and Harvey Crewe but by the time I finished my daily chores by 1 p.m. I thought it would be too late to go. I thought that unless you could get to the Crewe farm by 9 a.m. you would not be able to assist. I was busy at that time of the year as my cows start calving on 10 June. I do not know how many cows I had in when the search started. I suppose I could of helped for a few hours but I was fairly busy.

I know I have been a suspect all along in this case. I suppose I did use to chase Jeannette along a bit and used to write to her. I have read this through and it is true and correct. I have nothing to add.

A. Thomas, 25 October 1970

Arthur had just signed off on a document that proved he'd been officially "cautioned" – read his rights – a sure sign police were preparing to charge him with murder. Yet he had no inkling that this was in the offing. He thought that Hutton agreed someone was trying to frame him.

While Hutton and Johnston had the Thomases bailed up at Otahuhu that Sunday, Detective Bruce Parkes was doing the rounds at Pukekawa, looking for anyone who could demolish Arthur Thomas' alibi. Thomas had denied going to the local ratepayers meeting on the night of the murders, for example – proof to the contrary would show Thomas was lying, and could have been within five kilometres of the Crewe farm on the night.

"Where were you on the night of 17 June," Parkes asked farmer

Brian Murray. "Was Arthur Thomas at the meeting?" Murray had attended, Arthur had not, he told the police officer. As David Yallop points out, Murray was one of a number of Pukekawa residents living *within* the five mile gun radius imposed by police, whose guns were *never* checked.

Brian Murray is dead now, but in 1971 he gave an interview for the final issue of *The NZ Weekly News*:[59]

"From June until October last year the police vehicles were, as you can imagine, a common sight in Pukekawa. Even when they started going up and down the Mercer Ferry Road I thought they were going only to the river. So help me, they were going to Arthur's place – and I didn't know. I was questioned for the first time on Labour weekend. The police officer asked me if I was at the ratepayers meeting on the night of June 17. I said that I was. Then he asked me if Arthur Thomas was there. I said I wasn't sure. It was only then that I realised they were after Arthur.

"I called at their farm and asked Arthur and Vivien what happened. Then it all came out. How they had been grilled for hours by the police and how articles had been removed from the farm. I said, 'my God, Arthur, they are going to pin this on you'. And do you know what the poor trusting fellow said? He said, 'it's all right, Brian. I've nothing to worry about. I've done nothing wrong'.

"It took me ages to convince them that they should consult a solicitor. I told them I wouldn't leave the house until they gave me their word they would get a solicitor the next day. Only then would Arthur agree to do anything."

Brian Murray later added that Thomas genuinely believed police were trying to help him prove his innocence.[60] "Inspector Hutton knows that, he's helping me to find out who's trying to frame me... Mr Hutton will find out who's at the bottom of this'."

There's a Tui billboard in there somewhere, and evidently Brian Murray thought so too. "I didn't become concerned enough soon enough about a man who was too trusting, too honest, too naive to take care of himself," he told *The Weekly News*.

Remembering back on it now, Arthur's face takes on a sheepish look.

"Brian Murray come to see the ex and I. 'Arthur, get a lawyer, things aren't looking good. They wanna arrest someone, it doesn't

---

59 *New Zealand Weekly News* August 23, 1971
60 *Beyond Reasonable Doubt*, p71

matter who it is'. And I said it was no worries. But see I was pretty naïve. I just…"

Arthur's wife Jenny get's a sly smile on her face, and gently teases him again. "Arthur's a very much, like 'head in the sand' type of guy, who's gotta be knocked over the head with a mallet. He's still like that in many ways."

"Well," interjects Arthur, as if to prove he's learnt his lesson, "if the cops come to me now with a question about something, hang on, I'm seeing a lawyer straight away, first thing. I'm all changed. I'm a changed man now."

"Yeah, no, you would be with the cops," agrees Jenny, "but you've still got that 'hit over the head with a mallet' type personality."

Thomas cracks up. It's easier to laugh now, so long after the event. At the time he didn't appreciate the funny side. "Isn't it nice, my wife saying that? But anyhow, that's Jenny."

"I know you well!"

The irony was that even though Arthur and Vivien agreed to Murray's request to see a lawyer, and their lawyer instructed them to say nothing without him being present, Arthur nonetheless welcomed Bruce Hutton back onto his property two days after they read him his rights. I couldn't quite figure this one out – despite all the warnings why was Thomas still being so cooperative?

"You'd got hold of Paul Temm," I probed, "and he said, 'Whatever you do, don't speak to the police'?"

Arthur: Yes, yes. And I still…

Ian: Then along come the police.

Arthur: Yeah.

Ian: Did you think, didn't the little voice in your head say, "Errrrrrrrr"?

Arthur: No, I've got nothing to hide in my mind, my conscience – I stood up every time. My conscience – my conscience was the one that was telling me 'not a worry'. The police wanted to do some sortie – not a problem. Even with Brian Murray telling me till the very last minute, they arrested me and sheesh, it was quite a, then my faith went off the police."

As it would. What you see here is one of the reasons so many people swung behind Arthur Allan Thomas all those decades ago. They knew the careful, meticulous killer of the Crewes did not have the same personality type as gentle, trusting Arthur Thomas.

In contrast to the killer who'd removed all the incriminating evidence, even fingerprints, without trace, here was a man in Thomas who, when police had failed to search his house properly, he went around and picked up what detectives had missed that he thought might be relevant, like letters from Jeannette, and handed them personally to Bruce Hutton.

Here was a man who made no attempt to dispose of his gun or swap its barrel, and who happily handed it over to police twice. Here was a man who, if you believe the police, weighted down Harvey Crewe's body with an axle, yet kept other key identifying components of the axle on his property, even helping police look for them, and didn't bother hiding anything.

Here was a man with the noisiest car in the entire Pukekawa district. Every time the Thomases drove anywhere, everybody knew – the grinding whine of its worn out differential saw to that. If you believe the police, Arthur Thomas had to slip out of his house and drive sixteen kilometres through the heart of Pukekawa at night in a car people could hear coming a kilometre away. Not only that, he had to do it unseen on a night when half the town was on the roads going to or from the local ratepayers' meeting at the hall, just five km up the road from Jeannette and Harvey Crewe's place. Not only that, he had to drive back home in his noisy car, confess to his wife that he'd just murdered a childhood sweetheart he was secretly in love with, and ask her to come with him as an accessory after the fact to help clean up before morning. They then had to drive their noisy Hillman Minx back through the district to the Crewe residence, then back through town to the Tuakau side of the Waikato River to dump the bodies, then drive their noisy car back through town past all their neighbours, back home. All of this without disturbing anyone including Arthur's 17 year old cousin Peter, who was staying with them.

Not only that, here was a man who had to repeat that feat several times over the next few days, as he or Vivien drove to the Crewes to feed Rochelle on several occasions. All of it unseen, unheard. He also had to develop the *Star Trek*-like ability to teleport himself between a 21st birthday party in Pukekohe on the Friday night after the murder – alibi verified by police – and the lounge of the Crewe house at the precise same moment where someone was burning evidence, witnessed by the Flemings.

The scenario above is so implausible, so ridiculous, that you wouldn't buy a movie ticket to see it as fictional entertainment, because no one could suspend their disbelief on such a grand scale for 90 minutes. Yet, two juries swallowed this without so much as a gulp. Did we breed our jurors stupid back in the 1970s?

Ah, but I haven't given you the *piece de resistance* in this police fit-up of Arthur Allan Thomas on a double murder charge. On 26 October, Labour Day Monday, police and the Crown solicitors had gathered to decide whether they had enough evidence to charge Thomas. The decision was 'no'. One of the officers, the ever reliable Det. Sgt. Murray Jeffries, then purely coincidentally suggested out loud to Hutton that detectives had not searched one patch of the Crewes' garden properly back in August.

"Excellent idea, what ho!" replied Hutton in words to that effect, "send two of your best chaps and get it done, just in case there's something there we missed." So while Hutton was visiting Arthur Thomas on Tuesday 27th, down in the garden at the Crewe house Detective Sergeant Mike Charles and Detective Bruce Parkes were sieve searching the one tiny portion of dirt that their bosses had suddenly remembered they'd "overlooked" three months earlier.

Imagine Mike Charles' surprise when, a couple of inches under some clammy, soggy clumped dirt, his fingers felt a bullet shell. The Royal Commission report sets the buildup:

"About 10.30 a.m., the two officers began their search of the earth in the garden. They initially used a small garden fork and a sieve, but soon found that the soil was puggy and damp, and would not break up even if shaken. They therefore adopted the system of Mr Parkes moving ahead to loosen and break up the earth with the fork as far as possible, while Mr Charles moved along behind breaking the soil down with his bare hands.

"The soil was searched to a depth of about 6 inches. After between 1 – 2 hours of searching, i.e. some time between 11.30 a.m. and 12.30 p.m., Detective Charles found the shell case which was to become exhibit 350. The shell case was buried in the garden, and we accept Detective Charles' estimate that it was buried to a depth of approximately 2 – 3 inches.

"Despite the pugginess of the soil, the cartridge case, curiously enough, contained bone dry soil, which fell out as Mr Charles handled it.

"Having examined the shell case with Mr Charles, Mr Parkes went to their car to attempt to contact Inspector Hutton by radio-telephone. He was not able to do so, probably because Mr Hutton was interviewing Mr and Mrs Thomas at their farm at that stage. The two accordingly continued their search until 1 p.m., at which time Mr Parkes was able to contact him by radio-telephone and arrange a rendezvous at the home of Mr and Mrs Priest. There they showed him the cartridge case."

David Yallop obtained a delightful interview with farmer Owen Priest on this point, which is worth revisiting.[61] "They arrived back here about one o'clock. They had their cup of tea and with that Mr Hutton and Mr Toothill arrived. Mike Charles put on one of my daughter's hats and a pair of sunglasses and was dancing around the room like a kid. That was the kind of atmosphere. I said to Julie, 'Those jokers have found something'. The air was electric. It's hard to describe," said Priest.

More soberly, the Royal Commission report noted:

"Its importance was obviously realised by all of them; all three went back to the Crewe house; Inspector Hutton was shown the position where the shell case had been buried, marked by a stake by Mr Charles."

Two days earlier, Bruce Hutton had gloated: "Arthur, I have one other piece of evidence up my sleeve." This newly discovered cartridge case was the only new piece of evidence to emerge in the case. Hutton appeared to have known two days in advance that it would be coming to him. Hutton, true to his word, didn't tell anyone outside the police about the cartridge. Arthur, on the other hand, did tell his lawyer, Paul Temm (later Justice Temm) about the odd comment Hutton had made. Neither man knew what Hutton was on about, as neither knew about the shell discovery. Hutton would break the news. But not yet.

First, he was throwing everything he could into breaking Arthur Thomas' alibi. It wasn't good enough to throw fake evidence at him, Hutton needed to destroy his prey's credibility so that jurors wouldn't trust him when he legitimately protested his innocence in regard to the shell case and axle stubs.

It should have been a rock-solid alibi. Arthur Thomas was at home

---

61 *Beyond Reasonable Doubt*, p75

all night, corroborated by two witnesses. Normally, police would admit such an alibi is "cast iron", but not in this case. They tried, for example, to break 17 year old Peter Thomas – hauling him in for questioning three times.

"They pulled him up a few times to try and... yes, put the pressure on him, yeah," Arthur told me. "He knows he doesn't have to cover anything up. They've got nothing; that's where I was – at home – and that's it. He'd say to me, 'oh, the bloody cops!' and I said, 'Just tell the truth. You've got nothing to hide. Tell the truth'."

Peter Thomas was subjected to the same tour of police evidence at the Otahuhu CIB that Vivien and Arthur had endured, and Yallop writes how detectives "told him there was no doubt his cousin had murdered the Crewes." The teenager reportedly burst into tears, tears of frustration as he tried to explain that Arthur had been home that night of the murders with him and Vivien. "I told them there was no way Arthur could have left that farm without me knowing.[62]

"They showed me the axle and the stubs. They said it had come off Arthur's farm. I was very upset. Both Hutton and Johnston insisted that I had seen it on the farm. I insisted I had not, because I hadn't. They went on and on insisting that I had, and that I should say that I had, that I must say I had. I couldn't understand why they were so desperate to get me to tell a lie, it didn't make sense." His sobs fell on deaf ears. Bruce Hutton and Len Johnston, for their own reasons, needed Arthur Thomas hung out to dry, case closed, and a boy weeping in their offices wasn't going to change that.

Over at the DSIR, scientists quickly worked out that the shell found in the Crewes' garden had been fired in Arthur Thomas' rifle, the reason for which is probably no great surprise to intelligent readers. But the senior forensic expert, Dr Donald Nelson, had been in Australia and didn't get back until November 6, 1970. Police waited for his verdict.

It wasn't until 11 November that Hutton and Johnston pulled up in the Thomas driveway, and asked Arthur to accompany them to the police station. Thomas remembers it being a cloudy, foreboding day, and he was just climbing up on his tractor to do some farm work. "Don't worry about the tractor, just leave it there," warned Len Johnston. Vivien had taken their cat to the vet, and

---

62 Ibid, page 70

the bewildered farmer didn't think to ring his lawyer. Remember, Arthur had already signed a statement saying he'd been read his rights. That meant anything he said to the police was admissible in evidence against him, and without a lawyer present, well, Arthur *did* like to talk.

At the end of a wide-ranging game of 'bamboozle the suspect', peppered with "when did you stop beating your wife" type questions to provide police with plenty of fodder for his later trial, Det. Insp. Bruce Hutton reached up his sleeve and pulled out the trump card he'd been gloating about.

"Look, Arthur, a .22 shell was found near the rear door of the Crewe house by the police. Scientists say that that shell was fired by your rifle…Arthur Allan Thomas, I am arresting you for the murders of David Harvey Crewe and Jeannette Lenore Crewe, on or about June 17, 1970 at Pukekawa. You have the right to remain silent and the right to consult a lawyer. Anything you say may be taken down and later given in evidence against you in a court of law…"

Arthur was dumbfounded, and suddenly regretted not making that call to Paul Temm. "I just said to Hutton, 'Look, I told you where I was when it happened', and I fixed on that. My whereabouts – that's the only thing I've got: I'm home, I was bloody well home!"

Thomas remembers asking to go to the toilet, just thinking over and over, "I can't believe it. I said, as I went out the door, 'My whereabouts is important – where I was.' Hutton just shrugged. 'We don't believe you.' And that's it, so I remember going to the toilet. He had to get an officer to come with me," Thomas laughs grimly – "he thought I was gonna run away or something."

It didn't take long for word of the arrest to spread. Auckland came alive with newsflashes on Radio Hauraki, Radio I and 1ZB that a 32 year old man had been arrested and charged with the Crewe murders. Vivien Thomas arrived home from the vet to be greeted with a cocky Detective Sergeant Mike Charles.

"Mrs Thomas, I'm required to inform you that we have arrested your husband –" he began.

"What for?!" she snapped.

"The murders of Harvey and Jeannette Crewe."

"You must be bloody mad," exclaimed the 28 year old Englishwoman.

"She got stuck into him," says Thomas, leaning forward in his seat, "and his words... his words to her were something like 'Oh, I admire your loyalty' or some wording to the effect. She was sticking up for me, only because she knew where I was. That's not the way he interpreted it – she knew all about it and was covering up for me. That's the good thing about the ex, even though she divorced me. She knows where I was when it happened. If it was the other way, that I'd done it and she knew, she would've blown the whistle by now."

Indeed, it's only logical and that's exactly one newspaper reported of Vivien Thomas back in 1971:[63]

"You can use a lot of energy complaining and weeping". Her husband had no motive and no opportunity to do murder. But, according to the police view, he must have "sprouted wings" to get to the Crewe homestead unseen, suddenly acquired the "strength of Atlas" to carry the bodies, and kept his "obsession for another woman" from his wife during six happy years of marriage.

"For my part, I am supposed to have cleaned up a house in which my husband murdered a woman he had been smitten with for years. If it wasn't so tragic, it would be laughable."

"If you think I am annoyed now, you should have heard me when that police officer told me, after Arthur's arrest, that he "admired my loyalty"," she cried disgustedly.

"I hated him for that. As if I would be loyal to a murderer. If I thought for one moment that Arthur had done that, he could rot in prison and I wouldn't care ... I know it is nine months since my husband's freedom was taken away but I haven't got time to think about what his absence is doing to me. You can't dwell on yourself. The one thing on my mind is to get a retrial for him and have him cleared. He can't do anything by himself. We have to do it for him. No, he hasn't become bitter. He has a tremendous amount of faith. He has not become resigned because too much is happening right now. Someone knows something – they must come forward. I can't imagine who can hate us so much to do this to us," says Mrs Thomas. "To see an innocent man locked away in prison. Why, if capital punishment was still in force, he would be dead by now."

The vehemence, the strength of Vivien's conviction that Arthur was innocent, came from intimate knowledge: Vivien didn't just "believe" him innocent because she loved him, she *knew* he couldn't have committed the murders – regardless of the axle or the cartridge

---

63 *New Zealand Weekly News*, August 23, 1971

case – because he was lying beside her in bed all night. She *knew* it was a fit up.

Now Vivien Harrison and living in Australia, she hasn't spoken to Arthur in decades but this year said she still feels the same way. "I never deserted Arthur. Had that been the case, I would not be here, saying what I'm saying now...What I did was end my marriage to Arthur. But I did not desert him. I know Arthur did not kill those people and I will declare his innocence until the day I die."[64]

Another who felt equally aggrieved was Arthur Thomas' childhood mate, the shotgun kid Malcolm McArthur, who bowled into Bruce Hutton's Otahuhu police station office, jabbing his finger at the surprised Detective Inspector. "You've got the wrong man."

"He was a great guy, he really battled for me on the Retrial Committee," Thomas says sadly. McArthur died while Thomas was overseas. He and Jenny were unaware of his passing. "He was a true friend," Jenny adds.

After some additional processing at Otahuhu Police Station, Hutton bundled his catch into a police Holden and had him driven firstly to Oakley Mental Hospital for a standard opinion that he was fit to be charged, then to the Otahuhu courthouse for a quick remand appearance, and then to his overnight accommodation. For Arthur Allan Thomas, those first hours after his arrest were a nightmare he still occasionally revisits in the darkness, even now. He recalls how his mind raced as the police car sped from the Otahuhu CIB to his remand cell at the grim and foreboding Mt Eden prison, 20 kilometres away.

"Where am I going? What the hell's going on? My mind was kind of chewing it all over, and the only thing I kept coming up with was the fact the jury – I've got a trial by jury coming up – I've got to let the jury know. My faith was in the jury straight off, because I'd lost faith in the police. I couldn't understand why they arrested me. They'd got the wrong guy here, I knew that."

All the way, Thomas was protesting his innocence, telling his alibi to anyone who would hear him. The problem was, no one in the car with him could be bothered listening. "They didn't say anything in reply."

As the car pulled into the Mt Eden carpark, Thomas remembers

---

64 "A Life Sentence", *North & South*, July 2010

thinking, "righto, the twelve good men of the jury are going to hear all this and I'm going to get in the witness box – which I did, both times. Just tell them where I was."

Call it misplaced trust, call it faith in human nature, call it what you like – Thomas was convinced he'd be free once he got his day in court, and a chance to explain his alibi. At the processing desk of the prison, he felt his nerves jangling on edge. It's one thing to drive past Mt Eden jail, it's quite another to be driven to it. The farmer was acutely conscious that he was now inside, and couldn't get out. His freedom was gone. He was momentarily turned into a prison guard's wide-eyed glove puppet as they conducted an orifice search for weapons and anything else – like shoelaces – that he could use to harm himself or others with.

For his very first meal in the prison canteen, Arthur was served by a pretty thing dolled up to the nines with lipstick and a mod hairdo. "She looks very nice," he said approvingly to the guard beside him. "*She's* got balls," the guard replied. "There ain't no women in this prison, son."

"I remember the smell," he tells me, "and there's inmates everywhere." He found, thanks to Radio Hauraki, that his infamy had preceded him. "Oh, yeah. Once I was there, I was hot news. 'Arthur Allan Thomas, arrested for the double murders.' Yeah. Oh it's hot news and Hutton had been doing his big spiel – 'We got the guy.' And there it was. So inmates were saying as I walked past, 'Oh here's the Crewe murderer there'."

On that first night behind bars, though, the farmer from Pukekawa was left mostly alone with his thoughts.

"Well, I just hear the noise when they close the doors – steel, big cast iron door, you know, it blocks the sound out a lot. I heard a little bit of noise, not much. And my mind, it's just right through, right through. I kept going into it, over and over: where I was on the night, and Jeannette – particularly Jeannette, you know."

Arthur, so naive and trusting and archetypal country bumpkin that his fellow prisoners would soon nickname him 'Hayseed', began to realise that by telling police he'd once fancied Jeannette Crewe, he'd helped to weave the very noose detectives had placed around his neck.

"Lord, I... what I told the police about her, you know, a little bit of how we were acquaintances there. What's going on here you know?"

One thing Thomas decided was to tell his lawyers everything. Anything that could be used against him in court by police probably would be. So Thomas worked on a doctrine of 'no surprises'.

"That's how they found out that I had a child out of wedlock. I thought, well I'd better tell them that because they'll pick it up. All the terrible things in my life – tell my lawyers, so they're ready for anything that might come up. My mind was squeaky clean as far as the lawyers because they knew more about me than anyone else," Thomas laughs sadly, the cackle of a man whose life was eventually laid so bare that even he couldn't hide from it.

Mt Eden prison in 1970 didn't offer its guests TV, computers or Playstations. Nor did it offer writing paper. So Arthur Thomas turned to the only option available to him:

"I wanted to put everything in writing for my lawyers eh, so I had plenty of time to do it and I used toilet paper. They told me later, 'you can rewrite all that out on the foolscap paper'. I said 'No. Too late.'

"So I was doing this for my lawyers on toilet paper. I keep writing, writing, writing. There were pages and pages of stuff going back to all the nitty-gritties in my mind, of the past, all the bits and pieces. Everything."

For barrister Paul Temm and his Pukekohe-based associate Brian Webb, Arthur's life-story unrolled before their eyes on prison-issue grit-grade bog-paper. "I needed to get it out of my system," Thomas chuckles.

At his next court appearance date, Thomas – as a double murder accused – was shackled and handcuffed for his trip to the Otahuhu Magistrates Court, and the infamous 'walk of shame' in front of the press and their wall of flashbulbs. Thomas' lawyers nonetheless managed to get images that implied guilt suppressed as prejudicial to a fair trial. "Handcuffs. I was handcuffed from then on. Handcuffed to officers. They didn't publish it, that particular photo, yes."

The formal court appearances were short. Thomas generally had only a brief glimpse at his wife and family in the gallery before being led away to the cells again. His first chance to talk to Vivien didn't come until he was back at Mt Eden Prison.

"I went there with my brother-in-law Ray, and my mother-in-law," Vivien said in a 1970s interview. "I can remember Mum was sobbing in her throat. We were all in some kind of shock. So was Arthur when we saw him. He asked how I was. Asked if the farm was alright. He was groping for words. He told me about the baby that he'd fathered long before we met. It rocked me, but I told him there were more important things to worry about. He'd wanted to let me know himself as he felt it would come out in the hearing."[65]

Brother Ray, who obviously didn't have the absolute proof that comes from sharing a marital bed with Arthur on the night in question, therefore felt the need to ask Arthur to his face whether he'd killed the Crewes. Thomas said no, and that if he had done it he would expect to be punished.

There was such an expectation that the court would quickly see Arthur's arrest as the mistake it clearly was, that Vivien even optimistically packed a suitcase of clothes for Arthur to wear home once he was released at the first depositions hearing, in December 1970. It wasn't to be.

By all accounts, the depositions hearing was a shambles where the police and Crown were permitted to pull stunts left right and centre, designed to keep Thomas' lawyers in the dark. For example, an official diagram of the Crewe house layout was produced by the Crown, but lawyers only discovered as a result of cross-examination that the layout plan was only drawn after police had first moved furniture around to fit Len Johnston's windowsill gunshot theory – created to support the planted shell case. In other words, the official record of the crime scene had been doctored, and the Crown prosecutors would not have revealed it themselves.

Lawyer Paul Temm had also become aware that Len Demler's car contained a four inch long bloodstain in the front seat, so he was surprised to find no photos of this bloodstain in official photographs produced as police evidence at the depositions hearing.

Crown prosecutor David Morris chose not to give an opening address, meaning there was no overall narrative of the prosecution case against Thomas. Paul Temm was forced to sit back and see what popped out of the box each morning. One witness whose evidence needed checking was Beverly Batkin, a friend of Jeannette's who seemed chronologically confused. She talked of Arthur Thomas "pestering" Jeannette at dances in 1956 and 1957. The only problem with that was, as we saw earlier in the book, Thomas didn't attend the dances because he couldn't dance in those days and didn't have

---

65 *Beyond Reasonable Doubt*, p95

transport. His dancing lessons commenced in 1959, as diarised by the mother of his best friend Merv Cathcart.

It was little things like this that kept popping up, little fires that needed extinguishing, all the time. Batkin's evidence nonetheless became a front page headline in the *Auckland Star*: "*Victim 'Pestered At Dances'*, Witness Tells of Man's 'Passion'."[66]

The defence team got their first hint of some of the weakness surrounding crucial police evidence like the axle. The Magistrates Court heard from the first police officers who secured Harvey's body, floating in six feet of water, and how they hadn't seen or felt an axle underneath him and attached – the one that Det. Insp. Bruce Hutton had immediately felt while reaching from the comfort of his boat.

The Otahuhu depositions hearing was also the first chance for defence counsel to become acquainted with Exhibit 350, the cartridge case "found" in the Crewe garden. Paul Temm knew it was coming, because Hutton's final comment to Arthur before arresting him on November 11 was a gloat about the shell case police had just found, and which they'd traced to Arthur's rifle. But it wasn't until the week before Christmas 1970 that Temm got to hear the story allegedly behind it.

Detective Sergeant Mike Charles explained how he and Parkes had been sent back on October 27 to search a patch of garden police had forgotten to search properly back in June and August. He told how he'd found the soil too wet and clogged to sift, but that his fingers felt the shell case about two or three inches under the surface. Despite the wet soil it was in, he recalled "bone dry" soil pouring out of the shell when he tipped it up.

In cross examination, Paul Temm asked whether Charles had considered the possibility someone might have framed Thomas by putting a cartridge case from his farm, "where the police could find it?" Charles replied the thought, "hadn't occurred to me, not when I found the shell." There was a pregnant pause. "Has it occurred to you since?", probed Temm. "Yes," admitted the Detective Sergeant.

The cartridge case issue didn't go away. DSIR forensic scientist Rory Shanahan told the court he had some misgivings about the state of the case. "Had it been exposed to the elements for an

---

66 *Auckland Star*, 14 December 1970

extended period of time, I would have expected more corrosion to be present." He clarified that "extended period of time" as "in terms of months". Funnily enough, Thomas' lawyers harboured exactly the same misgivings. For a bullet case supposedly buried in a wet winter garden for four months and ten days, it was remarkably shiny. Under further cross examination, Shanahan would later admit at the first trial that it "had no corrosion".[67]

The single bullet found by Detective Stan Keith in Arthur Thomas' shed, in an old apple box full of nuts and bolts, was also presented into evidence as Exhibit 343. The significance of this particular bullet is easily explained. When Stan Keith took it back to base, police removed the lead from the shell. On the base of the lead, the bit with its backside stuck in the shell case, the number "8" was stamped. The bullets that shot the Crewes were also Number 8's. A hundred and fifty-eight million of them had been produced by munitions company ICI, but production of the Number 8's had ceased in 1963, seven years before the killings.

This was the only bullet that could link Arthur Thomas to the Crewe homicides because, as would soon become clear, the other cartridge, the one in the garden planted by police, had an Achilles heel that would eventually prove devastating to the police case – a spectacular own goal on the part of Hutton and Johnston. In fact, at the risk of one too many clichés – you could say they shot themselves in the foot with the shell case they planted. All that, however, was in the future.

On 22 December, 1970, the justices of the peace hearing the depositions determined there was enough evidence to send Arthur Allan Thomas to trial for the murders of Jeannette and Harvey Crewe. Vivien went home without a husband, and still carrying that full suitcase of clothes.

---

[67] There was a footnote to this. The *Auckland Star*, on 5 August 1971, published a story where a Retrial Committee spokesman challenged the state of the cartridge, on the basis it showed no corrosion despite being buried in wet, peatish soil for four and a half months. The following day, the *Star* published a retraction: "The spent cartridge found outside the house of the murdered Crewe couple at Pukekawa was, according to a DSIR scientist at the subsequent murder trial, corroded, consistent with its having been exposed to weather and dirt for a long time." The newspaper said its retraction was published "at the request of the Police". The journalist behind both stories was long-time *Star* columnist Robert Gilmore, who said Hutton had phoned him. The retraction wasn't factually correct, the DSIR scientist did not say the cartridge was "corroded, consistent with its having been exposed to weather and dirt for a long time". The DSIR's Rory Shanahan in fact said: "I could not say for certain how long this had been outside." He added the shell, "*had no corrosion*". It seems the *Star* fell for the silver-tongued Hutton's bluff.

CHAPTER 7

Life On Remand

For Arthur Thomas, adjusting to the pecking order of prison life came quickly. "I was very nervous. Early days – very nervous. But that was it, there was no serious trouble from the other inmates. They would give me a smile sometimes and that made you feel a little bit better, that I'd see a smile sometimes."

Nonetheless, there he was, remanded in companionship with some real killers in what was still known as 'the capital wing', even though hanging had been abolished a decade earlier. There was, of course, a natural curiosity about the high profile crime.

"Some of them asked me, 'well why did you do that' or whatever else, but I cannot remember anyone specifically putting the question to me you know? And like it did matter to me, I said, 'Well I was just home that night, and the police got the wrong person'."

Thomas remembers there were chuckles over his answer. "They laughed at that because most of them in there are guilty of their crimes, you know. But I have spoken to some inmates that said 'Oh, I'm innocent here to a point. I was guilty of this particular crime, but there are other crimes similar and they just put the ring right around the lot and charged me with them', and so they're doing someone else's crime and time, because the police wanted to get them off the books.

"A lot of that goes on. And a few of the inmates came to me about that. They're guilty of a particular crime but they've got their added ones, police would say 'this is a similar crime to your one', and they'd be charged for those ones too."

Once everyone had worked out who Arthur was, and where his story fitted in the jail's grand tapestry of "I never done it, guv'nor!" tales, life quickly fell into a routine.

"You just do what you're told. If it's four o'clock, whatever time it is, they come inside, 'do this, get the dishes, shower there' – you can have a shower two or three times a week. Not every day. And the visiting was at certain hours. The lawyers come in from time to time to talk on some issues and things, and get ready for the trial at its set time and everything."

At this early stage, if any guards were sympathetic to the Pukekawa farmer, they didn't let on.

"No, no, they kept pretty quiet. But I didn't get a good report on Justice Henry from the inmates. 'Oh, who's going to be your judge?' 'Justice Henry,' I told them. 'Ahhhhhh. You're buggered'. That's what they said. I didn't want to believe it. 'No, no. I'll be right'. But so many inmates told me, 'Justice Henry – you're under'."

New Zealand's court system in 1971 was slightly different from its current construction. Ordinary criminal cases were heard in the Magistrates Court, and indictable offences like murder or other serious crimes were tried at what was then called the Supreme Court. In a revamp of the courts a decade later the names were changed: Magistrates became District Court judges, and the Supreme Court was abolished, its place taken by what we now know as the High Court. More recently, the Supreme Court has been brought back as an actual Supreme Court, sitting above the Court of Appeal.

Sir Trevor Henry had been knighted in 1970. A keen athlete in his day he'd served on the Olympic selection panel that sent Jack Lovelock to Berlin for the 1936 Olympic games and his gold medal win in front of Hitler. At the time of the Arthur Thomas trial in February 1971, he was nearing his 69th birthday,[68] and had a reputation with criminals as "the hanging judge". Arthur would have plenty of time to ponder this from his cell, late on those summer nights over the Christmas break of 1970.

Sir Trevor's views on police infallibility were made clear in a newspaper article:[69]

A senior judge of the Supreme Court, Sir Trevor Henry, praised the

---

68 Sir Trevor Henry retired in 1974, but survived to the age of 105, passing away in 2007. He had a keen legal mind and took particular interest in the detail of the Winebox inquiry – his grandson Brian Henry was Winston Peters' counsel at the inquiry. At the time of the Thomas trial in 1971 it's fair to say he still trusted police and law enforcement agencies to do their job ethically. By the time the Serious Fraud Office and IRD had been hammered for failing to investigate the Winebox frauds in 1995, he was no longer labouring under such illusions.
69 *New Zealand Herald* June 29 1972

police yesterday and criticised the undisciplined members of society who brushed aside tradition. "Today, said Sir Trevor, tradition appears to be abruptly brushed aside even by people who ought to know better." Sir Trevor said that at no time had disciplined action – which was the essence of police training and police tradition – been so closely scrutinised and challenged, frequently on the slightest and most tenuous pretext. Today people freely assumed the mantle of judge and jury in cases they had never heard. Many freely aired their inexpert and uninformed views and got undue publicity. "They substitute their opinions (on evidence they have never heard) for the judgement of the constitutional tribunal which has seen and heard every witness," he said. Some did not hesitate to impugn the police, or the tribunal, to leave the veiled suggestion that all was not well.

"He was the one that brought the police in to look after the jurors; the jurors weren't allowed to go home – never, ever in any other trials. He wanted the jury to bring a guilty verdict, that trial judge. And it worked," Thomas mutters.

In a normal jury trial, and I've covered far too many of them, the jury is selected from a pool of 60 people called to make themselves available on the day of the hearing. Once the 12 jurors are selected, they hear evidence from 10 am to 11.30 am, break for morning tea, resume at 11.45 and continue until 1 pm. Lunch is held until 2.15 pm and the case resumes until afternoon tea at 3.30 pm, back at 3.45 pm through to 5 pm when the juror gets to go home for the night. That's a normal jury trial. In all cases, the judge will remind jurors to disregard anything they hear in the media because it may contain information not relevant to the case or be a distortion of what they themselves have heard. They are reminded not to discuss the case with anyone, not even spouses.

Up until 2009, it was routine for juries, *once they finally retired to consider a verdict* at the end of a case, to be "sequestered", or locked up together in a hotel for the night. A change in the law has abandoned that practice except if the judge deems it necessary in a particular trial. It is far less common, in fact almost unique in New Zealand, *for juries to be put up in a hotel together for the entire trial.*

But that's what happened to Arthur Allan Thomas, twice. Instead of locking the jury away only for the few hours while they considered a verdict, the juries were locked away for three weeks at a time.

It happened like this. In the summer of 1970/71, police criminal intelligence agents from the CIS unit – the New Zealand equivalent of the Bodie and Doyle roles in *The Professionals* – were scouring through the lists of potential jurors in line to be called for Thomas' mid-February 1971 Supreme Court murder trial. Their task was to work out who on the jury list might have a negative view of police or a positive view of a small town farmer like Arthur Thomas. On a list of hundreds of people, names were being struck off by police long before they ever got a letter advising them of jury service. That week, police wanted to make sure that only pro-police jurors were picked for the Thomas case.

It was a staggering and audacious perversion of justice, but it was also the way the New Zealand court system ran, in a nudge, nudge, wink, wink fashion. The skulduggery did not end with stacking the jury, though. That was only the beginning. The second stage of what happened is more murky in origin.

It is hard to know whether the cunning Crown prosecutor David Morris made some seemingly offhand comment to Thomas defence counsel Paul Temm in order to plant the thought in his subconscious, or whether Temm came up with the idea entirely on his own, but the record shows Thomas' own lawyer asked the court to sequester the jury for the whole duration of the trial. It later emerged, however, that the Crown solicitors had booked hotel rooms for jury members weeks in advance of the trial, lending credence to the suspicion Temm had been set up by the crafty Scotsman heading the prosecution.[70] With 96 witnesses being called – seventy seven on behalf of the Crown – that trial was expected to last three weeks.

"This practice of keeping juries incommunicado is generally regarded as bad from a defence point of view," wrote *Sunday Times* journalist Terry Bell in his small book on the case, "since there is evidence – mainly from American courts – that jurors, kept in this way, tend to develop feelings of resentment toward the accused. However, there were no complaints from the defence – in fact they proposed the move."[71]

Faced with three weeks away from husbands, wives, children or work, locked up in a hotel room, many potential jurors understandably bailed out on the day of selection, telling the court they simply could not commit to being away from home and office that long.

---

70 *Beyond Reasonable Doubt*, by David Yallop, p113
71 *Bitter Hill*, Terry Bell, Avant-Garde Publishing, 1972, p32

Naturally, the already pro-police jury pool was drained of nearly half – 29 – of its 60 candidates. Of the remaining 31, most were retirees who, as a rule, were conservative and pro-Establishment. In those days, the idea of "police corruption" was a foreign concept. As Terry Bell paraphrased the general community mood at the time:[72]

"We have to have faith in the police and the courts or our whole society will totter...the mere idea that the mighty monolith of the justice system could have been guilty of a gross error is too hideous a concept to even toy with; they believe in the system and in its infallibility."

It's an interesting exercise on the side to see how much damage the police have inflicted on themselves and society in general in the 40 years since the Crewe murders, how much that loss of faith Bell warned of has actually cost New Zealand. I often hear police top brass lamenting that youth have no respect and don't trust them, yet I never hear those same apologists ever acknowledge their own role in destroying that fragile public trust. While 95% of police are good, hard-working and honest, many of the top brass at Police National Headquarters and the senior old-boys network they preside over behind the scenes would not look out of place in the Queensland or New South Wales police forces. Until Police Minister Judith Collins summons up the will to clean out the Augean Stables she nominally controls, nothing is likely to change.

Back in 1971, however, gaining a murder conviction was a cakewalk. The police had a ready-made constituency who believed they could do no wrong, and eight men and four women of them were on that first jury. But the jury stacking didn't end there, as a funny thing happened on the way to sequestration.

Normally, a jury is locked away under the protection of the court itself – the whole point being to show independence from anything that could taint their judgement:

"Once a jury is sequestered, strict measures are imposed to insure their objectivity," advises one US legal website.[73] "For example, jurors are not allowed to use a public restroom without a court bailiff or marshal being present. Receiving and making telephone calls is forbidden but will not result in a trial verdict being reversed by a higher court so long as the court officer can hear the conversation

---

72 *Bitter Hill*, page 84
73 http://courts.uslegal.com/jury-system/issues-pertaining-to-the-jurys-performance-of-its-duties/jury-sequestration/

and nothing pertaining to the case is mentioned. Jurors must also be transported as a group, eat together, and sleep at the same lodging."

You couldn't object too much to that – the jurors are under the direct protection and supervision of court bailiffs and or the Marshalls Service. In the Thomas trial, however, the jury found they were guests of police inspector Bruce Hutton and his officers, after the court ordered they be sequestered at one of the Auckland Police Station's favourite watering holes, the Station Hotel in Anzac Avenue, across the road from the courthouse.

"Oh, that hotel was a favourite haunt of police," remembers lawyer Gerald Ryan, who acted as one of Thomas' lawyers in the second trial. "The cops would regularly entertain jury members, and one policeman ended up in bed with a woman on the jury!"

All of this, remember, whilst the jury were sitting at the trial. You could call it the judicial equivalent of Stockholm Syndrome, where jurors held captive begin to sympathise with those holding them – in this case the police officers whose evidence they would hear and weigh up during the trial. Arthur Thomas, too, is still livid that his juries were corrupted by the police and the court.

"How much money was spent on the jury for champagne each night, given to them by the police – They had heaps of champagne to drink. And of course, when the juries… when they came to retire, to reach a verdict they said 'Thank you very much police officers. We now return the compliment'."

Readers will recall I have previously itemised the main police allegations against Arthur Thomas, in the absence of any other evidence linking him to the murders.[74] Those allegations were:

1. BULLET FRAGMENTS COULD HAVE BEEN FIRED BY THOMAS RIFLE
2. CARTRIDGE CASE DEFINITELY FIRED BY THOMAS RIFLE
3. AXLE UNDER HARVEY CAME FROM THOMAS FARM
4. WIRE ON BODIES MATCHED WIRE ON THOMAS FARM
5. THOMAS LIED ABOUT MEETING HARVEY CREWE
6. WATCH STOLEN FROM HARVEY TAKEN BY THOMAS TO LOCAL JEWELLER

---

74 There were no clothing fibres, hair strands, blood, body fluids, bootprints, mud, tyre tracks, fingerprints or any other forensic evidence pointing to Arthur Allan Thomas ever having been in the Crewe house.

7. MOTIVE & OPPORTUNITY
8. MYSTERY WOMAN WAS REALLY VIVIEN

Stripped of everything else, those allegations form the whole case against Thomas. Let's see how they panned out at his first trial as it began on February 15, 1971, at the Supreme Court building (now the High Court) in Auckland.

BULLET FRAGMENTS
One of the key issues to come up at that first trial was the bullet fragments found in the heads of Harvey and Jeannette, and whether forensics experts could match them to Thomas' pump action Browning rifle.

There were nine bullet fragments retrieved from Harvey's head (Exhibit 289), and on the largest of those nine fragments was a "figure 8" on the base. This identified the fatal bullet as one of ICI's Number Eights, which ceased manufacture in 1963. It was old ammunition, and given the Thomas family's keen firearms use – Arthur had learnt to shoot properly and been taught ballistics at the Young Farmers Club, and regularly shot rabbits and possums on his property – any 1963 ammunition is likely to have been used up years earlier.

From Jeannette's head police obtained fifteen fragments, but one large enough to provide some useful forensic evidence. It too was a Number Eight.

The DSIR's Donald Nelson told the court of "certain markings" he'd found. "On the 'Jeannette Bullet' (Exhibit 234) there were four land marks, most of a fifth, and judging by the position of the marks that were there, these indicated that it had been fired from a rifle with six broadly right hand twist lands. This is commonly called the 'rifling'.

"In 'Harvey's Bullet' there was [only] one good land marking, portions of two others, but their width and spacing was consistent with this bullet being fired from the same rifle as Jeannette's bullet."

The DSIR had test fired bullets from 64 rifles, and compared their markings to those found in the bodies. Placing the Jeannette Bullet (the best preserved exhibit) under a microscope, Donald Nelson photographed the rifling marks and then looked for similar marks going in a similar right-hand direction on the test rifle bullets. Under Crown examination from prosecutor David Morris, Dr Nelson told the court that four "landing", or rifling, marks on Jeannette's bullet were "identical" in spacing to marks found on bullets test-fired from the Thomas rifle. But he also admitted under cross examination from Paul Temm that the results didn't prove Thomas' gun had fired the fatal shot, because parts of the bullet were missing. He also conceded that a Remington rifle in the care of Crewe neighbour Mickey Eyre had the same "identical" rifling pattern. The fatal bullets were in small fragments, so "identical" could be creative license. Nonetheless, he admitted he couldn't distinguish between either rifle:

"And these bullets might or might not have been fired…from that Browning of the accused?" questioned Paul Temm.

"Yes, sir," confirmed Donald Nelson.

"Might have been fired from that Remington," offered Temm after a second or two.

"Yes, sir."

"And might have been fired by another weapon altogether, that you have not tested?"

"Yes, sir."

Game, set, match. Or it should have been. The police star witness was admitting the fatal bullets could have been fired by literally any old gun. Two rifles out of 64 tested provided "identical" markings to the fatal bullet from the limited reconstruction the DSIR could do, but that meant around 2,500 guns in the wider Auckland region could have each given "identical" markings as well under the same test. Hardly the smoking gun the prosecution claimed it was.

But there's more to bullet forensics than just the rifling marks. After all, a particular brand of rifle uses the same mass produced rifle barrel, and if your only test is rifling marks from the rifle grooves then all rifles in that product line should match. Makes sense, really. So what scientists are also supposed to look for are "striations" – tiny imperfections created by dust, lead-scoring or micro-grit inside a particular gun barrel. The damage caused inside the barrel never gets repaired and leaves its imprint on every bullet subsequently fired. It is these unique striations that, when analysed in conjunction with the rifling marks, actually provide the exact link between gun and bullet.

Donald Nelson gave no evidence about whether he found striations on the fatal bullet fragments or on those test fired from Arthur Thomas' rifle. Nor did he provide high resolution photos of the bullets so lawyers could compare for themselves the striations on the genuine Thomas bullets with the striations on the fatal bullets. That evidence was never revealed and appears to have been largely overlooked. Certainly on the Jeannette Bullet – the largest fragment found – the DSIR had been able to locate and photograph four complete land marks. There should have been striations which, if the bullet had come from Thomas' rifle, the police would have fallen over themselves to highlight. But they never did.[75]

However, police did have something else to definitively link Arthur Thomas to the fatal bullet fragments: Exhibit 343, the only No. 8 bullet found on the Thomas farm. This is the one found by Detective Stan Keith in an old apple box full of odds and ends, the day after Detective Len Johnston had been at the property.

While obviously not the fatal bullet itself, its presence apparently proved that Arthur Thomas had the same ammunition as the type that killed the Crewes. Or does it?

Exhibit 343 appears to be another planted bullet. A strong clue to this effect is that while police records and Detective Stan Keith's testimony all show that 343 was found on October 21st, police and DSIR records all show that a bullet presented as Exhibit 343 was *handed to the DSIR for forensic testing on October 19* – two days prior to its "discovery".

During the depositions hearing, at page 134 of the evidence, Detective Keith describes what he found on October 21st:

"In an apple box which was fixed to the wall of the garage, I found one .22 cartridge amongst the nuts and bolts in this box. The cartridge has the letters ICI stamped on the shell and is hollow nosed. [Shown Exhibit 343], that is the bullet and shell case which were together as a single cartridge when I saw them and now produce as Exhibit 343, and I labelled and retained that cartridge (referring to Exhibit 343) as a single cartridge, I was present when the bullet was separated from the cartridge case and after that had been done I noted a figure 8 imprinted in the lead."

At page 135 of the evidence, Keith says:

"On October 19, 1970 I took Exhibit 343, that is the .22 bullet and

---

[75] In fact, it went the other way. The Royal Commission later discovered there were striations on Thomas' test bullets that didn't match the fatal bullets. Police chose not to reveal this.

shell case to Dr. Nelson of the DSIR and received it back from him that same afternoon."

At page 172 of the Supreme Court first trial transcript, he states:

Detective Keith: "On October 21, 1970 …in an apple box fixed to the wall of the garage amongst nuts and bolts I located a .22 cartridge."

Prosecutor: I show you now the cartridge, is that the one you found?

Detective Keith: "Yes"

Prosecutor: I noticed the case has the lead bullet apart, is that the condition you found it?

Detective Keith: "No, later at Otahuhu police station I was present when the cartridge was dissected. After this was done I noted the figure 8 imprinted on the lead on the bullet. That is the base of the lead bullet. I produce that as Exhibit 343."

At page 173 of the Supreme Court transcript:

Prosecutor: On October 19 did you take Exhibit 343, the .22 shell case, to Dr. Nelson of the DSIR and receive it back the same afternoon?"

Detective Keith: "Yes sir."

By the time the DSIR's Dr. Donald Nelson was testifying at the Supreme Court, he was asked at page 202:

Prosecutor: "You refer to receiving on September 19 from Detective Keith unfired bullet bearing figure 8 on concave base, together with a fired shell case, is that correct?"

Nelson: "I haven't made a note in my book about the shell case." [Note: he didn't challenge the date, but instead the status of the case]

Prosecutor: "Was the number of the exhibit you received 343?"

Nelson: "Yes"

Now clearly the good Dr Nelson had his months wrong, but the consistent date the DSIR claims to have received and examined exhibit 343 is the "19th". Remember, the bullet was not found until the 21st.

It doesn't take a garbologist, let alone a rocket scientist, to know that you can't hand something over for forensic testing before you actually discover it. So here's my hypothesis: Police knew the Crewes had been killed by Number Eight bullets. They made a decision to plant one in Thomas' shed, probably intending to discover it by October 19. Fate or bad planning intervened, and it wasn't "found" until the 21st, but in the meantime a sister bullet had already been sent to the DSIR for "forensic testing" because the police didn't actually need it to be the bullet they recovered. Through a typical bureaucratic public service bungle, police forgot to correct their error and couldn't exactly confess to the DSIR that they'd cheated and were using them as patsies.

There were *two bullets* masquerading as Exhibit 343. This would also explain confusion at the second trial[76], where defence expert Dr Jim Sprott appeared to have examined a different version of Exhibit 343 than the one the DSIR had looked at, of which more later in this book. Proof of these different versions of 343 is also found in the evidence disposal notes, which described Exhibit 343 as "a live whole .22 shell and bullet found by Detective Keith".[77] Keith has already testified he watched the bullet being dissected, how could it be "live" when later disposed of?

I'm confident readers can now safely assume that the only bullet found on the Thomas farm capable of linking him to the bullets that killed the Crewes was just as much a plant as the shell case you're about to read more on. That main course, Exhibit 350, the cartridge case planted in the flower bed, was about to be served up.

THE PLANTED CARTRIDGE CASE

History, of course, has well and truly established the cartridge case known as Exhibit 350 was evidence fabricated to frame Thomas. Jurors at the first Thomas trial did not know this, so let's examine what they were told.

The implication was that the empty cartridge case was one of those that contained a fatal bullet, and it fitted the police scenario of the stormy-night windowsill shooter.

Under cross examination from Paul Temm, however, the DSIR's Donald Nelson admitted he couldn't make that link. "Turning to the cartridge case (Exhibit 350) found by Mr Charles[78], are you able to say that the bullet (Exhibit 234) that killed Jeannette Crewe came from that cartridge?" asked Temm.

"No sir," replied the scientist.

What the scientist *was* certain of was that the shell case found in

---

76 *Beyond Reasonable Doubt*, p284
77 *Auckland Star*, 14 September 1973
78 It is interesting that at one tricky point when Det. Sgt. Mike Charles was being cross-examined about his shell case, someone in the building tripped the fire-alarm switch, resulting in the evacuation of the court. Charles was spotted conversing with Crown Prosecutor David Morris during the break – something he wasn't allowed to do. "You know better than that!" snapped Paul Temm QC when the trial resumed. *Courier Times Advertiser*, 19 April 1972

the garden was indeed identical to one test-fired from the Thomas rifle. Ergo, the shell case Exhibit 350 came from Thomas' gun.

Justice Sir Trevor Henry's summing up focused on this seemingly important point:

"The two scientists, Dr Nelson and Mr Shanahan, swear that it was a shell fired by the accused's rifle. They have scientifically examined the test shell and the shell which Detective Charles said he found, and they say categorically that the same rifle fired both...No expert evidence was called to the contrary...but it is still for you [the jury], as Mr Temm says, to say whether you accept their evidence."

The implication from Justice Henry was that you would have to be a very stupid juror indeed not to believe that the cartridge case had come from Thomas' Browning pump action rifle. The further implication was that the defence lawyer was just trying to con jurors by challenging the DSIR evidence.

Henry would take this aspect even further, as a sign of just how crucial the shell-case was to the prosecution argument:

"Now, if you are satisfied...that the shell found by Detective Charles was fired by the accused's rifle, then the question arises...was it fired at the home of the Crewes on that night, and, if so, who fired it?"

The judge has linked the shell to the Thomas rifle, and is basically saying, 'to get himself out of this hole, Thomas has to have convinced you that someone else had his rifle that night and shot the Crewes with it'. But Sir Trevor actually says it even more bluntly:

"Is the only reasonable explanation on all the evidence that the accused fired that shell at the Crewes' place on that night?"

There was in fact a very good reason the cartridge found in the garden could *not* have contained either of the fatal bullets, but that reason did not emerge until after the first trial and will become clear later in this book. As far as the jury were concerned, the fact that the DSIR could not prove it fired the fatal lead didn't overturn the obvious circumstantial implication that a shell case in the bushes was worth two bullets in the head.

Even Justice Sir Trevor Henry got sucked in by the police ruse, and he neatly but naively told the jury to effectively put aside any conspiracy theories that the real killer had "framed" Thomas:

"The accused himself said that someone was framing him. Now that would entail a visit to his farm and the search for and the finding of a spent shell to be planted by somebody of whom we do not know anything at all, and again, the shell will not involve the accused unless the bullets found in the heads of Jeannette and Harvey Crewe were No. 8, the same as his and had the same rifling 'marks' as would be made by his rifle.

"How would an unknown person know that his [Thomas's] rifle and spent ammunition from his farm would give that result?"

No one, neither the judge, nor jurors, nor Thomas himself, knew that police officers Bruce Hutton and Len Johnston had indeed planted the cartridge to frame him. Only Hutton and Johnston, watching the summing up from the front row of the ornate courtroom's public gallery, knew what they had done – even as the judge scoffed at the very idea.

"You may well think that any suggestion of the planting of a shell has little merit or validity," Henry added.

Little wonder, given such persuasive summing up from Justice Henry, that the jury bought the police argument on the cartridge case in trial one.

Yet there was more jiggery-pokery in the chronology of DSIR forensic testing that emerged in evidence but wasn't hit for the home run by defence lawyers. Rory Shanahan, a DSIR forensic scientist who examined the planted cartridge case, told the Supreme Court he didn't make a positive ID that the case came from Arthur's gun until October 29, 1970. Fair enough. Why then did Bruce Hutton call off the search for the murder weapon at 3pm the day before? Up until then Inspector Pat Gaines had his men trawling the Waikato river for a rifle used in the shootings. Gaines testified to receiving a phone call from Hutton at 3pm on October 28, telling him they could stop searching for the gun.

It's reminiscent of the DSIR receiving and testing the Number 8 bullet found in Arthur Thomas' shed, two days before the bullet was actually found there. In this case, Hutton was getting sloppier the more evidence he planted. What other explanation exists for a murder inquiry boss who calls off the search for the murder weapon 24 hours before the DSIR have officially made the link? Pride comes before a fall, but Hutton's fall was still a long time coming.

THE AXLE CAME FROM THE THOMAS FARM

Another rort from police was the axle allegedly found underneath Harvey Crewe's body in the river. It was from a 1928/1929 Nash

Standard Six car, supposedly via a trailer once owned by Arthur Thomas' father, Allan.

Police came a cropper in the December 1970 depositions hearing at the Otahuhu Magistrates Court when Crown Prosecutor David Morris tried to fit the trailer wheels and stub axles Len Johnston had "found" at Thomas' farm, onto the ends of the axle "found" underneath Harvey Crewe. In a moment of great theatrical embarrassment, Morris couldn't make them fit.

"The bolt-holes in the wheels did not fit on to the bolts of the Exhibit car axle," wrote Robert Coombridge in a 1979 review of the case sent to Prime Minister Rob Muldoon,[79] "and therefore [Morris] failed to link the car axle with having come from Thomas' property. This was a serious weakness in the Crown case involving the Exhibit car axle allegedly retrieved from the bottom of the Waikato river from beneath the floating body of Harvey Crewe.

"However, this serious weakness was 'fixed' by Det. Insp. Hutton at the trials of Arthur Allan Thomas…in his own words upon oath in the witness box. This is what he said: 'After showing Arthur Allan Thomas how the stub axles fitted to each end of the main axle, I then said, 'Well, what do you think of these particular parts?' and he replied, 'I must say they go together'.

"At no stage of Inspector Hutton's evidence was he cross-examined on whether he was able to match the wheels to either the stub axle or the Exhibit car axle. Further to this, Mr D S Morris made no attempt to demonstrate in front of the two juries whether he could fit the wheels to either the stub axle or the Exhibit car axle," wrote Coombridge.

"No reasonable jury having heard the verbal evidence of Inspector Hutton saying that the accused had remarked, 'I must say they go together' could have arrived at any other conclusion…After all is said and done, the accused Thomas was never asked whether he made such a remark to the inspector. What is a jury expected to believe when an accused person does not deny such evidence?"

Coombridge argues Thomas' lead trial lawyers failed in their duty to rebut weak Crown claims, leaving their client dangling on the end of a prosecutor's mostly illusory rope. To be fair to the lawyers, they were battling police corruption and would probably never have won.

Then there's the mysterious provenance of the axle itself. Arthur

---

79 *The Crewe Murders at Pukekawa*, by Robert Coombridge, p56

Thomas had never owned the trailer that the axle came from – the axle had been disposed of as rubbish in 1965, a year before Thomas moved onto the farm. It's possible it could have been dumped at the Tuakau tip in the mid 1960s, or alternatively taken by scroungers in 1965 – of which more later in this book. There's also no guarantee it was actually ever attached to Harvey Crewe's body at all. The body was discovered by a police officer, not a member of the public, and none of the first police responders reported feeling an axle attached to Harvey.

We only have Hutton's word that it was attached to the body, and frankly readers will already know my view: Hutton's testimony is worthless. The man was found by the Royal Commission to have lied on oath.

The stub axles were a plant, like the cartridge case. They weren't at the Thomas farm dump when Len Johnston and Arthur Thomas first searched it. The Royal Commission's account of how the stub axles were found during a second search is worth reading again:

"Inspector Parkes gave evidence that they collected their wire samples and that Detective Johnston then borrowed a spade and began foraging around on the tip. He said that, of three tips on the farm, Detective Johnston was concerned to search only *one*. After only a few minutes, to use Inspector Parkes' words, 'Detective Johnston located two stub axles. One was probably partly uncovered, but the other was buried.'

"Inspector Parkes said that Mr Johnston knew what they were, and seemed quite excited by his find. He did not search the tip any further that day. Inspector Parkes very fairly agreed that it was an extraordinary piece of luck that the two stub axles, which were to become such significant exhibits, just fell into Detective Johnston's hands."

Three tips on the property, but Johnston went to search only one, and knew exactly where to dig for a "buried" stub axle and retrieved it after only a minute or two. If you want to see how this improbable clutched straw was spun into a golden thread of conviction by the Rumplestiltskin of the Bench, you could do worse than read the words of presiding judge Sir Trevor Henry summing up: "The axle is part of an assembly and the wheels, the studs, the stub axle, all the rest of that assembly is found on the accused's farm."

Pity the judge didn't mention how police couldn't make the wheels fit the axle assembly, but then how would the judge know? The lawyers forgot to cross examine on it.

THE WIRE CAME FROM THE THOMAS FARM

The bodies of Harvey and Jeannette Crewe had been wrapped in, alternatively, a pink blanket and a bedspread, and then wrapped in wire. The killer used a combination of galvanised wire and copper wire to truss his prey before dumping their bodies in the Waikato river.

Samples of wire were taken from a few farms in the Pukekawa district after the bodies were found, including 11 samples of galvanised wire and four of copper from the Arthur Thomas property.

Four of the 11 Thomas galvanised wires were said to be in 'excellent agreement' with one of the wires found on the bodies – "and that wire was of a type and gauge common to [nearly all] farms," wrote journalist Terry Bell in his analysis of the case in 1972.[80] In other words, the wire wasn't a drop-dead slam-dunk either – it could have come from virtually any farm. Of the copper wire also used to tie the Crewes, *none* of it matched anything found on the Thomas farm.

Wire is a primary fencing ingredient on all farms, and rural supply stores hold enough stock to satisfy all farms in their wider area. Metallurgists confirmed that a single batch of fencing wire from the same smelt would produce about 70 kilometres of wire. That's a lot of coils of wire for a district to chew through before they've cleared the shelves of that particular batch.

Assistant prosecutor David Baragwanath wanted to know whether DSIR scientist Harry Todd was able to refine his "excellent agreement" and "indistinguishable" comments about the matching wire sample:

"You referred to wire 1 as being indistinguishable within the limits of your tests, are you able to say categorically whether [they came] from the very same coil?"

"No, I could hardly say that," replied Todd. The tests were not that accurate. In other words, he could say it was thin number sixteen gauge carton wire, but the metal tests the DSIR performed wouldn't tell you which batch of number sixteen it was.

Now, to give matters even more perspective, Harvey's body was wrapped in *three different kinds* of galvanised wire, and some copper wire. Of the 11 galvanised wire samples taken from Arthur's farm, four of them were the same type of wire (presumably taken from four rolls of the same wire on different parts of the farm) which collectively matched only *one* of the samples on Harvey – and that

---

80 *Bitter Hill: Arthur Thomas, the case for a retrial*, by Terry Bell, p38

wasn't an exact match as we've seen. Of the copper wires, forensic tests showed the copper used on Harvey and Jeannette had come from the same batch, but it didn't match anything police had seized from any of the farms, and didn't match the copper wire stores in Arthur's barn.

No wire found on Arthur's farm matched the wire used on Jeannette's body.

Sir Trevor Henry, summing up, said of this: "The wire on that bedspread, although it could not be positively identified, had some similarity, although not full similarity, with the wire samples."

THOMAS LIED ABOUT MEETING HARVEY

But it was Det. Sgt. John Hughes' evidence that made Arthur Thomas sit bolt upright, when Hughes read out to the court his version of a conversation with Thomas on July 2:

"[Thomas] said that he had visited the Crewe farm while working for an agricultural contractor three or four years before. He said that he had met the person whom he believed to be Jeannette's husband, Harvey Crewe *there*, and said he thought he was a decent sort of bloke. He said that he had morning and afternoon teas in the Crewe house and had never been back since."

Police argued in court that Thomas had prior knowledge of the Crewe house layout because he'd helped aerial topdress the Crewe farm. Further, Det. Sgt. John Hughes committed perjury by stating that Thomas had met Harvey Crewe while doing this, and that he'd told Hughes Crewe was a 'decent chap'.

In and of itself this wasn't significant, but it grew from a bone of contention to a baseball bat of contention over credibility. When Thomas protested in court that Hughes was mistaken over his testimony or lying, Crown prosecutor David Morris sneeringly invited the jury to 'behold a man' who claims everyone else is lying but him. As a farmer, Thomas should have appreciated what was happening. The wolf was separating the vulnerable one from the rest of the herd, destroying any sympathy the jury might still have for him. Its impact was devastating.

As history in fact records, the police officers were lying. It was a very effective wind-up to make Thomas look even more guilty in the eyes of the jury. Thomas had indeed been at the Crewe farm – but four years before the Crewes lived there. He was assisting with the

Barr Brothers topdressing operation when they did the Chennells estate farm in 1961 and 1962. He could not have met Harvey Crewe there and had morning tea with him, because Harvey lived 450 kilometres away at the time and didn't move north until 1966. The aviation company records, which were not raised in court, showed Thomas had not worked on the Chennells topdressing flights after 1962, and had left the employ of Barr Brothers in 1965, a full year before Harvey and Jeannette Crewe moved back to the area.

Yet Sir Trevor Henry understandably sided with the affable and charming John Hughes, summing it up thus:

"You may think – it is a matter for you – that the accused has not always given consistent accounts on this. He told Det. Sgt. Hughes he had met Harvey Crewe, and that he, Harvey Crewe, appeared to be a decent type of chap. In his statement of the 15th October he says this: 'I spoke to Jeannette several times etc. I never saw her husband to speak to. The times I spoke to her she was alone.'

"Only a small thing, but I just draw your attention to that," remarked Sir Trevor. Thomas was damned for calling Hughes a liar, and equally damned for his statement to Hutton denying he had spoken to Harvey Crewe.

The theme continued during evidence about the brush and comb set Thomas had given Jeannette for Christmas in 1962. It hinged on a comment Thomas didn't remember making to Detective Len Johnston that the gift may "still be wrapped up for all I know". Knowing Johnston's modus operandi, it was probably a fabricated comment, particularly as it became pivotal in the first trial. Initially, Detective Bruce Parkes told the first trial that he was the man who found the gift tucked away in a spare bedroom. "The paper was not wrapped, but there was a card attached."

Somehow, by the time Det. Insp. Bruce Hutton took the stand, so had the state of the gift. "The wrapping was in a perfect state at the time and I actually opened it to see what it was."

Even if Hutton were telling the truth, and a Royal Commission has already figured out that's something Hutton has immense difficulty with, the wrapping paper couldn't have been in "perfect" order because Crown witness Claire MacGee testified Jeannette had told her in 1963 that Arthur "gave her the brush and comb set". Clearly the gift had been opened – Jeannette was talking about it way back in 1963.

Thomas told police the gift had cost him four or five pounds which, to put it in context, was around one third to half a week's wages. So it wasn't a cheap plastic brush and comb set.

Significantly, in the second trial, Parkes also admitted he'd told Thomas the gift had been wrapped up.[81] This development in the second trial, Justice Sir Trevor Henry later admitted privately,[82] took the sting out of the debate about the brush and comb set and made Thomas' alleged remark "irrelevant".

Nonetheless, at the first trial, under Henry, it was taken as more proof that Thomas was lying.

THOMAS TOOK HARVEY'S WATCH

One of the most bizarre side issues of the court trials – but again one that was used to paint Thomas as a liar in the juries' eyes – concerned a wristwatch. Pukekohe jeweller William Eggleton approached police partway through Thomas' first trial, telling the story of how a big man in a black singlet underneath a white shirt had come in with a watch needing repair. The timepiece was made of rolled gold, and Eggleton was surprised to see it covered in what appeared to be blood and mucus.

When he'd seen a picture of Arthur and Vivien published in a newspaper in November 1970, he believed it was Arthur Thomas who had come into his shop with the bloody watch. But Eggleton didn't make contact with police until 23 February 1971.

Assistant Crown Prosecutor David Baragwanath assessed the witness statement, and then joined defence counsel Paul Temm in the judge's chambers to discuss the admissibility of this late witness. Justice Henry picks up the story in an interview he gave to David Yallop in 1977:[83]

"They told me, Temm and Webb, that they had no objection to the evidence going in. I just about fell through the floor. I had

---

81 I actually suspect the change of evidence in the second trial was a deliberate attempt by police to get their stories straight. Hutton's evidence had contradicted Parkes in trial one, and I believe what really happened was that Len Johnston and Bruce Hutton had cooked up themselves the comment allegedly made by Thomas and included it in Johnston's notes for later use in court. Parkes, who actually had found the gift in an unwrapped state (after all, we know Jeannette opened it because she talked about it to her friends and she kept it), was unaware of the stitch-up in the first trial and told it like he saw it, but was forced to change his story for the second and in doing so left himself open to defence cross-ex on whether he might have told Thomas himself the gift had been wrapped up. For reasons I began this footnote with, I don't think Thomas actually made the comment to Johnston anyway. I'm confident it was just part of the perjured evidence Hutton and his team were providing.
82 Interview with David Yallop, *Beyond Reasonable Doubt*, p190
83 *Beyond Reasonable Doubt*, p159

expected them to object strenuously to Eggleton's evidence being heard. If they had objected I would have upheld that objection."

It wasn't the first strategic lapse made by Paul Temm, sadly, but it was one of the more controversial errors of judgement.

"There is no question about it," continued Sir Trevor Henry. "The lateness of the statement. I also considered Eggleton's evidence unimportant. The probative force was so small, the prejudicial effect so great...[but] if there is no objection from the defence then it goes in."

Sir Trevor kept wondering if Paul Temm had some kind of "ace" up his sleeve with which to undercut Eggleton's testimony and thus weaken the prosecution case. But it never came. Temm was relying on Arthur Thomas to deny it on the witness stand, but the only problem was Arthur's credibility had already undergone a serious hit because of the "so Det. Sgt. John Hughes is a liar?" issue. It was easy for David Morris to thunder across the courtroom in his Glaswegian burr, "Mr Eggleton, the jeweller who gave evidence, you heard him identify you as the person with the watch...you tell us he is entirely mistaken in his identification?"

"He is definitely mistaken," grumbled Arthur Thomas, adding Eggleton to his published list of liars, while a knowing Morris suppressed a triumphant grin.

Sir Trevor Henry made no mention of the watch in his summing up, but David Morris certainly did, referring in his closing address to "the vital evidence of the watch".

"The jeweller, Mr. Eggleton, was a patently honest man," Paul Temm told the jury as he summed up, "but his identification of the accused was a case of mistaken identity." It was true, but it simply wasn't tough enough to unravel what some have called the rope of circumstantial evidence the Crown was weaving around Thomas' neck.

"The case is not decided by a series of separate and exclusive judgements on each item or by asking what does that by itself prove, or does it prove guilt," intoned Sir Trevor. "That is not the process at all. It is the cumulative effect. It is a consideration of the totality of the circumstances that is important."

Never mind the quality of the facts, feel the width of the grand narrative the Crown constructed. Personally, I strongly disagree with Sir Trevor's approach. Yes, the big picture is important, but when the big picture relies on core facts as its sole foundation, those facts had better be true. Otherwise the big picture becomes a movie rather than a documentary. In Thomas' case, the narrative was plausible only if jurors ignored the mistakes and fabrications behind each of the so-called facts.

So what was the story behind the damning wristwatch evidence? The first jury made their decision based on Eggleton's testimony above, they never got to hear an effective rebuttal. I'll tell you what happened to the watch, shortly.

MOTIVE & OPPORTUNITY

The key issue in the trial, was whether Thomas had the means, and a motive, to kill the Crewes. We've dealt with the motive pretty extensively in earlier chapters – it was non-existent. So let's concentrate on the opportunity aspect. In any ordinary case, Arthur's alibi – that he was home all night with his wife and cousin – would normally be accepted, especially if the two other witnesses were not being charged as accessories.

Indeed, when Sir Trevor Henry referred to other potential suspects in the case, like 28 year old Mickey Eyre whose rifle also could not be ruled out of the investigation, he was absolutely happy to accept Eyre's alibi. "She [Eyre's mother] told you that John Michael was hard of hearing and had suffered from a speech impediment from birth and that not surprisingly, due to these impediments, he did not go out at night unless accompanied. You will also recall, I am sure, that she told you that he was at home with other members of the family that night....The possibility that Eyre was involved in any way with the deaths of the Crewes can safely be disregarded by you," concluded Sir Trevor.

Another witness, Jeannette Crewe's former boyfriend from 1963, Derek Booth, told the court he'd been in Whangarei until 6pm on the night of the murders. His alibi was accepted without any other witness corroboration at all.

So why did the judge not apply that same standard to Arthur Thomas' alibi? Sir Trevor had already admitted no one could have entered the Thomas property to take his gun at night without alerting the household: "It is perfectly plain that no intruder could have entered the Thomas property at night, uplifted the rifle, committed the murder and returned it without alerting either the members of the household or the dogs who were nearby. This suggestion you may think is plainly to be rejected."

Quite. And yet, the Crown case was essentially that Thomas was able to leave the house, just after going to bed with his wife at 9pm, start up his old clunker of a Hillman Super Minx with the loudest differential whine in the district, and drive off with the trailer attached without waking up the dogs, his wife or Peter Thomas, and then slip back equally undetected by wife, cousin or dogs in the early hours of the morning, creep back into bed and resume life as normal.

You can't have it both ways. If the idea of someone sneaking *on* to the Thomas property is so fraught with difficulties for the judge that it's "plainly to be rejected", then surely the idea of someone sneaking *off* the property in a noisy car and coming back is even more so.

David Payne, secretary of the local Ratepayers Association, told the court in that first trial that Arthur's differential whine was so bad you could hear his car coming from two miles away. I know what he means. I live on the city fringe. Behind me are hills, and behind them, seven kilometres away at the bottom of the valley on the other side, a railway track. Late at night I can hear the rumble of the locomotive and rolling stock going through on its regular schedule. Sound carries long distances in the country, particularly at night.

"His car was known, so was its noise," agreed Pukekawa resident Brian Murray, who lived on the road the Thomases travelled.

"These are the things city people don't understand," said his wife Eileen Murray,[84] who'd been waiting up that night for the late return of her husband from the ratepayers meeting. "In an area like this, with the quiet and the lack of traffic, we do notice things like that, and we know. The Thomas car did not go up this road that night."

Merv Cathcart, another of Thomas' neighbours and friends whose farm Thomas would have had to drive past, also swore the car never left the property.[85]

"You knew every time that car of his went by. I was in that night. I went to bed about 9.30pm. We slept right on the front of the house, about fifty feet from the road. You could hear the noise of his car over half a mile away. It was such a well known noise. I never heard it that night."

Apart from the noise that everyone knew, it was a particularly busy night in the community.

---

84 *Trial by Ambush*, p57
85 *Beyond Reasonable Doubt*, p177

"There were around sixty people on the road that night – 31 at the meeting, 12 at table tennis at Opuatia beyond the Crewe farm and 16 playing indoor bowls at Glen Murray. That's a lot of people in a community of about 200 adults," Brian Murray added.[86] And Thomas had to drive nearly 16km each way, let alone an extra trip to the river, all without being seen or heard.

I said it at the start of this book and I'll repeat it here so readers can get some distance perspective. The distance between the Crewe farm and Arthur Thomas' farm was about the same as the distance between Newtown in Wellington, and Tawa north of the city. In Auckland terms, it's almost the same as the distance between Queen Street and Manukau City. The Crewes and Thomases were not neighbours.

"It's unbelievable, to be honest," says Arthur Thomas to me from across the sofa. "I'm at one end of the district, they're in the other. Now if I'd done that, someone's gonna see it, someone will catch me. I don't know what's going on with their life or anything; they mightn't even be home or whatever it is, you know. You just think of all those scenarios. Now for me to go all the way there… where they're just waiting there for me to go and shoot them – that's unbelievable.

"I don't know how they'd actually think I'd put the bodies in the river – it's another, what, more than probably 15 miles to the wherever, whatever part of the river. And how would I, on me own, put them in the river? You know – bodies. If we did have an axle – bit hard if we did have an axle because in court they said he was a big 16 stone guy, he's a big guy."

One aspect that's always been controversial is time of death. On the police version of events, the Crewes were killed late at night, possibly after the TV had closed down for the night at 11pm. Police preferred a late night murder because it meant Thomas could have snuck out after his wife and cousin fell asleep around 9pm. On the Crewes' kitchen table the meals still had not been cleared away and the dishes had not been done, however, throwing a discordant note into the symphony police were trying to compose against Thomas. The Crewes were normally in bed by nine, according to those who knew them, Demler told the Court they usually ate around 7pm, and they weren't great TV watchers at all. How likely is it that on

---

86 *Trial By Ambush*, p58

this Wednesday night, after a hard day of running around, Harvey and Jeannette were still up after 11pm, with dinner still on the table and dirty dishes on the bench?

What if the killer did not turn up to the house after dark, but in fact was already in the house when the Crewes arrived home from Tuakau sometime around 5pm on the evening of the 17th, just around sundown?

The house had suffered at least two break-ins – the burglary of Jeannette's jewellery in 1967 and the arson on baby Rochelle's bedroom in December 1968. What if the man who torched the haybarn on June 17, 1969, had returned on June 17, 1970 while the family were out, and got trapped in the house when they arrived home? That would make early evening killings much more likely, and explain why the meals had not been cleared from the table.[87]

Julie Priest, living across the road about 300 metres from the Crewe residence, reckons she heard three rifle shots in quick succession sometime after 8.15pm and before 8.45pm on the Wednesday night. Her husband Owen didn't hear them. Police doubted she would hear shots taking place in another house, from within her own house 300 metres away, on a squally night, and they never called her to give evidence. As one with a country outlook, however, I can confirm hearing shots up to 800 metres away and over the other side of the hill from within my own home – admittedly from hunters in the outdoors. With the wind in the right direction, or paused at the right moment, it's possible Julie Priest heard those night shots, even if unlikely.[88]

Priest did, in fact, hear daytime gunshots when police were test-firing at the Crewe house in late October, and she confronted Hutton over it.

---

[87] David Yallop tried to argue the flounder was a midday meal, but my inquiries with Jeannette Crewe's last visitor, Thyrle Pirret, show that's simply not possible. There was just not enough time between Pirret leaving and the Crewes being seen arriving at the Tuakau stock sale, for Jeannette to have also cooked a flounder lunch. On the evidence in front of me, the Crewes would have left just a few minutes after Pirret. The fish had to be dinner, not lunch, unless the 'lunch' had been cooked on their return from the sale, around 3.30 or 4pm. The QC Muldoon hired, Robert Adams-Smith, speculated it could have been breakfast. Again, not possible. It wasn't on the table when Pirret arrived for morning tea. If it was indeed a very late lunch, then the killer struck before Jeannette had even begun to think about preparing dinner.

[88] For the record, Julie Priest wrote to Rob Muldoon after the publication of Yallop's book claiming she'd been misquoted as to the time and direction of the shots. She told Muldoon she could not be as specific as Yallop had made her out to be. *NZ Herald*, 30 January 1979. For his part, Yallop told Muldoon he had Julie Priest on tape, and offered to play the recordings. He suggested she had obviously been pressured by someone. *The Dominion*, 31 January 1979.

What does this mean? It means the Crewes were probably dead by 8.45pm, while Arthur and Vivien Thomas were still cleaning up after dinner and getting ready for bed.

Police could not find a single person who heard or saw the Thomas car on the road that night. They couldn't find a single tyre track from his car or trailer in the mud at the Crewe house. They couldn't find any mud from the Crewe farm on Thomas' car tyres. They couldn't find a single fibre from the pink blanket or bedspread used to wrap the bodies, when they searched Thomas' car and trailer. Nor did they find any blood, any hair, anything at all.

There was no evidence, and police didn't push it, that Thomas had ever been to the Crewe house in the days after the murders. Additionally, on Friday night, when a father and son saw smoke and sparks coming from the Crewe chimney as someone burned evidence, Arthur and Vivien were at a family 21st in Pukekohe, partying with more than a dozen witnesses.

Turning to the alibi itself, it wasn't just the word of Arthur, Vivien and Peter Thomas. Rosemary Thomas testified that she'd rung Arthur and Vivien at 7.30pm to ask if they were going to the ratepayers meeting,[89] and was told they were too tired as they'd been dealing with a sick cow – exactly the point the Thomases had tried unsuccessfully to make to police. So it was OK to rule out Mickey Eyre on the strength of his mother's assurance, yet Arthur Thomas had the direct witness support of three other witnesses and the police treated it as a grand conspiracy. "In this case, this is the stupidity of the thing," declared an exasperated Vivien at one point. "How many people do you need to have an alibi?"[90]

Part of the Crown's conspiracy theory was trying to create disbelief and suspicion over the fact that the Thomases should have discussed their whereabouts with each other regarding the night of the 17th.

Yet, newspaper reports from the morning of June 23rd – the day

---

89 You'll recall much earlier in the book I mentioned how Len Demler revealed at the second trial how he'd received a call from stock agent Joe Moore on the night of the killings. Moore, presumably following up from the stock sale the Crewes had attended earlier in the day, told Demler he'd been ringing the Crewes but getting no answer. Demler told the court he thought no more about it until he got more calls from stock agents the following Monday. The most significant fact about this phone call? Demler says it was 7pm on the night of the 17th June. If the Crewes were already dead by 7pm, which other evidence like the half-eaten meal supports, and Arthur Thomas was home with his wife and cousin taking Rosemary Thomas' phone call at 7.30pm, there's more hard evidence proving it was impossible for Thomas to be the killer. This first trial jury didn't hear this revelation. A dinner time killing is a better fit with the evidence at the scene. It just didn't fit the police case against Arthur Thomas, which is why Hutton had tried to argue so strenuously for an 11pm murder.
90 *Hawkes Bay Herald Tribune*, 8 April 1972

the Thomases discussed the case – reported Harvey and Jeannette Crewe had been "missing from their blood-spattered farmhouse since last Wednesday". The *Herald* went on to note, "The baby, 18 month old Rochelle Crewe, is believed to have been alone in the house since Wednesday night."

I suggest it is human nature, in such circumstances, for people in a small community to automatically think, 'Last Wednesday… what were we doing last Wednesday love?'. We all look for reference points around big news events. Subconsciously we wonder if we might have seen something, if there might be some snippet of information that could be useful to police.

The judge however spun it totally differently in his summing up to the jury: "Shortly after the news of the disappearance was made public on 22 or 23 June, they and Peter Thomas say they had a discussion to fix their movements for the nights of the previous week. You may indeed think it remarkable that innocent people should have such a discussion."

The implication? That Arthur and Vivien were in this crime together, and that the failure to charge Vivien was a courtesy, rather than because of her innocence. In this way, the alibi was brutally deconstructed.

Vivien Thomas, stressed and out of her depth, didn't perform well on the witness stand under cross examination from David Baragwanath over the precise details of the sick cow she'd told of helping Arthur with on the night of June 17. "It is evident, even from a reading of the trial transcripts," wrote David Yallop, "that Vivien Thomas, self-composed when questioned by her own counsel, gave way under Baragwanath's questions, becoming a hesitant, bewildered woman. Despite the hesitancy, the brittle element which is an aspect of Vivien Thomas still shows through. It is an aspect which cannot have helped her husband's position during the trial. Juries are often very emotional, irrational and illogical. They will take a dislike to a particular witness and bring in a verdict based on that dislike."[91]

At issue was a conflict in dates surrounding the cow and its calf. Vivien, when hauled into Otahuhu police station, had told the police a date for the shooting of the sick cow, and then checked when she got home and read the farm records for that day. She'd then advised

---

91 *Beyond Reasonable Doubt*, p171

police of the correct day, and Baragwanath used the change to paint her as a woman altering her story to suit her husband's alibi.[92]

"Well," says Thomas today, "I thought she did very well – but Kevin said, 'No, didn't do too well at all from a jury's point of view'."

It can't have helped, either, that Sir Trevor was even more blunt in his barely veiled claim that Vivien was the mystery woman. "It is true that Mrs McConachie said that on the Saturday afternoon she had seen a child running about inside the road gate, and also a light-coloured car. On the Saturday, Mrs Thomas had returned from a cat show before midday; and she had travelled to and from it in her husband's light-coloured vehicle."

This insinuation only gained traction because defence lawyers, again, had failed to cross-examine witnesses properly. In this case, a simple question of Bruce Roddick, who had actually seen the mystery woman, would have quickly established that the mystery woman was not Vivien Thomas, whom he already knew and who was no mystery to him. Temm and Webb left that door open by failing to ask whether the woman he had seen was Vivien, and judicial innuendo galloped straight through it.

Crown prosecutor David Morris added his ten cents' worth: "This is not a trial of Mrs Thomas," he purred, in a voice oozing insincerity. "The Crown does not suggest she knew anything about the murder. She may have visited the Crewe farm on the Friday to feed the child, to minimise the tragedy, this would explain the apparent inconsistency of the careful and meticulous planning by the murderer and the seemingly foolhardy behaviour in feeding the baby and attempting to clean-up.

"You may well think she is a determined, resourceful and loyal wife," said Morris, patronisingly, hoping the jury would get the hint. Of course it was a trial of Vivien Thomas; shoot her down and Thomas crashes and burns as well. Listening from the bench, the judge sure got it.

"The defence claims that the accused never left his home on the night of June 17th," opined Sir Trevor Henry, "that is, at any time when these killings could happen…The Crown claims that when this evidence is properly evaluated and weighed, it proves that the

---

92 If the defence had asked Pukekohe dentist Garth Brown the right question at trial, he would have testified that when he saw Vivien and Arthur for an appointment at midday on the 17th of June, 1970, he had invited them to visit his new house in the district and have a cup of tea, but the couple refused his hospitality, telling him they had a very sick cow they had to get back to. Thus, the alibi builds.

accused, despite what he and his wife say, did leave his home that night and that it does enable you – it is a matter for you – to exclude the reasonable possibility that anyone else could have done it."

The one thing that the prosecutors, the judge and jury all failed to grasp was the total implausibility of Vivien Thomas being involved in any way. As you read earlier, she told a reporter that if Arthur had really committed the crime he could "rot in prison" forever. This was a crime of passion involving a former girlfriend, at a time he was supposed to be happily married to Vivien. What wife, if she knew her husband was lying about his whereabouts in such a crime and that he had nursed an uncontrollable lust for another woman for six years, would stand by him for the rest of her life, for decades longer than their actual marriage lasted?

If Thomas' lawyers had done a half decent job, and the police had not been corrupt, Thomas would never have been convicted. The Crown case was a conspiracy theory that required Vivien not just to stand by her cheating murdering man, but to help him cart off bodies and clean-up. It defies belief, and defies logic.

The jury, however, ignored this gaping hole in the prosecution fairy story, and in doing so were left with little option at the end of trial one. Faced with what appeared to be cast iron evidence on the cartridge shell in the garden having come from Arthur's rifle, and the bullets in the bodies matching the number eight bullet found in Arthur's shed, and Arthur clearly lying (in their view) about detectives John Hughes, Len Johnston, Stan Keith, Bruce Hutton and virtually everyone else who testified, it wasn't exactly a difficult choice. When the "hanging judge" Arthur's fellow inmates had warned him of pointed out that Vivien's alibi evidence probably couldn't be trusted because she'd got her cow dates wrong, that was the clincher.

Of course, as Arthur Thomas adds, the three weeks being locked away together in the Station Hotel, in the company of police officers who took the jury on weekend trips to the Parakai hot pools, the movies, sailboat excursions and so on, probably assisted the jury's deliberations as well.

The jury retired to consider its verdict on March 2, 1971. During sixteen working days of evidence, a total of 96 witnesses had traipsed through the courtroom doors. Seventy seven of those witnesses were called by the Crown.

If Arthur Thomas was expecting a jury deliberation to carefully consider all that evidence, he was sadly deluded. After less than two hours, the jurors were back.

"You know, when I was found guilty I could remember I just absolutely, I had no words to talk, you know. My lawyers, I looked at them, I said, 'Well what the f***?', I was sort of going on, I was swearing a bit and going on, but this – I shouldn't swear but you know, 'Why has this happened? Where are we going? What appeals have I got? The judiciary's failed me!"

Lawyer Paul Temm tried to reassure his client. "We'll appeal. We'll take it to the Court of Appeal."

Thomas didn't really hear it. The prison guards flanking Thomas ordered him back down to the dungeon under the old courtroom. "I just turned to the side, tried to blink away the tears in my eyes and walked down into the hole in the floor. I was just blown away."

For Arthur Thomas, it was the beginning of his full incarceration as a guest of Her Majesty in New Zealand's toughest prison, and it wasn't going to be pleasant.

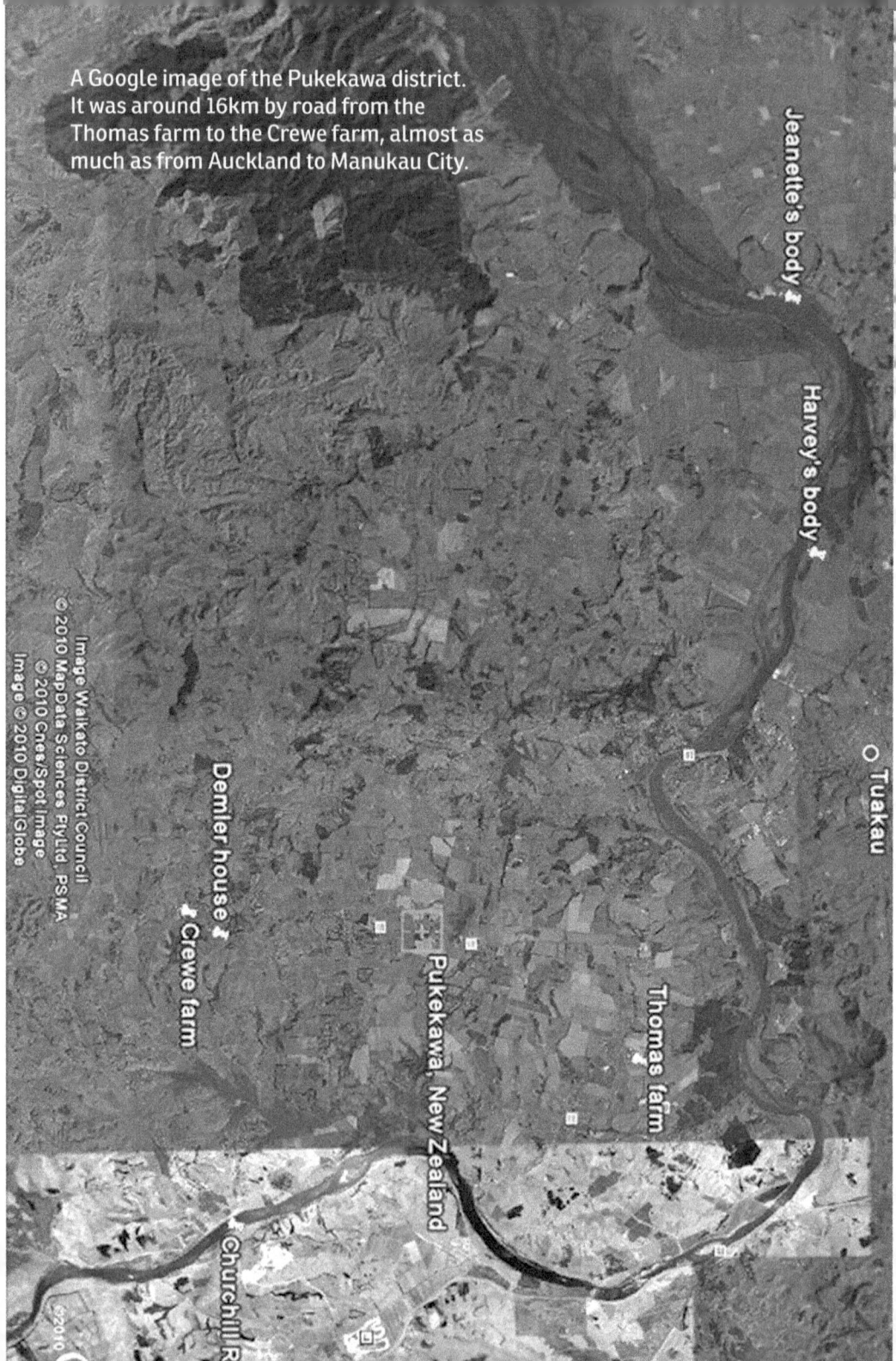

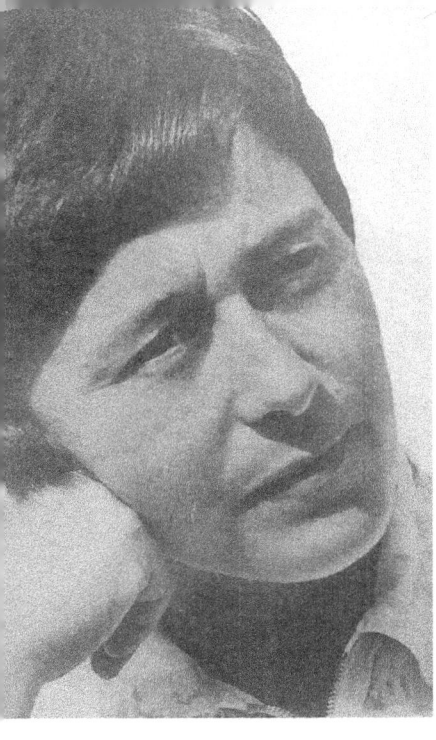 

THE CAST, Clockwise from top left: Vivien Thomas (now Harrison); Jeannette Crewe; Harvey and Jeannette on their wedding day, 18 June 1966; Arthur and Vivien on theirs, 7 November 1964.

CLOCKWISE FROM TOP LEFT: Detective Inspector Bruce Hutton; Detective Sergeant Len Johnston; Bruce Roddick; Len Demler.

ABOVE: the crime area marked on Google Earth. The red line equates to 100 metres. **BELOW, left:** The Crewe farmhouse today, and; **BELOW, right:** A police aerial photo of the Crewe farmhouse on 25 June 1970. The house sits around 30 metres back off the road. **FACING PAGE, Top:** Bruce Hutton holds the axle obtained from underneath Harvey Crewe, whose wrapped up body remains floating in the water immediately below Hutton. **LOWER, left:** Bloodstains on the lounge floor. It was later revealed this photo was taken after police had re-arranged the furniture. **LOWER, right:** Rochelle Crewe, taken two days after her rescue from the house. Not exactly emaciated.

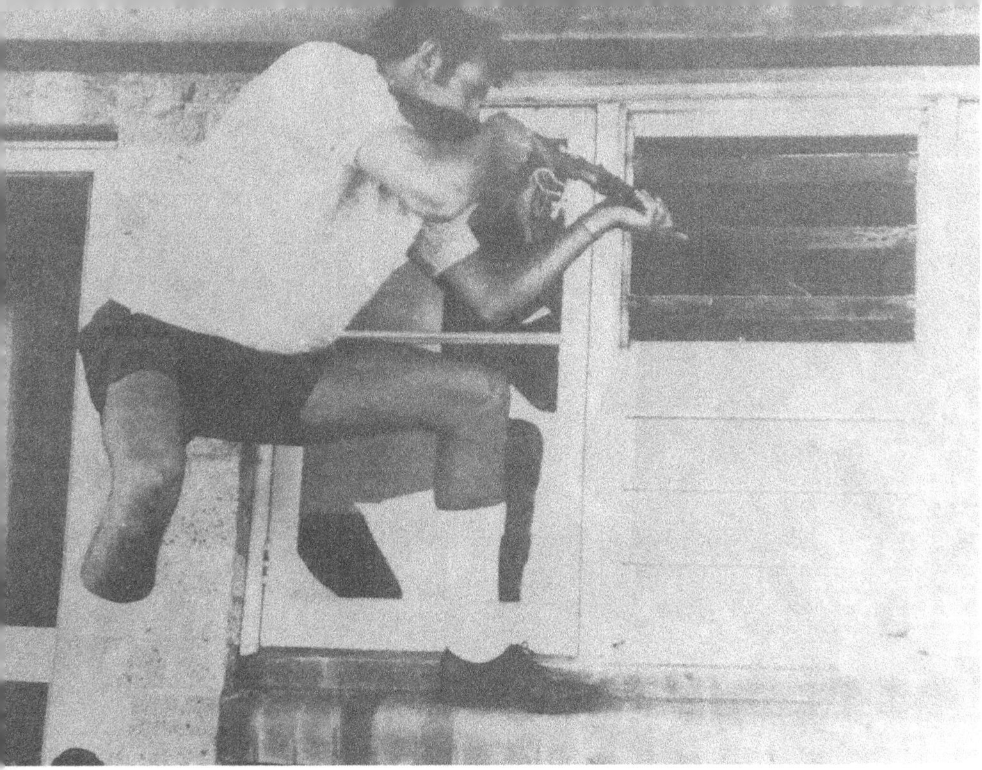

ABOVE: A Thomas retrial committee member re-enacts what police claim was the killer's position, perched on a wall and windowsill. **BELOW:** The position where the planted cartridge case was found, a full 16 feet from the windowsill.

ABOVE: A case of two halves. The top half of the image is the planted case, and the bottom half is an ordinary number eight bullet of the kind that killed the Crewes. You can easily see the typography differences between the two cases. The top case never held number eight bullets. **BELOW:** A graphic illustration of the difficulty Bruce Roddick faced in identifying the mystery woman. The distance across the rugby field from left to right is 75 metres, the distance he believes stood between him and the woman he saw. He could easily distinguish clothing and hair colour, but facial definition?

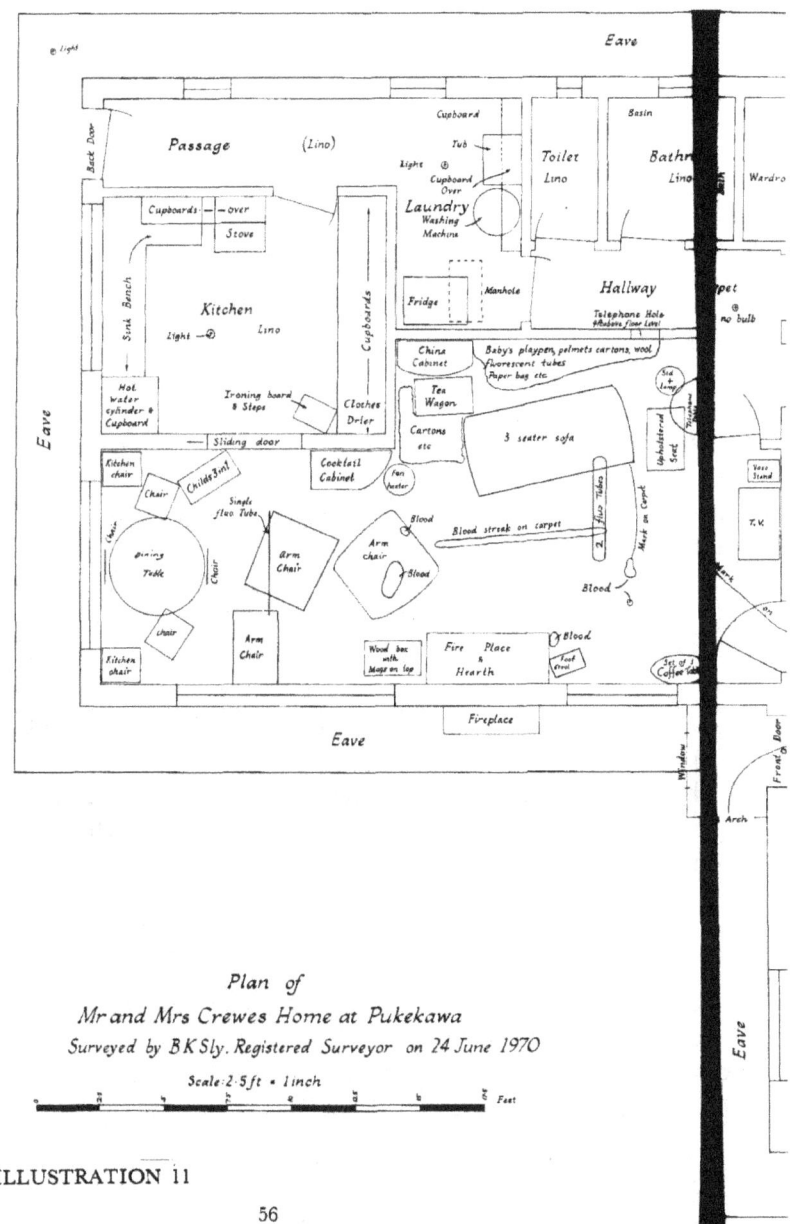

Plan of
Mr and Mrs Crewes Home at Pukekawa
Surveyed by B K Sly, Registered Surveyor on 24 June 1970

Scale: 2.5 ft = 1 inch

ILLUSTRATION 11

CHAPTER 8

The Push For A Retrial

In 1971, the workload of the courts was small compared to today. Appeals rolled around quickly. Arthur Thomas, convicted on March 2nd 1971, was back in the Court of Appeal in May 1971. One of the issues was the weight to be given to what was an entirely circumstantial case against Thomas.

The Court of Appeal took its cue from an 1866 court ruling on circumstantial evidence.[93]

"It has been said that circumstantial evidence is to be considered as a chain, and each piece of evidence as a link in the chain, but that is not so. For then, if any one link breaks, the chain would fall. It is more like the case of a rope comprising of several cords. One strand of the cord might be insufficient to sustain the weight, but three strands together may be of quite sufficient strength...the three taken together may create a conclusion of guilt with as much certainty as human affairs can require or admit of."

Paul Temm QC argued that trial judge Sir Trevor Henry had failed to fairly point out in his summing up that the Crown's rope was massively frayed, with many strands stretched to breaking point. Out of a multi-thousand word summary, Sir Trevor "summed up the defence case in only five lines," complained Temm to the appellate judges in Wellington.

Temm argued that the possibility of Thomas' rifle being used by someone else had "been ignored" by Sir Trevor, but this latter point wasn't quite correct – as we've seen, Henry didn't ignore it but instead told the jury that it was "plainly to be rejected".

---

93 Queen v Exall, (1866) 4 F&F 922, 929

Finally, Temm argued there was a clear absence of motive, and Sir Trevor should have pointed that out to the jurors.

One of the things that emerges from the summing up is the incredible number of times Sir Trevor stung Thomas like a viper, and then immediately qualified it with a comment to the effect, "but that is a matter for you [the jury] to decide". The lawyers counted up 70 or so occasions in the speech where that occurred – 70 jabs at Arthur Thomas from behind the bench.

"A trial judge cannot take refuge after making an unfair remark by saying 'but that is for you to decide'," noted appellate judge Justice Sir Alex Turner, soon to be appointed President of the Appeal Court. "In this instance the trial judge has only put forward the one interpretation on the remark and this was unfavourable to the accused."

Despite this, and in fact despite Temm's entire submissions, the Appeal Court threw Thomas' case out, declaring, "Having studied the summing up carefully we are of the opinion that there really is no substance in this complaint" that Sir Trevor's comments were unbalanced. As the newspapers of the day record, they weren't impressed either with a late claim in the first trial by Temm that perhaps Harvey and Jeannette had died in a murder suicide. We've covered in this book why this was an impossibility, and most commentators also saw it as a desperate clutch for an elusive straw by Temm. "We are surprised he thought it worthwhile to make this suggestion," said the judges, "which we think would be immediately rejected by the jury."

The Court of Appeal delivered its written judgement on June 18, 1971, what would have been the Crewes' fifth wedding anniversary had they survived, and a year and one day after their murders. It's clear the learned judges relied on evidence we now know was fabricated, such as the testimony from a ballistics expert on the cartridge case found in the Crewe garden.

"He gave a confident opinion that the cartridge could have been fired only by the appellant's rifle. His opinion was based on a microscopic examination of the cartridge," wrote Justices North and Haslam in their 44 page ruling. Of course, we now know why the shell matched Thomas' rifle – police had used Thomas' gun to fire it.

While the judges admitted being unimpressed at the "somewhat slender evidence as to the existence of a possible motive", they didn't think this was material to the trial verdict.

Once they realised the judicial system was dealing them a dud hand, Arthur Thomas' family and supporters ramped up the pressure, setting up a Committee for the Retrial of Arthur Allan Thomas and whipping up public support. "God knows the truth," wrote Thomas from his cell at Paremoremo maximum security prison, where he'd begun a life sentence for the murders. In the newspapers and magazines, Vivien was everywhere.

"A lawyer remarked to me," Vivien told a local newspaper,[94] "that the general public attitude following a case such as this is that people, regardless of their feelings on the outcome, are inclined to want to forget the whole thing and shun the case and even relatives of the convicted man completely, and he said that he found the growing and seemingly unprompted interest uncanny.

"I feel that this is the gradual realisation growing from facts being exposed now … things such as the incredible irregularities in the trial itself, and the inevitable exposure of evidence apparently not followed up. I think that we probably got some unwitting assistance from the Crewe murder magazine published by Wilson and Horton. Anyone studying the story and pictures in that closely must see the incredibly flimsy evidence with which my husband lost his freedom. This magazine has turned the people of New Zealand into a jury," Vivien Thomas said.

Indeed, if it had not been for Vivien's strong stand on her husband's whereabouts and innocence, Arthur Thomas would never have had the public support he came to enjoy. Pat Vesey, Vivien's Wellsford-based uncle, became chairman of the Thomas Retrial Committee on the strength of Vivien's assurances that Arthur was with her, in bed, that night.[95]

"Look, I am extremely fond of that girl," said Vesey in August 1971. "I discussed the murder at their home many times before Arthur's arrest, just as other people did. Do you think for one moment that I would have left her there with a double murderer? If it was proved conclusively that Arthur did this horrible thing, I would hate him. But he didn't do it. He couldn't have done it.

"I say 'go and talk to Vivien'. I think you must accept that if Arthur committed these murders, she would know. If you still believe, after talking to her, that he is guilty, then you will never be convinced."

---

94 *County News*, 28 July 1971
95 ibid

Without Vivien and cousin Peter Thomas as a firm alibi and an anchor point for the Retrial Committee to rally around, the public would have given police the benefit of the doubt – simply because of our need to believe the police don't cheat by framing innocent people for murder. Vivien has continued to tell the truth for 40 years, long after her relationship with Arthur Thomas ended. Those wedding vows, "for better or worse", have in this particular sense transcended the destruction of their marriage.

For local farmer and Thomas family friend Brian Murray, the realisation that perhaps the police do cheat epitomised the loss of innocence many people felt. He explained he'd always brought his children up to cooperate with the police, but if cooperation meant leaving yourself open to being framed, it was now a bad idea. "From now on they are being told[96], 'the minute a police officer questions you, say nothing and get a lawyer'. This is how this shocking business has affected me," said Murray, a father of eight. "Goodness only knows what it is doing to poor Arthur and Vivien. She has been doing a day's work before she goes to the prison for an hour every Saturday and another day's work when she comes home."

A straw poll by the *Auckland Star* newspaper found 15% of Pukekawa residents supported a retrial, and 15% were vehemently against it. The remaining 70% were apparently sick of hearing about the case, with many telling the newspaper "the police do not make mistakes".[97]

Others, like farmer David Payne, were turning their attention to the Number Eight bullets that killed the Crewes, and the lone Number Eight found in Arthur's shed. "After much thought and investigation I came to the conclusion that whoever fired two bullets at the Crewes farm either used or had access to an ammunition supply that was rarely used. Arthur Thomas used a rifle a lot. Shooting at possums and so on," said Payne.[98] Arthur was likely to have used up any 1963 ammunition years previously, he pointed out.

"Much was made of Arthur's not attending the ratepayers meeting on the night of the murder and of his not taking part in the search. I can name about 50 men who didn't attend the meeting and about 20 who didn't take part in the search.

---
96 *NZ Weekly News*, 23 August 1971
97 *Auckland Star*, 5 August 1971
98 *Auckland Star*, 5 August 1971

"I know Arthur well and I feel his naivete – he's a country boy with a standard six education – harmed him. Much was made of his saying something to the effect that 'if the police think I'm guilty, I must be'. That might sound damning. But it is Arthur all over. We have in the area a senior and responsible agriculture Department inspector who was ready to testify that when he told Arthur his milk lines and inflations – in the milking shed – were not clean, Arthur said: 'if you say they are dirty, they must be'."

Police, meanwhile, told reporters they were still trying to find out who fed baby Rochelle during her five day ordeal. [99]

"The police enquiry into one aspect of the Crewe murders – who fed baby Rochelle from the time of the killings to when she was found in the farmhouse five days later – is still not closed.

"This was confirmed yesterday by the head of the Southern division CIB, Detective Inspector Bruce Hutton, who led the five-month long investigation into the murders of David Harvey Crewe and his wife, Jeannette Lenore Crewe, at Pukekawa in June last year.

" 'The child was obviously fed during the time between the killings and when she was found', said Mr Hutton. 'The file on this aspect of the enquiry is not closed'."

"Mr Hutton said information as to the identity of the woman had been coming into the police for some time. Recent information was helping detectives to establish who the woman might have been. He appealed to anyone with information to offer to notify the Otahuhu CIB immediately."

It is highly significant that Detective Inspector Hutton said this in August 1971, but in 1977 he lied to David Yallop in these words: "I personally believe, and *have always believed*, that *the baby was never fed and could not have been fed*."[100]

One of the first acts of the Thomas Retrial Committee was to circulate 700 copies of a petition asking the Prime Minister, Sir Keith Holyoake, to grant a retrial. It was badly targeted – the Governor-General was the man with that power, not the Prime Minister, but nonetheless it guaranteed publicity for Arthur's case. His 23 year old blonde sister Lyrice was photographed on the streets of Hamilton in a miniskirt collecting signatures.

They eventually collected 22,500 names nationwide, including 150

---

99 *NZ Herald*, 9 August 1971
100 *Beyond Reasonable Doubt*, p23

from prisoners at Paremoremo jail who also believed Arthur was innocent. It was, in its time, the largest petition of its kind on record anywhere in the British Commonwealth. The petition was handed to Governor-General Sir Arthur Porritt in November 1971, along with a plea to the government. Just before Christmas 1971, acting Justice Minister David Thomson and the Governor-General appointed a retired Supreme [High] Court judge, Sir George McGregor, to "sift through the evidence presented at the trial" and review the case. The retrial committee chairman, Pat Vesey, called it "a Christmas present for Mr and Mrs Thomas"[101], but when McGregor later delivered his verdict Vesey wouldn't be quite so chipper.

McGregor spent his summer going through the court transcripts, and on February 17, 1972, announced to a waiting nation, "In my opinion there has been no miscarriage of justice". It was a strong, defiant start, but as you read through his report it quickly becomes apparent he had no handle on the case at all, peppering his document with factual mistakes.

He talks, for example, of a mystery woman seen by a "Brian Michael Roddick", when in fact it was Bruce Roddick. McGregor agrees that Roddick's description "does not implicate Mrs Thomas in any way", and added that "The trial judge in his summing up put it to the jury that this person was unknown and that the description given by Roddick did not correspond with a description of Mrs Thomas."

Great. Except here's what the trial judge said in his summing up: "It is true that Mrs McConachie said that on the Saturday afternoon she had seen a child running about inside the road gate, and also a light-coloured car. On the Saturday, Mrs Thomas had returned from a cat show before midday; and she had travelled to and from it in her husband's light-coloured vehicle."

Sir George McGregor further claims that "the evidence for the Crown does not identify this person as being Mrs Thomas." To which I respond with this from Crown prosecutor David Morris: "She may have visited the Crewe farm on the Friday to feed the child, to minimise the tragedy." On this issue, McGregor was away with the fairies, clearly.

On the issue of the bloodstained watch raised by a late witness, Pukekohe jeweller William Eggleton, he was more useful. Sir George

---
101 *NZ Herald*, 20 December 1971

noted some sworn affidavits proving that Eggleton had confused Thomas with another customer, who'd now come forward, and he stated: "If these affidavits are correct the person who delivered the watch to Mr Eggleton could not have been the accused. I am not impressed by the evidence of Eggleton...[he] was mistaken. [But] I think this doubtful evidence would not have influenced the jury in its decision." Although McGregor went on to say the new evidence "completely refutes" the Crown case on the watch, the retired judge couldn't bring himself to allow a retrial, despite trial judge Sir Trevor Henry's own belief that the watch evidence was hugely "prejudicial" to Thomas.

The new evidence was, in fact, decisive. Arthur Thomas' uncle Bill Thomas, who bore a facial resemblance to his nephew, was a client of Eggleton's and had brought in a watch for repair in early September 1970, just a couple of months after the murders, and to add to the jeweller's confusion another man, pig hunter Jon Fisher, had brought in a rolled gold watch for repair after it was damaged in a pig hunt in January 1971 – about six weeks before Eggleton decided to contact police. Fisher's watch was covered in blood and mucus and had a broken facia.[102]

Despite this terminal blow to Bruce Hutton and the Crown prosecutors on the watch, it didn't stop them from trying to resurrect it at Thomas' second trial in 1973.

On the issue of the mysterious cartridge case found in the Crewe garden McGregor, like the Court of Appeal, found the ballistics evidence proving it had been fired by Thomas' gun was overwhelming. He took note of a fresh affidavit from a man named Graeme Hewson, who testified he'd helped police search the flower bed where the shell was eventually found, and the cartridge was not there back then.

"The effect of the affidavit," stated McGregor, "is that the flower bed where the cartridge case was found had been previously and thoroughly searched and sieved by police officers, one Graham (sic) Robert Hewson assisting them. It is now suggested that as the flower bed had been previously searched the cartridge case must have been

---

102 Staggeringly, Fisher had come forward after hearing of the ruckus about his watch and made a statement to police on 2 September 1971 confirming it was his watch, not Thomas', that Eggleton repaired. I say "staggeringly" because Bruce Hutton and his team suppressed the statement as "irrelevant" to the Thomas trial, and then had the gall to pull the Eggleton stunt again in the second trial in 1973.

placed in the garden after the first and second searches by police."

Having stated that, however, McGregor rejects it because he can't believe anyone would have had access to Thomas' gun.

"It is difficult to accept that some other person obtained access to Thomas' rifle after the first two searches and before the third, and 'planted' the cartridge case in the Crewe garden."

Reading McGregor's report, and the Court of Appeal ruling, with the benefit of the evidence uncovered by the Royal Commission, it's hard not to conclude that Bruce Hutton, multi-millionaire, should be sued to within an inch of his life for the tens of millions of dollars he cost taxpayers by fabricating evidence and wasting the time of more than half a dozen judicial inquiries who accepted his corrupt testimony at face value and denied Arthur Thomas justice. There is no statute of limitations on this. As I understand it, the Solicitor-General could bring charges against Hutton in a heartbeat. In my opinion, this should be done.

It is probably relevant that a police witness in one of Bruce Hutton's cases once admitted, under cross-examination, that the police officer had asked him to plant evidence, in this case gelignite, on a suspect police wanted to and subsequently did arrest.[103] In my view the man could not be trusted running a chook raffle, let alone a murder investigation.

McGregor concludes his report by making some fundamental errors of fact. For starters, he says:

"In the first place the ballistics evidence identifies the bullets found in the brains of the two victims as having been fired by the accused's rifle."

No it doesn't. Find me one piece of court testimony in this book that proves that. The ballistics tests found the bullets could have been fired by 3% of the rifles police tested, which included Thomas', but the bullets were not in good enough condition to narrow it down any further. On those averages, around 2,400 guns in the wider Auckland area could have fired the fatal shots and given the same rifling marks. Sir George McGregor was wrong.

"In the second place," he writes, "the axle which must have been attached as a weight to Harvey Crewe's body came from the accused's farm."

---

103 *Readers Digest*, "Who Killed The Crewes?" November 1979

No it didn't. Careful readers will have noted this was the Crown insinuation, but they had no evidence to prove it and in fact had to plant stub axles on the Thomas property so they could make the insinuation mud stick in court. The origins of the axle itself remain a mystery to this day. Nor does the evidence prove the axle was "attached as a weight" to Harvey Crewe. We only have Bruce Hutton's word for this, and his word is worthless. Justice Sir Trevor Henry, in his summing up, explicitly stated, "There is no evidence, of course, which can directly show to you that [the axle] was on the accused's farm."

Strike two for McGregor.

"In the third place," finishes McGregor, "the cartridge shell found in the garden at the third search is identified as having been ejected from the rifle of the accused. These matters...seem to me to identify the murderer as the person who had at all times possessed the rifle, who possessed Number Eight cartridges and who had the axle on his farm.

"These three matters must have satisfied the jury that the only inference beyond any reasonable doubt was that the accused was the guilty aggressor. In my view, from the legal aspect, no further reference to the Court should be granted."

Can you begin to now see why Arthur Thomas deserved his million dollar compensation payout? The entire case, in the eyes of all judges, hinged on fabricated evidence that the courts believed was real. Judges ruined their reputations because Bruce Hutton and his team lied to them. The New Zealand Police took a PR beating they've never recovered from, because they endorsed and encouraged officers like Bruce Hutton to lie in court cases. By the time of the second Thomas trial in 1973, Detective Inspector Hutton himself announced the case had already cost taxpayers between $6 million and $8 million in 1973 dollars, and that figure did not include the cost of the second trial which had not yet been tallied up.[104] By the time the case eventually ended in 1980, the actions of Bruce Hutton and Len Johnston in framing Thomas had cost New Zealand taxpayers somewhere north of $50 million in today's money, based on a conversion of Hutton's 1973 figure plus three million 1973 dollars extra to cover the cost of the second trial, further appeals, indepen-

---

104 "Murders costs put at $6m-$8m", *NZ Herald*, 18 April 1973

dent reviews, compensation and the cost of the Royal Commission, as well as the cost of Arthur's incarceration – about $100,000 a year in today's money). And for that, Bruce Hutton was promoted and commended by New Zealand Police Headquarters. Nothing changes, evidently, although criminal charges should now be laid in my view.[105]

The National Government's Attorney-General in February 1972, Sir Roy Jack, quickly welcomed McGregor's discredited report, declaring, "We have been fortunate in having the benefit of a very careful and thorough examination of all the papers made by the Hon. Sir George McGregor, a recently retired Supreme Court judge. No ground has been shown for reference of the case back to the Court of Appeal for further review. Justice has been done."[106]

For good measure, he added, "I hope that the public will share my confidence that justice has been done in this case and are now prepared to accept the verdict and the decision of the Court of Appeal."

Vivien Thomas, who unlike the media had not been given an embargoed copy of McGregor's report in advance, was also quick to react. "It has been a big shock to everyone. Everyone has been stunned. There is no justice in New Zealand. I honestly thought that we would get a retrial."

Truth newspaper, later to become one of the key players in Thomas' retrial bid, was carrying a major story that week: "A large wife-swapping ring has shocked residents in and around Gore, in the

---

105 Under the Crimes Act 1961, I believe there is sufficient evidence for Hutton to still be charged and sent to jail for the rest of his days. The police don't hesitate to prosecute sexual offences dating back to the 1960s so I can't see why this would be difficult. I don't have the 1961 version at my fingertips, but I'm sure there was an equivalent provision to the current s115, which reads: **Conspiring to bring false accusation.** Everyone who conspires to prosecute any person for any alleged offence, knowing that person to be innocent thereof, is liable...(a) to imprisonment for a term not exceeding 14 years if that person might, on conviction of the alleged offence, be sentenced to preventive detention, or to imprisonment for a term of 3 years or more. I'm sure Hutton's lawyers might try to argue he didn't 'know' Thomas was innocent when he framed him, but I think a jury can reasonably be left to determine whether a cop who has to fake evidence to push the balance from 'innocent' to 'guilty' is deemed to know it by definition.
There's also section 113: **Fabricating evidence.** Everyone is liable to imprisonment for a term not exceeding 7 years who, with intent to mislead any tribunal holding any judicial proceeding to which section 108 applies, fabricates evidence by any means other than perjury.
Or section 116: **Conspiring to defeat justice.** Everyone is liable to imprisonment for a term not exceeding 7 years who conspires to obstruct, prevent, pervert, or defeat the course of justice in New Zealand or the course of justice in an overseas jurisdiction.
And there's always that old standby, s109: **Punishment of perjury.** (1) Except as provided in subsection (2), everyone is liable to imprisonment for a term not exceeding 7 years who commits perjury. (2) *If perjury is committed in order to procure the conviction of a person for any offence for which the maximum punishment is not less than 3 years' imprisonment, the punishment may be imprisonment for a term not exceeding 14 years*
106 *NZ Herald*, 18 February 1972

South Island. People fear that the group's activities could herald another outbreak of venereal disease. *Truth* knows the names of many couples allegedly involved in the wife swapping. They include some of the district's leading business and professional men, as well as sports identities. Wife swapping is not illegal..."[107]

Again, some things never change. Entertaining as that article may have been, *Truth* nonetheless interrupted its programme to deliver a front page story on the Thomas case. "An anonymous telephone caller might hold a trump card in renewed efforts to win another trial for Arthur Allan Thomas." The newspaper revealed that a man claiming to be a juror had rung the Thomas Retrial Committee "several months ago" and said jeweller William Eggleton's evidence about the bloodstained watch was the clincher in the jury's eyes, just as Justice Henry had feared it might be.

The call had suddenly become relevant now that McGregor had admitted Eggleton's evidence was wrong, but denied a retrial because he claimed the jury would have paid no notice to Eggleton. Although it was illegal to poll jurors, the Committee was hopeful the caller might ring back and offer to testify about the influence of the watch evidence.

Inside its pages, the newspaper devoted significant column inches to the previously unpublished affidavit of Graeme Hewson, Harvey's best friend and the man police had asked to stay with Len Demler early on and spy on him. Hewson's new affidavit contained intriguing allegations that the area where police "found" the incriminating shell case on October 27 1970 had actually been searched twice previously, with nothing found at all.

"During this time (after Jeannette Crewe's body had been found on Aug. 16 1970)...I offered to assist the police in any way I could," testified Hewson. "I was invited to form one of the search parties in the grounds of the Crewe farmhouse...This party examined the ground around the house very thoroughly and we were instructed to look for .22 calibre shells.

"The garden alongside the wall of the house and along the fence lines of the enclosure around the house were thoroughly searched by me and police officers...In these (court exhibit) photographs can be seen the site of the flower garden which was planted alongside the fence outside the kitchen.

---

107 *NZ Truth*, 22 February, 1972

"I am quite positive, because I myself was involved in the work, that this garden was stripped of vegetation and then carefully sieved in the two or three days after Jeannette's body was found. I am quite sure, from the thoroughness with which the work was done, that if a cartridge case had been in that garden at that time, it would not have escaped notice.

"I am informed and believe that it has been said that the garden alongside the fenceline outside the kitchen was not searched with a sieve in the August search. I can say quite positively that that statement is wrong. The garden in question was searched and the earth as sifted as I have described, and I helped to do it," swore Hewson on oath.

So here were two key points – the significance to the jury of Eggleton's mistaken watch testimony, and a sworn affidavit suggesting police had lied when they said on oath the Crewe garden flower bed had not been searched. "Surely," asked *Truth*, "this affidavit alone is grounds enough for a new trial?"

The Thomas case was, by now, making international news. In Britain and the United States, there was interest in this classic whodunit and the baby left behind. The man at the centre of the growing media storm, Arthur Thomas, described himself as in "shock" at the McGregor report findings.[108]

"I still have not got over the shock yet. I'm not doing much work as my mind is going round and round. I can't make out what's hit me or believe that this is happening to me. Last night I was thinking in my bed about 12 o'clock, how can we let the people know the inside story of why they turned me down?"

Thomas told his lawyers in the letter he was happy to meet McGregor or any other judge and answer their questions directly. "I'm fighting fit in here, my blood is boiling, yet I can't do a thing to help. I feel so bloody hopeless, but I still have faith that this will come right in the end."

Arthur's mum, the late Ivy Thomas, also weighed in to the public debate.[109]

"I know my boy … he's innocent … he would never stoop to such a horrible, dastardly crime. We feel very strongly about this. You can't tell a mother what her children are like. Arthur didn't do this

---

108 *Sunday News*, 27 February 1972
109 *Sunday News*, 5 March 1972

... it is not in him ... he's a good boy and I'm proud of him, proud of my whole family. Nothing on earth would ever convince me that Arthur is guilty of this horrible crime."

Mrs Thomas said she and her husband would continue the fight for a retrial despite McGregor's report. "We're going to battle on ... you don't just leave an innocent man to rot in prison. What frightens me most, is that the murderer is still free and the person who committed this crime is being protected by others."

What she didn't know, and which is only now being revealed a little later in this book after 40 years, is that two new suspects in the Crewe murders both had extremely strong ties to the police. And yes, the killer appears to have been very well placed to escape detection.

Evidently, all this public and media pressure was beginning to have an impact. By late April 1972, the Thomas Retrial Committee had been invited to submit fresh evidence to Attorney-General Sir Roy Jack, who promised to reconsider whether to re-open the murder case. "The door to justice is always open and has in fact never been closed," Jack told committee members.[110] It's interesting to note, four decades later, that politicians back then seemed far more willing to re-open criminal cases under constitutional conventions than the timid 'hands-off' approach taken by governments today.

Arthur Thomas was praying he'd get the right outcome. "I've got my faith – it will all come right. I've always been religious. I've always believed in God, I don't go to church, but you don't have to do that to believe in God. It's what's in your heart and mind and soul that matters."[111]

Thomas' prayers were answered. On June 19, 1972, Attorney-General Sir Roy Jack recommended to the Governor-General that Arthur Thomas' case be referred back to the Court of Appeal in light of the new evidence that had come to light, which by now included not just the affidavits on the watch and shell case, but also one from Bruce Roddick where he categorically confirmed Vivien Thomas was not the mystery woman. The Government also agreed to a Thomas Retrial Committee request that the bullet fragments from the bodies of the Crewes be sent for further forensic analysis to Britain, along with the controversial shell case, to see if Arthur Thomas' gun could be definitively ruled out or in as the murder

---

110 *Sunday News*, 23 April 1972
111 *Trial By Ambush*, Booth, p62

weapon. "Clearly the result of the tests could have a very important bearing on the case," admitted the Attorney-General.

As it turned out, the bullet tests in England couldn't prove or disprove Thomas' gun was involved, although the British scientists were reported by the *Herald* as "amazed to learn that the cartridge case had been found in the garden more than four months after the killings. The shell apparently was not as badly corroded as might have been expected after such a period."[112] The Governor-General handed the entire file to the Court of Appeal on August 21, 1972, for reconsideration, and Thomas' lawyers began drafting their formal appeal submissions.

Stuck in Paremoremo jail, however, Arthur Thomas couldn't know that his marriage was falling apart. Vivien had taken a lover, and was drugged up on Valium and Mogadon as her life and dreams collapsed around her under the stress of the case. "I was living on pills and smoking like a chimney," she would later confess.[113] She'd shot through to visit her parents in England for several months, and took advantage of that time to clear her head, ditch the drugs and try and work out where her life was headed.

In the newspapers, the only hint Arthur Thomas received of marital problems was a veiled reference by Pat Vesey in an article defending Vivien.[114]

"Strangely enough there are people far more interested in spreading malicious gossip than trying to reason out whether Arthur Thomas should get a new trial," wrote Vesey. "Secondly, Vivien's health has suffered under the strain of keeping the farm going and fighting to prove her husband innocent, and her doctor has ordered her to take a complete rest away from all the present atmosphere of struggle and tragedy.

"The extent some people will go to hurt this already cruelly maligned woman knows no bounds. These rumours are the lies of a deranged mind or the work of someone who wants to divert attention from the questions they themselves will have to answer about their conduct throughout this case, and should anyone be found to instigate such rumours, no stone will remain unturned to see that they are legally dealt with," Vesey wrote.

---

112 *NZ Herald*, 2 August 1972
113 *Sunday News*, 26 November 1972
114 *Courier Times Advertiser*, 10 May 1972

For gentle, naive Arthur Thomas, talk of rumours about his wife must have been largely unfathomable. Those months without Vivien found him deep in the heart of Paremoremo jail, at the centre of all kinds of trouble, stories he's now telling for the first time in nearly 40 years.

CHAPTER 9

The Inside Story: Prison Life

While family and friends battled for Thomas' release on the outside, behind the bars of Paremoremo prison Arthur Thomas was forced to conform to the prisoners' code: don't complain, do what you are told, and don't rat. As wife Jenny jokes today, "He went into jail an innocent man, and came out a criminal!" It's true what they say – prison is a university degree in crime.

One of those experiences saw Arthur hospitalised.

"Ah, deary me," remembers Thomas, pausing to gaze at the sun on the pasture outside. "I was bringing cigarettes and chocolate in through an officer. And this other inmate had money and I didn't have any money. But he had a bit of money inside the prison. This is going back to Paremoremo now, when I was convicted. And the inmate found out that I had a way of getting stuff into the prison through a prison officer."

"Arthur, I'll do a deal," said the inmate. "Chocolates and cigarettes and things, for double the price, cos I've got plenty of money," he said. "I've got plenty of money, and we'll double it, so the rest of it is yours."

Okay, thought Arthur, what's the catch. "So what do you want – cigarettes, chocolate? I don't do drugs."

"No, I'm not interested in that."

Thomas' new client promised to pay, and on the due day told Arthur he wanted to meet him down at the prison kitchen. "At certain times in the kitchen, no one's there see, and I thought oh, there's no conflict here. But instead of paying, he hit me in the jaw there –" Thomas breaks off to rub his jaw where he got blindsided. "He walked up to me. There was no threatening, no warning. Bang!

Hit me right there. He knocked me over, and walked away."

As Arthur picked himself up, he realised there were hard bits of stone in his mouth. Only, they weren't stones. "I got up and oh, blood was coming out of my mouth, and when I talked I was spitting blood and teeth, and it was just like that. I looked up, there was no one around, see. No cops or no one, no inmates to help me out."

He staggered to the door and the intercom.

"I just asked, pushed the button I think, and this camera comes on and they can see me and push the button so I can go through."

Thomas, who'd gained privileges including making tea for the prison superintendent, couldn't hide his injuries when he wheeled in the tea trolley a short time later. "He seemed to know something's happened. And I said 'Oh, I'll have to see a dentist. I think I've got a lost tooth there; I had a falling out with an inmate'."

When the dentist arrived, he took one look at the mauled mouth and ordered Thomas' immediate dispatch to Middlemore Hospital. Arthur couldn't believe the media circus that quickly followed. "The Minister of Justice in the Labour Government ordered a full enquiry into this. Big news. Front page. 'Thomas King Hit' while in Paremoremo. But there I was, waiting to go to the surgery and a nurse came in and said 'Oh, your brother, Desmond, can't come and see you'.

" 'See me?,' I said. 'What's going on? He doesn't know about this.'

" 'Yes', she said. 'It's on the News'." Thomas roars with laughter at the thought that a punch in the chops made the national news. " 'What?,' I said, 'The whole of New Zealand knows about this?' Of course the Minister of Justice made two statements, a big enquiry."

In fact, his jaw had been broken in the attack, and all of it was caused by Thomas opening up a sideline business in the jail, smuggling chocolates and cigarettes in through a prison officer. The fracas ultimately cost him his perks for a while. "I shouldn't have been dealing with an officer, you know. I shouldn't have got into that.

"When I got fixed up, after a few days in there, and got back to my cell – I'd had a good job there. I had the set of keys. I was looking after the superintendent's cups of tea – any VIPs, some judges, yeah. Cuppa teas. Had a good job. And I'd been given the keys so as to keep the officers out of the biscuits and things, locked up in my cupboard, in the guard room.

"Anyway, the superintendent says to me, 'Righto Thomas'. He

wanted the name of the officer who was bringing in the goodies. And I said 'Oh no, I don't want to', because the guard had a family and all that, you know. So the superintendent says, 'Righto, hand your keys into there. Go back to the workshop'. I lost me job. I don't care. It didn't worry me. Back to the sewing. I was sewing hats and things back there."

But even something as simple as sewing couldn't ensure Thomas stayed out of trouble. He'd been assigned light duties making shirts and rain hats, but found his sewing desk became ground zero for a prison rebellion.

"The other inmates sometimes, if they had a little problem or something, I tried not to know anything about it – just kept me head down. Anyways, underneath this big long table in the sewing room they used to keep all the stores of materials, and beautiful materials too. And someone said, 'they're going to light a fire here'."

Arthur froze, looking at the materials table beside his sewing desk. He knew there was nothing he could do, nothing he could say. It was a Sergeant Schultz moment. "I know nothing! Nothing at all."

He nervously watched as the culprit crept away, leaving a little flame licking up the desk beside him.

"Ah they lit it, the inmates. They got behind and lit the bastard. I knew they were doing it, but you don't poke your nose in and say, 'No don't do that.' No way, or they'd smash the living daylights out of you – oh yeah."

Like a scene from a comedy movie, all he could do was sew harder, hoping his intensity would attract the attention of guards over the side of the room, and letting his eyes dart and gesture, without moving a single facial muscle. All the while, the flames were getting bigger.

"There I am, at my sewing machine, the fire couldn't have been any closer; we knew the smoke was going up. And I thought, carry on sewing. And anyhow the smoke got thicker, this guard, I was hoping he'd see it you know."

With smoke now stinging his eyes, Arthur just sewed even harder, trying to judge at what point he should cut and run, mindful of the consequences if he did.

"Like I said, they'd smash the proverbial out of you. Inmates are… there's no officer will help you man, you're just on your own… and I knew that. There's a thing with inmates; you 'know nothing' eh?

And I learnt that very quickly with inmates telling me, yeah."

Finally, the guard turned around. He looked at the smoke cloud now creeping across the ceiling, and the flames now keeping Arthur Thomas toasty and warm, then he looked at Arthur. "He knew I knew," remembers Thomas, "but I couldn't tell him."

Then, the guard grabbed the phone and rang through the first alarm.

"At this particular time, they did not see the person who lit the fire. But everyone was taken out, the fire engine came with the fire hoses, put the flames out, a lot of damage done."

Even though Arthur was sitting beside the blaze, the superintendent realised he wasn't to blame. "They knew I wasn't that sort of guy," he jokes now. "Arthur Thomas is a farmer. He might be a murderer, but he's not an arsonist! I'm sure that's what they were thinking," he laughs.[115]

The rough justice Thomas spoke of didn't happen often, but when it did it was usually brutal.

"I remember one time, a person had cornered a child molester or something it was, and they put a blanket over him and then beat the crap out of them. And I remember I just walked the line, but that's terrible that, put a blanket over them first and then whatever weapon that they've got…"

His voice fades away as the memory of the terrible beating plays out in his mind.

"Yeah when you see these things, you just tell the guards, 'No I didn't see it you know'. That's the ruling with inmates in the prison; you don't say nothing. You just say nothing about it."

Thomas was still in the thick of it when his fellow inmates decided to stage a full riot. Word came, as it always did, through the grapevine that prisoners in D-Block – the section of Parry reserved for the worst offenders – were staging a revolt over conditions in their wing. In sympathy, other prisoners stormed the gymnasium, breaking chairs and repeatedly bending the steel legs back and forth until they broke off, creating crude but effective clubs. Arthur found himself sandwiched in the gym between angry inmates and a delegation led by the superintendent trying to calm the crowd down.

"Some of those inmates who went to D Block said 'Right-o. If

---

[115] In the case of fire, the wardens' offices at Paremoremo jail now have "emergency escape chutes", according to journalist Rosemary McLeod in the *Sunday Star-Times*.

there's nothing done about it we're going to burn this gymnasium down right now'." Across, the auditorium, Thomas could see superintendent Jack Hobson, flanked by a priest and two familiar faces – his own lawyers Peter Williams QC and Kevin Ryan. "Gee, I thought, I've got Peter Williams and Kevin Ryan up here, I'll walk with them and walk out of here while she burns down here."

Thomas had already considered bolting to the toilet block. "The toilet won't burn, it's all concrete blocks and things, I might as well hide there, but I might get smoked out, see? I was worried, you know, I was only a farmer. I didn't know, where are we going to go here. But the inmates had these chair legs for their defence."

Journalist Rosemary McLeod was the first female journalist to tour the prison, and wrote of the design instructions, "When a government architect set out to design Paremoremo he was told to imagine each prisoner had a gun, a hacksaw blade, a ladder, rope, and a stick of gelignite. So it's the safest place in New Zealand to be locked up."[116]

Evidently they hadn't factored in chair legs.

Order was restored without Thomas needing to dash for the toilets, but not before the ringleaders had been identified and noted down for later arrest and transfer to D-Block to join their compatriots. Superintendent Hobson decided to try and improve morale by distributing *Playboy* magazines.

"Jack Hobson I think was a better superintendent; he was more lenient, and I remember him allowing inmates to have *Playboy* … do you remember *Playboy* magazine, you can see the old 'how's your father' and everything, the old upside down birds nest," Thomas cackles, as wife Jenny rolls her eyes and shoots him a look. "And Supt. Hobson said, 'Yeah, why not have those books,' where the other superintendent wouldn't allow that. So he just was a bit more lenient. But my favourite superintendent was Sid Ward. He's dead now. I sent a card when he died, when I heard he'd passed on."

But it wasn't all riots, beatings and birds nests. The prisoners liked their cups of tea or coffee, but they weren't permitted to have kettles in case they used boiling water as a weapon against the guards. That didn't stop good old kiwi ingenuity. Using two razor-blades sandwiched either side of a lump of wood or matchsticks, with a

---

116 Originally published in *The Sunday Times*, reprinted in the *Sunday Star-Times* February 14, 2010

wire from each blade running back to a jerry-rigged shaving cord, inmates built what became known as 'tea-bombs'.

The logic was that you dumped the razor assembly of the tea-bomb into water contained in the porcelain basin of your cell, or in a cup, and you flicked the switch. As 240 volts surged through, the blades quickly heated and boiled the water (Don't try this at home, it will probably kill you). They were highly dangerous, and highly illegal, and Arthur Thomas was the proud owner of one, in his capacity as purveyor of fine teas to the inmates; in particular, to the man in the cell next to him, one George Wilder – the prison escaper immortalised in a Howard Morrison Quartet song, *George the Wilder Colonial Boy*. Wilder captured the public imagination on the run by leaving apologies and thank you notes at homes he burgled for food or cash.

"So I have to boil the water for George and give him a cup of tea as well as me, that's our little system," recalls Thomas. "Anyhow, sometimes I'm a bit slow in giving George his cup of tea, and next thing, tap tap tap on the floor, and oh that's George!"

Thomas looked down, to see a hand reaching underneath the bars at the front corner of his cell. In the hand was a piece of paper.

"Because the wall's only a thick, concrete block between his cell and mine, there's a gap where you can sweep the floor and all that stuff – anyway, he's passing me this piece of paper: Georgie Wilder out in the desert, the hot sun and the tongue hanging out [laughs] and he's trying to grab his bloody drink, and he looks so real. By heaven, he's good."

Arthur looked at the picture, and then it dawned on him what it meant. "Oh George. Struth! What a joker. I'm a bit slow here, he was asking me to put the jug on, see? He had a really dry sense of humour eh."

But with illicit rewards always lurks the risk of discovery.

"Yeah I was charged. I was caught with one, with that particular one here. And okay, the officers searched your cell and found this little matchbox; mine was in the matchbox and, 'Yeah Arthur, I found a tea bomb in your room. I'm charging you with it', – because I had to go to Jack Hobson, the superintendent. And I lost five days' – loss of pay. So I'd work and get no pay, see."

Oddly, however, the prison's 3iC, a man named Jackson, evidently unaware of Thomas' culpability in procuring tea-bombs, and assuming he was trusted because of his job in the superintendent's office, took him aside a short time later.

"Oh Thomas, won't you come in here and help me tidy my room up."

When Thomas entered the office behind Jackson, he could hardly believe his eyes – a desktop covered in seized tea-bombs.

"Oh could you get rid of this please?"

"Yeah okay."

"And this one, just dump this one here. Okay, you get rid of it."

Thomas had died and gone to tea-bomb heaven. Here were the confiscated illegal items, and the jailers were handing them back to him to dispose of. Only in the New Zealand justice system. Naturally, the Pukekawa farmer found good homes for the tea-bombs.

It's unbelievable," he grins, leaning back in the sofa and taking a sip from a kettle-made cuppa. "Then there was the monster tea-bomb made by my good mate Murray." Murray, who'd been shot and wounded in a home invasion that left his beautiful bride dead, had nonetheless been charged and convicted with her murder; all the while protesting his innocence like Thomas. But Murray didn't believe in half measures. If everyone else was using razor blades for tea-bombs, he wanted something more powerful. His tea-bomb was constructed from two metal plates – industrial strength.

But with power, whether temporal or electric, comes responsibility. And Murray made a crucial mistake one night while trying to boil his cup of tea in the handbasin.

"He was caught with the big one. What happened, he had a couple of quite big plates, you know. But what happened, he just touched the plate on the steel bench there, and it blew the flaming fuse. Arced it. Bang! And the prison lights went out."

The short circuit didn't exactly escape the attention of surprised guards at Paremoremo maximum security prison.

"Yeah, they had to get an electrician. It cost nearly $100 to get the electrician to check the fuse, and then the prison officer walked past Murray's cell and the dumb bastard, he still had his big tea-bomb sitting there in plain sight. They unlocked the door and he was taken to the ground eh, straightaway."

You'd think all this might have put Arthur Thomas off any idea of further messing about with illegal potboilers, but no. "I got caught a second time with a tea bomb. The first time it was Jack Hobson and I lost a week's pay. The second time I was caught with a tea bomb, I went up to Sid Ward. And instead of giving me like two weeks – because it was the second time caught – oh no, he gave me about two or three days' loss of pay. At this rate, I thought, the next time I get caught I'll go free!"

But it wasn't only tea. Arthur Thomas and George Wilder quickly realised they could also make moonshine in prison: Japanese sake – rice wine. In Arthur's portion of the wing, there were ten cells in a row, and a corridor running along them. At the end of the corridor, a shower with a barred window grate above eye level for ventilation of the steam to the outside air.

Below decks was the prison kitchen, with "rice to make bread there, see the yeast is very important," explains Thomas matter-of-factly, "so they had rice and sultanas and all to make this sake. So we were pretty good at it, some of the inmates and myself, because I used to make it in Pukekawa – that's another story."

It was all very well having the ingredients, but they needed containers to brew it in. They decided to use bottles of toilet cleaner. "Yeah," – laughs Thomas as I look at him dubiously. "Oh, she's well-rinsed out in the water and…"

"You haven't died of cancer yet," quips his wife Jenny.

Having assembled the ingredients, and some rinsed-out poison containers to ferment the brew, Thomas and George Wilder needed somewhere to store it where the guards wouldn't find it. Which is where the showers came in. There was a cavity in the blocks that formed the outer wall of the shower – the perfect place to lower the bottles into, secured by a piece of string.

"And in to the cavity went what tools we used, to be able to lever, to pass it out you know. And we were able to put the string inside and down near the side where you can't see and have the string holding this and then you push the loop in and held the string, that holds this cleaning bottle. And of course, no worries, the screws can't see the bottle and things."

Arthur's problem was that he hadn't been much of a drinker, but George Wilder was and he held his liquor much better. "We went on drinking it and I tell you what, he was very good. He was a wiry guy, he didn't look like he was drunk at all, but he was.

"Anyhow, I was into this drinking from a half-gallon and I shared with some of the inmates, but I drank most of this. Now, I hadn't drunk for years, drinking spirits you know. I went down below to have my... and I thought I was pretty good, I was staggering but I'm really... but anyhow, I went down below to have my meal in the dining room. All the meals are down below. You grab your plate and you go and grab your food and everything. Anyhow, we had plastic knife and forks, and I had problems."

The more Arthur Thomas – 'Hayseed' to his mates – tried to cut the potatoes the more he missed and stabbed the table, or almost up-ended his plate.

"So I thought, stuff the knife and fork, I start grabbing the potatoes with my hands. The screws always need to check everyone's behaving you know, but he noticed old Thomas is not eating like he should. And anyhow I was stuffing potato and everything down my gob and I walked out, but then the officer said, 'Thomas, if you don't make the stairs, you're in the pound' [solitary confinement].

"Mate, he knew me, because I was out to lunch at dinner time and he could tell... you know. This is the story, but anyhow, so what I did, I went to stagger towards the railing of the step. He said if I fall down... you know, if I do fall down, I'm in the pound. So the idea was, don't fall down. So I grabbed the handrail you know. Whoops, missed a step. But I never hit the ground."

It was a long, lurching trip up the stairs, and into his cell, fighting the urge to just drop to the ground and laugh his head off, all under the watchful eye of a knowing guard. Georgie Wilder, on the other hand, who'd had even more to drink, didn't display a single sign of inebriation.

From making moonshine sake, Thomas then turned his talents to trading in tobacco. He was brought in – as a trusted lifer – to assist another inmate in making up official tobacco allowances – known as "figs" – for later sale to prisoners up and down the country. It was a prison-organised operation, the idea being that inmates could use their prison wages to buy smokes through this Justice Department programme. Paremoremo had the contract to pack and fill the orders for all the jails nationwide.

"They'd buy a big box of tobacco from WD & HO Wills, and us inmates had to weigh what they call figs for the inmates. Put it in a little plastic bag, weigh it, seal it and send it off around the country, round all the prisons round there. When you buy a fig – you call it a fig – it costs you so much money. But we were also smuggling out tobacco in our socks and anywhere in the areas that they don't search too much, and giving it to inmates around the prison, see.

"But the thing is, the wardens know that when one box comes in it's gonna be so many thousand figs for one box. So what we did," – Thomas begins giggling uncontrollably here – "we're adding a bit of water. [laughter] We were adding water [laughter] to the thing to get the right weight."

Knowing the officers would randomly weigh the figs, the inmates realised they could manipulate the weights by adding a drop of water to each fig to make up the weight of the few strands of tobacco they were stealing from each unit.

The officers couldn't tell, because the weight was correct, and it was too soon for the damp tobacco to go mouldy. By the time it reached its destination in Invercargill, however, the quality of the fig might not have been so crash hot. The Pare inmates, meanwhile, had a secure stock of illicit, dry tobacco over and above the official quota.

Physical fitness could be an issue in the prison. In the main wings, prisoners had access to the jail's gymnasium. But in the classification section, where prisoners were held until authorities had determined whether they were dangerous or harmless, there was no gym equipment. Necessity, again, was the mother of invention.

"Every inmate that goes to maximum security goes to classification. When they get classified, some go to another prison or whatever it is. In the long term just like me, life imprisonment, you enter the blocks. Some of the young fellas in the classification wanted to build their muscles up a wee bit, while they're inside, in the prison see. So anyhow, there was none of this in the classification block. None of this weightlifting at all. So what they did – they used the broom, you know we were allowed to sweep the floors and everything and keep it tidy and everything."

But while a broomstick was the right length, it needed weights. Thomas and his colleagues quickly twigged that the massive cast-iron sewing machines used in the workshop could be slung onto the broomsticks, one on each end.

"These big, special, heavy-duty sewing machines – they were quite good. We could lift them out and they're quite a bit of a weight... by jove they were heavy. And the broom is bending," says Thomas, re-enacting the moment and making a panting sound. So far, so good, but then the next inmate tried it.

"He lifts it right up high, and one of the sewing machines slipped off, eh. They're cast iron, and under the lino is concrete floor, so she's solid, eh. It was all going so well until the stick broke and there was a massive crash as this machine hits the floor. Struth, did we scatter. Because we were all watching, and next thing we ran back to our... lucky it wasn't my sewing machine anyway!"

Prison guards working in an office up the corridor came sprinting.

"What the f***'s goin' on here? What's happened here?," they said, staring at the battered black machine on the floor.

"Oh, it just dropped," someone said. Arthur can't recall what the final excuse was. The next day, though, he found his own sewing machine had been appropriated to replace the broken one.

Arthur's sewing skills came in handy the month that convicted killer Dean Wickliffe enjoyed a brief taste of freedom during an escape from Paremoremo. Wickliffe had been imprisoned in 1972 for the manslaughter of a Wellington jeweller, and achieved notoriety for becoming the only man to have twice escaped from New Zealand's highest security jail. On his second outing, I played a small role as the TV3 journalist left alone in a dark field in the middle of the night while police evacuated and left the media behind with the comforting words, "You'd better get out of here, he's on the loose with a gun." On Wickliffe's first outing, however, Arthur Thomas was the prison superintendent's go-to guy in figuring out how it was done.

It turned out many of the floor mats in prison common rooms and showers had disappeared, and no one had really paid too much attention. Late at night, Wickliffe would unravel the stitching on the mats and weave the strands together to make a rope. On the day of his escape he'd thrown his rope over the perimeter fences and scarpered.

Acting superintendent Sid Ward asked Arthur Thomas to help categorise the escape rope into court exhibits. "We were sitting there on the floor of the superintendent's office, and there were bits of thread all over the place from different mats. You couldn't see the floor for all the strands of rope they'd recovered. Anyhow, the main superintendent Jack Hobson came in, took one look at how much rope Wickliffe had managed to hide and use, swore loudly and said, 'Did they use a bloody truck to carry the rope into the yard?'"

Hobson wasn't happy that his prison officers had missed such an audacious escape plan, and stomped out of the office slamming the door. Arthur Thomas and Sid Ward cracked up laughing.

"I couldn't believe how the hell they'd hid all the ropes for two days' straight," chuckles Arthur.

It would be easy to assume life in maximum security jail was a cake walk. Thomas says however the stories are the stand-out bits – those isolated days that broke the boredom of staring at three cell walls and bars.

"I lost my freedom. For nine years, I was locked away. I was innocent, and it didn't matter what anyone else thought – I was doing a life sentence and I knew I hadn't done it. I lost a lot of things outside."

He lost his farm and, of course as we now know, he would soon lose his wife, Vivien.

CHAPTER 10

On The Cover Of The *Rolling Stone*

In October 1972, a newspaper headline reported, "Thomas – most trusted inmate". For the first time in three years at Paremoremo, an inmate had been awarded the job of cleaning the visiting room after visiting was over. He disclosed his promotion, which included cleaning the toilets, in a letter to friend and Retrial Committee chairman Pat Vesey.[117]

"It will take about two hours to clean but they will pay me a full day for it. About three years ago an inmate had the job until they found 22 bullets in a toilet. That was the end of it until now. I'm very pleased to be regarded as a trusted inmate."

Despite the huge media attention on his case, however, it's staggering how many basic errors crept into media coverage that showed journalists just were not fact checking properly. Despite calling herself "Jeannette" with two 'n's on official documents like her Will, almost without exception the media spelt her name with one 'n'. The New Zealand Press Association occasionally referred to a murder victim called "David Henry Crewe" – presumably if such a man existed he would be surprised at reports of his early and violent demise. Vivien was most often called "Vivian" or "Vivienne" in newspaper reports. And Arthur Thomas, who'd been aged 32 when he was arrested in November 1970, was evidently the Peter Pan of Paremoremo – still aged 32 according to the *Levin Chronicle* in February 1973[118], even though he'd just had his 35th birthday. The *NZ Herald* in December 1972 had a front page story about "Thomas, aged 32", even though he was about to turn 35 in less than a month.

---
117 *Sunday News*, 29 October 1972
118 *Levin Chronicle*, 5 February 1973

There were continuous references to the "Chennell estate" even though the family name was Chennells – which I've cross-checked with Births, Deaths & Marriages (that error even crept into the books by Pat Booth and David Yallop probably as a result of police error, but not that of journalist Chris Birt who appears to have done an exemplary job of getting basic factual information correct).[119]

It wasn't until September 1972 that the Thomas Retrial Committee engaged the services of forensic scientist Dr Jim Sprott, to analyse the shell case found in the Crewe garden. His investigations would soon play a pivotal role in turning the case around.

November that year saw Vivien's return from her five month English sojourn, visiting her parents and kicking a sleeping pill habit. Her first stop was the prison. "We went to Paremoremo to see Arthur this morning, and he has still got enough faith left to believe that everything will turn out all right. If we didn't have this faith, we just couldn't keep going. The biggest factor is the knowledge that Arthur didn't commit that crime ... so we will keep going until justice is done."[120]

In January 1973, the *Sunday News* led with a front page story on Len Demler's decision to quit the Pukekawa district forever, after nearly 40 years there.[121]

"A leading player in the Crewe murders drama has sold his Pukekawa farm and is leaving the district. And already rumours are starting to fly that he has been hounded from his home and is planning to settle in America. But Len Demler, father of Jeanette (sic) Crewe, who was gunned down with her husband Harvey in their Pukekawa farm house in June 1970, told the *Sunday News*:

" 'I've sold my farm and I'll be moving out. I don't know where I will be going yet, but I reckon we've done enough farming'.

"On the doorstep of his neat, green and white painted home he said his decision had nothing to do with the Crewe murders or any of the rumours in the district. 'Me knee's crook and I've had enough. And that's all there is to it', he said. The interview was then brought to an abrupt halt by the new Mrs Demler whom the 64-year-old Pukekawa farmer married last year.

---

119 Undoubtedly, in unleashing my inner pedant, I have invited similar scrutiny of this book. So be it. In my criticisms however I do delineate between mere typo's and constant repeated errors. I just can't believe how someone could remain 32 for three years and no-one ever thought to question it!
120 *Sunday News*, 26 November 1972
121 *Sunday News*, 28 January 1973

"When Len Demler informed her that he was talking to the *Sunday News* she moved quickly to the door and slammed it shut. 'We've had enough publicity', she said."

Just a week later, Arthur Thomas' lawyers were back in the Court of Appeal in Wellington for their second appeal hearing seeking a new trial. The Court suppressed the contents of all affidavits they had presented, so media coverage was sparse. All the Thomas family could do was wait, and hope.

"Vivien Thomas was huddled before a radio in Mangamuka Bridge in the far north yesterday morning when she received the news she has been awaiting for two years," began a *Herald* front page story late February. "It came in a telephone link from Matakana Island – a call from her father-in-law to announce that her husband, Arthur Allan Thomas, had been granted a new trial. Thomas, a 32 (sic) year old Pukekawa farmer..."[122]

The Court of Appeal had indeed ruled Thomas deserved a new trial, based on the new evidence, although at this stage details of that evidence remained suppressed. There's a subtle difference between a retrial and a new trial. A retrial forces the Court to re-hear exactly the same evidence as the first trial. A new trial allows fresh evidence to be presented.

"The judges said that after hearing the new evidence, they were not satisfied that, if that evidence had been before the Supreme Court [High Court today], a jury could have come to no verdict other than guilty. 'That being so, it follows that there must be a new trial,' they said."

"I am absolutely thrilled," Vivien told reporters. Secretly, she knew her marriage to Arthur would survive or die on the outcome of the second trial. If she could just get him released. Just days later, the pressure came crashing down on her.

"Vivien Thomas 'cracked up' yesterday," reported one newspaper, saying she'd been forced to take bed rest.

"I'm going away for a few days, I just have to get away from it all. I won't tell you where I'm going, maybe you can understand why," Vivien told the journalist. Arthur, on the other hand, was dumbstruck by the news from the court.

"He was walking up the main corridor [of the prison] when we

---

122 *NZ Herald*, 27 February 1973. Matakana Island, incidentally, is near Tauranga. Matakana, where Arthur's father farmed pigs, is not an island but a region near Warkworth, north of Auckland.

first saw him," Kevin Ryan told the paper. "We gave him the big 'V' sign through the iron grilles that separated us. When we got within talking distance Arthur's first words were, 'I can't believe it'. All Arthur could say was 'gosh'. He must have said it a dozen times. Really, he was speechless."[123] Paremoremo superintendent Jack Hobson had already organised Thomas' transfer back to the remand unit at Mt Eden jail, making it his first car ride and view of the outside world in two years. It was reported as "an exciting experience for him".[124]

Across at the Thomas farm in Pukekawa, however, someone had set stock loose, busted a diesel pump and set fire to the farmhouse. Things were getting nasty in the intimidation stakes. Vivien was no longer living at the farm.

Within four weeks, the case was back in the Supreme Court, day one of the second trial, Monday 26 March 1973. This time around, it was Justice Clifford Perry and, just like the first trial, his first move was to order the sequestration of the jury in police custody at the Station Hotel.

Unlike his predecessor Paul Temm QC, who'd been fooled into suggesting the idea, Thomas' new defence lawyer Kevin Ryan strenuously objected to jury isolation, on the grounds that it would unbalance the demographic of available jurors, and that he could see no reason for keeping the jurors together as guests of the police. Justice Perry, while noting the objections, dismissed them.

Once again, police intelligence agents had pre-selected the jury pool after being given the potential jury list three weeks earlier. Thomas' lawyers had received the pre-vetted list (although they didn't know police had rigged it) only on the Thursday night before the Monday trial, leaving them one working day to research more than 90 names. Kevin Ryan later told how Hutton boasted to him about it: "We had the jury list three weeks before the trial...It doesn't matter [how we obtained it], we just had it three weeks before, and of the jury that were put on eight of them were category A. Eight were A.1. We had them down as A.1."[125]

Interestingly, the man who became jury foreman, Bob Rock, was one of those who applied to be excused from the jury service and

---

123 *Auckland Star 8 O'Clock Edition*, 3 March 1973
124 *Sunday News*, 4 March 1973
125 *Beyond Reasonable Doubt*, p275

three week trial[126], but the Crown and the court turned down his request. Not only did Rock become foreman, but it would later transpire he was an old naval buddy of police officer John Hughes, and the judge, Clifford Perry, knew it and did nothing. What are the chances, eh?

When Detective Inspector Bruce Hutton was on the witness stand in that second trial, he lied like a flatfish[127], at one point provoking such a reaction from Thomas that doctors had to be called.

Hutton was reading the court details of his November 11 interrogation of Arthur Thomas, the day he charged him with murder. "I said, 'Look Arthur, a .22 shell was found near the rear door of the Crewe house by the police. Scientists say the shell was fired from your rifle'. The accused replied: 'The murderer must have got hold of my rifle out of the house somehow. I am not a fortune teller. I cannot help you on that one'. He then went on to say…"

And at that moment, having just absorbed that Hutton was lying about the planted shell case, Thomas lost it, crying out in the courtroom, "No!" and collapsing in the dock. The courtroom was adjourned for the day, and medics were called in.

"Mr Ryan had assured me," writes Robert Coombridge, "that he was going to 'rip Mr Hutton apart' over all that evidence by saying to me that he was going to ask Arthur Thomas in the witness box whether he made such statements or not…[but] it all went unchallenged by the accused Thomas. Of course, that was no fault of the accused himself. Defence counsel had a duty and obligation to represent his client adequately."[128]

An example of defence counsel leaving Thomas hanging came when Crown prosecutor Morris threw a 'have you stopped beating your wife' type of question at him: "Do you know anybody with more reason than you to be jealous of Harvey?"

I mean, seriously. If he answered 'yes' he'd have to name some-

---

126 *Auckland Star*, 26 March 1973
127 A perfect example of Hutton's deceptive conduct was his testimony on oath at the December 1970 depositions hearing at the Otahuhu Magistrates Court. Hutton read an alleged statement he had taken from Thomas which contains the incriminating comment: "I have been told of overalls found in the boot of my car. I have been told of bloodstains on them. But I cannot remember getting blood on them." Despite Hutton's admission that he told Thomas of bloodstained overalls, no overalls were ever produced in evidence, and as Robert Coombridge points out no detective ever testified about finding bloody overalls in the boot of Thomas' car. Like John Hughes, Bruce Hutton wasn't above fabricating comments and weaselling them into an official statement – a statement later read by the juries.
128 *The Crewe Murders at Pukekawa* by Robert Coombridge, p53

one and explain why, and of course by answering 'no' he walked straight into the Crown prosecutor's linguistic trap. While many readers might have paused more and answered "I had no reason to be jealous of Harvey at all, so there must be someone else", that's you, and Arthur's Arthur. This was the kind of badger-baiting the prosecution indulged in virtually every hour of the trial, and it's another illustration of why and how he got stitched up.

Even now, Arthur remembers that question above all others.

"Oh, that was dirty! 'Can you think of anyone who had more reason to kill Harvey than you?'. I just sat there and I couldn't think what to say, and I just said 'no'. That bastard!"

It's something that should have been picked up in a re-examination of his client by Kevin Ryan, and clarified. It appears not to have been. When I question Thomas about the efforts of his lawyers, he's exceedingly grateful for their efforts, but he admits hindsight has shown things that could have been done very differently. Those issues, he says, were out of his hands at the time.

"They're the ones who were jacking up the trial and I just did what I was told to do by the lawyers. The defence lawyers, they're the guys running the show."

He does believe Kevin Ryan and Paul Temm didn't do enough to fight the jury sequestration idea. "I think where Kevin Ryan failed was the jury being locked up by police. He should have jumped on that very hard, to say, 'I'm defending my client', and walk out of the court. He should have done that," he says softly, pausing.

"Because that's what happened, I couldn't say anything. I could see what was going to happen, but I couldn't, I wasn't allowed to speak up. It happened with Paul Temm at the first trial; the cops were all set with their bottles of champagne – 'get this man convicted again.' It didn't matter what cost. He should have done more."

In truth, however, watching senior counsel storm out of court in protest might have provided great theatrics, but it would have been a gesture of impotent and irrelevant rage. The machine would have rumbled inexorably over Arthur Thomas regardless.

Thomas' supporters should have realised by this time that corrupt cops like Bruce Hutton and Len Johnston had no intention of losing, no intention of letting the facts get in the way of their good story. "The supporters of Arthur Allan Thomas, who saw the Pukekawa farmer crucified more than two years ago, hoped for a resurrection before the Easter of 1973," reported journalist Terry Bell in *Rolling Stone*, in a piece he wrote as a media spectator to the second trial.[129]

"Instead, they witnessed yet another crucifixion in a courtroom environment that had the atmosphere of a heads or tails lottery... But there was more to it than a simple lottery with a single prize. Bets on the one side were backed by careers, futures and the edifice of a judicial system.

"Confused, battered and bewildered he tearfully pleaded his innocence in the wake of the jury's guilty verdict. The voice was plaintive, cracked – and all but drowned out by the sobbing, angry roar from the public galleries. In the chill confines of the Auckland Supreme Court's basement holding cells he again pleaded – as he had done since his arrest – for a lie detector test.

"His confusion was complete. The second trial had largely been a repetition of the previous Supreme Court fiasco. To him, his family, friends and a growing band of supporters, he had a cast-iron alibi. He was at home on the night of the murders. His wife confirmed the fact, as did his cousin, Peter. Either they are lying, or he is innocent.

"The Crown evidence against this seemingly granite-like alibi was, by the court's own evidence, circumstantial, 'like the strands of a rope'."

One piece of evidence the jury was not allowed to hear was the track record of Bruce Thomas Newton Hutton, star police officer, but Terry Bell laid into the cop with a whip in the magazine:

"Detective Inspector Bruce Hutton has on at least two previous occasions caught the wrong man – and had seemingly cast iron cases on both occasions. In one, the Jury killing at Ponsonby, he actually had a signed confession from a drug addict later found to be completely innocent. In another, involving the Bower brothers and an alleged break-in at an Army arsenal in South Auckland, Inspector Hutton put on a good performance in the witness box reading from his notebook incriminatory statements allegedly made to him by the Bower brothers. The brothers subsequently denied ever having made the statements and it was subsequently proved that they had no responsibility for the arsenal break-in."

As Justice Sir Trevor Henry might have said: "I can offer no opinion on this – it is a matter for you, the good men and women

---

129 *Rolling Stone*, 10 May 1973, presented in evidence at the Royal Commission hearings for investigation under its terms of reference.

of the jury, to decide as to the accused's, Hutton's guilt."

Copies of *Rolling Stone's* NZ edition from May 1973 are probably lost to posterity now – indeed, police ordered all copies seized nationwide when it was published[130] – but one was tabled in Parliament, so for the sake of completeness it's worth also recording the key points of Terry Bell's biting account of what happened when police took the jury under their protective wing:

"When the jury confinement move was made, defence counsel Kevin Ryan protested impotently. He had good reason not to want the jury confined – especially at the Station Hotel. For the Station Hotel, with its cosy sixth floor house bar, is a regular haunt of the local constabulary. Police wanting to create the best possible conviction atmosphere could not have chosen better than the Station Hotel.

"The atmosphere was one thing. Precisely how the jury would act, another. The element of gamble existed; the police merely wished to load the dice as much in their favour as possible. In the end, the police had the jury wallowing in beer, Tia Maria and Coruba rum, eating out of their hands. And according to hotel staff, the transition from nervous jury members to high-living cop-lovers was remarkably rapid.

"Fuelled by crayfish mornay, and 'every conceivable type of drink', they deliberated the fate of Arthur Allan Thomas...The Auckland Jury players accorded themselves a series of boozy ovations almost every night throughout the three weeks of the show."

Bell told of one particular party, marking a jury member's birthday, where the entire cast and their police hosts adjourned to the hotel cabaret. "Their performance that night reached cabaret proportions, shocking the hotel staff and sparking off rumours about a game called 'musical beds'. But what of Arthur Thomas? Every night he was taken back to a bleak dinner in the brooding grey stone fortress that is Mt Eden prison, and meanwhile jury members would retreat for cocktails.

"Every day, Arthur Thomas would sit – a pallid and nervous looking figure – placing his trust in the attentions of the jury – who sometimes yawned, occasionally dozed and whiled away the hours between the pate and the parties. However, there were some similarities. During the course of the trial, Arthur Thomas collapsed,

---

130 *Beyond Reasonable Doubt*, page 277

passing out in court. During the course of a party a jury member also collapsed and passed out – on the carpet.

"Which is not to say that the jury paid no attention to the proceedings during the days. The obviously did, from time to time. When Vivien (Thomas, playing her self-imposed role of tough, unbending battler), gave evidence she verbally sparred with prosecution counsel W.D. Baragwanath. Flickers of annoyance at her nerve slipped across the faces of several jurors...a weepy, broken woman goes down better with juries.

"The same flicker of annoyance registered on jury faces during the cross examination by the defence of DSIR scientist Dr Nelson. The aura of respectability surrounding a scientist being assaulted by a blunt, forthright lawyer with an obvious personal interest in the case, was obviously a bit too much for some jury members to take.

"Living in such intimate surroundings with the police, the jury could not be expected readily to accept allegations – even when backed with some evidence – that the police or other members of the judicial establishment could conceivably be guilty of a deliberate or accidental warping of the truth. They were certainly not going to be very receptive to accusations that Bruce Hutton had actually planted evidence.

"According to Auckland University psychologists, there is substantial literature available on conformity experiments, and the effects on groups of people in enforced close proximity living conditions. The tendency in such conditions is to conform. And when the element of gratitude is introduced – the police did much to assist in the hotel hanky-panky – the direction the conformity will take seems distinctly weighted.

"Even in cases where police do not participate in the frivolities, this would apply. But when the police are active participants, the effects are incalculably increased. Unless the evidence of the eyes and ears of astonished Station Hotel staff is mistaken, police escorts played an active supporting role in the Bruce Hutton show.

"One hotel worker, asked about the final grand hooley on the eve of the verdict, says: 'The whole lot of them were in it. They were paralytic'. And that was the night *before* Arthur Thomas received his second life sentence.

"It was also the night that saw mattresses being flung into the hallway of the first floor, with its lounge 'like a well-stocked bar'.

When, on the following day, the jury went to complete their duty... in court the jury looked bored, tired and impassive. Kevin Ryan was worried when they retired to consider the verdict. He whispered to his brother Gerald, 'The jury could be hung'.

"They weren't. Only hung-over," concluded Terry Bell.

As an eyewitness himself to the court case, and a first-hand investigator into the jury hijinks, Bell's account gives us a useful insight into what was in fact another crime police officers need to be held accountable for: corruption of a jury.[131]

Against a background of such serious jury tampering by the Commissioner of Police and his minions, it wouldn't have mattered if the defence had actually wheeled in the real killer with a handwritten confession in the victims' blood and photographs he'd taken at the crime scene of himself posing beside the bodies – Arthur Thomas was still going down for it.

Rolling Stone's acerbic cartoonist skewered Justice Perry at the bench, telling Thomas in sentencing: "I'm afraid your wife's testimony to the effect that you were in the North Island at the time is no defence – I hereby find you guilty of the [South Island] murder of Jennifer Beard as well!!"

Pat Booth reported how the police had taken jurors out to entertain them at times:[132] "The films, the shows, the boxing, the fishing trip" – all just some of the activities the eleven remaining jurors (one fell ill early in the trial) had enjoyed at the hands of their hosts.

In the courtroom as the jury delivered their verdict – after just *two hours* of deliberation – hell broke loose. People who'd sat through the three week hearing and actually paid attention to the evidence knew the ruling was wrong.

---

[131] **Section 117, Crimes Act: Corrupting juries and witnesses**. Everyone is liable to imprisonment for a term not exceeding 7 years who—(a) dissuades or attempts to dissuade a person, by threats, bribes, or other corrupt means, from giving evidence in any cause or matter (whether civil or criminal, and whether tried or to be tried in New Zealand or in an overseas jurisdiction); or
(b) influences or attempts to influence, by threats or bribes or other corrupt means, a member of a jury in his or her conduct as such (whether in a cause or matter tried or to be tried in New Zealand or in an overseas jurisdiction, and whether the member has been sworn as a member of a particular jury or not); or
(c) accepts any bribe or other corrupt consideration to abstain from giving evidence (whether in a cause or matter tried or to be tried in New Zealand or in an overseas jurisdiction); or
(d) accepts any bribe or other corrupt consideration on account of his or her conduct as a member of a jury (whether in a cause or matter tried or to be tried in New Zealand or in an overseas jurisdiction, and whether the member has been sworn as a member of a particular jury or not); or
(e) wilfully attempts in any other way to obstruct, prevent, pervert, or defeat the course of justice in New Zealand or the course of justice in an overseas jurisdiction.
[132] *Trial By Ambush*, by Pat Booth, p29

"Screams, tears and angry protests threw the Supreme Court at Auckland into an uproar late yesterday," reported the *New Zealand Herald* in a story and photos taking up most of the front page. "Pandemonium continued, with fists being waved from the public galleries at the jurors."

A pelting with rotten crayfish may have been more appropriate.

As the crowd in the courtroom grew louder and more violent, Arthur Thomas remembers crying out to the jury. "I had nothing to do with this, this terrible murder. I was at home with my wife!" He doesn't remember hearing as the crowd roared, Vivien Thomas adding her own wrenching scream from the heart, "He was, he was!" The convict was led away to the dank, 1860s vintage dungeons below the old court, while above him pandemonium reigned.

"What sort of people are you?!" Vivien, now well beyond breaking point, wailed at the fleeing jurors. "He's innocent – you're murdering him!"[133]

So what was the fate of Bruce Hutton after all this, and knowing his track record as we now do? He was awarded, a few weeks later, the highest internal honour in the NZ Police, the Certificate of Merit. Police Commissioner Angus Sharp, himself about to become 'Sir' Angus, wrote that the award reflected Hutton's "devotion to duty...particularly for diligence and zeal shown during the Crewe murder inquiry."

You'll laugh at the next paragraph.

"His meticulous care in preparing the file for prosecution, and the outstanding assistance he gave the Crown prosecutor during the trials, combined to bring a successful conclusion to an extremely difficult and arduous inquiry and was in accord with the highest traditions of the New Zealand police."

Plus ça change, plus c'est la même chose.[134]

It's not that Thomas' defence lawyers made a bad fist of it in the second trial. Sure, they could have slammed a few more homers, but it wouldn't have made any difference. Not to Arthur, nor to his marriage.

"That second trial jury ended our marriage," Vivien Harrison told

---

133 *Auckland Star 8 O'Clock edition*, 21 April 1973
134 The more things change, the more they stay the same. See *Investigate* magazine, June 2007, http://www.thebriefingroom.com/archives/2007/08/to_serve_and_pr.html and also *Investigate* magazine, July 2007, http://www.thebriefingroom.com/archives/2007/12/police_minister.html

author Chris Birt this year.[135] "I had always thought, in my own head, that if Arthur had been freed, we would have picked things up. At that time, it was still retrievable, for me anyway. I had not talked to Arthur about that. But when he was convicted again, I knew it wasn't retrievable and that was the end of my marriage. I had made that decision inside me, but I didn't do anything about it for another two years.

"When he went back to Paremoremo, we carried on fighting for Arthur, but I could not carry on in our marriage. Our plans for the future were completely and utterly gone."

Vivien's first affair had begun in January 1972, lasted a short time and was one of the reasons she'd left the country to clear her head. In 1974 she met a new man and began an 18 month relationship. She later described it as a time of great confusion. "There were always fresh developments happening. They did indeed happen, but none of them got Arthur out. In the meantime I had a life to lead. I was living in a limbo world. We both were."[136]

For Arthur, despite what the news clippings say, he insists he didn't really see it coming until virtually the moment it happened. Vivien didn't tell him herself, she left it to Pat Booth to deliver the bad news. Apparently Pat didn't get there quickly enough.

"Arthur heard all about it on the radio," his mother Ivy told reporters after a jail visit to comfort her son. "I believe the acting prison superintendent Mr Ward was with him when it came over Radio Hauraki...I have never seen my son so upset."[137]

"It was back in 1975, yeah," nods Arthur Thomas. "Yeah, and I still wasn't too happy. I wasn't happy about that. Okay, I had nothing else, you know, just my mate-"

He pauses, then continues quietly. "I was buried as an inmate, I was a prisoner and I need something when I get out, you know, just beside me, you know?"

"No, that's it," interjects Jenny. "It would have been late in the piece. Everyone around Vivien and Arthur would have picked up the fact that Vivien was quite evidently drifting away, but to Arthur he would be late in the piece picking up on that I would have thought. Because... he's an ostrich, he's a head in the sand type of guy; he

---

135 "A Life Sentence", *North & South*, July 2010
136 Interview with David Yallop, *Beyond Reasonable Doubt*, p283
137 *Sunday News*, 4 May 1975

would not want to face that possibility, so he would probably not want to tell himself, no, and he would be the last to keep holding onto it. It probably hit him like a sledgehammer," Jenny adds.

The night the news broke, Thomas took it hard.

"I refused visitors. That time was the lowest of the low and I was just absolutely blown away. I remember I was so down in my cell and the padré arrives and I don't know who told him – it didn't come from me – but someone, padré, comes and talks in my room there for hours – and he doesn't normally come and see me."

One visitor Thomas did not turn away was the prison superintendent, who came bearing a suggestion: "Thomas, go in the room and smash everything up and get rid of your pressures," said the jailer.

"And boy, did I smash things," remembers Thomas with a grim chuckle.

It's an insight into how a man copes with the trauma invading his life. He doesn't like to admit to crying. "Oh yeah, a bit of that too, yes. Yeah, I don't want to talk so much about tears and things, but by crikey I tell you, I wasn't a happy man for months in that time. Months I was down in the … oh I don't know what words to use, just how I was. Everything had let me down. Everything's let me down, so that's why I refused visitors. That's how bad it was."

There was a popular hit on the radio at the time, *Tie a Yellow Ribbon Around the Old Oak Tree*, a song about a prisoner being released and a US folk tradition of sweethearts wearing yellow remembrance ribbons. Every time he heard Tony Orlando and Dawn belt that song out over the prison radio, Arthur Thomas just felt more and more broken.

"Oh well that was just a pipe dream, yeah. I often hear that song. I thought it would be nice if I had that, but… no."

Thomas feared that people would think he had done it if Vivien broke up with him – an understandable reaction given that she was his alibi – but the public came to understand it was the pressure of the case that blew things apart, not a change of heart. As Vivien has said many times since the divorce, the break-up did not change the factual reality that Arthur Thomas was in bed beside her all night on June 17, 1970. She didn't just believe he didn't do it, she *knew* he didn't do it.

"What it boils down to," she told one journalist, "is either I'm telling the truth or I'm lying. If I'm lying, why haven't I been charged?

And if I was lying, I don't think I'd still be here doing what I am."[138]

One of those Thomas turned to in his darkest hours was a fellow prison inmate named Archie Banks, better known perhaps as the father of Auckland mayor John Banks. Archie – a chemist by trade – had been in and out of prison frequently on various charges, but he provided a sympathetic ear for the wounded Thomas. "He had a heart of gold," Arthur explains. "He was very, very fond of his son John."

Banks was one of the inmates Thomas stayed in touch with after his release, but Archie died in March 1984. "A scallywag and a true friend, that's how I'd describe him" says Jenny Thomas. "He's probably the one who kept Arthur sane when he hit rock bottom."

The important thing to know about Arthur Thomas, however, is that he's never been a "victim" in the classic sense. Throughout his arrest, prosecution and incarceration, there was an inner strength, fuelled by faith, and a belief the Truth would, somehow, set him free. Stripped of his freedom, he readjusted, and never gave up.

The image the Retrial Committee presented to the outside world was very 'victim-centred', but from their point of view it had to be. The public attention span was short, stories had to be told in soundbites, in a way easily understood. The media were having grave difficulty with little things like ages and names, so a more complex and nuanced narrative would have been lost on them and probably counterproductive. In a sense, the Arthur Thomas story became Everyman's Story, a there-but-for-the-grace-of-God morality tale for a generation losing its innocence. Arthur Thomas the Man became lost behind Arthur Thomas the Icon. Lost, but not defeated or overcome by it; the real Arthur was always there.

Arthur's wife and partner of nearly 30 years, Jenny, agrees. "A really dear friend who's passed over a long time ago, Keith Christie, was the ag pilot when Arthur was involved with topdressing. And Keith knew Arthur really well prior to prison and then he came back afterwards and he became a really good friend of ours. He told me, 'Arthur's the same. His inner being's the same. He's the same guy I knew prior to him going inside'. I think that's quite astounding. And I believe him," says Jenny, looking across at her husband.

Given what he had to go through, it is indeed astounding.

---

138 *Sunday Times*, 23 September 1973

CHAPTER 11

Shootout At The ICI Corral

It would be easy to wade back into the minutiae of the second trial, and actually look at some of the key evidence presented. You'll find however that most of that key evidence has already been alluded to throughout the book. The main points against Arthur Thomas have by now emerged as a sham, and the second trial or indeed the subsequent appeals added little to the sum of human knowledge on the Crewe murders.

It was more notable, perhaps, for one remaining evidence strand still under development – where did the cartridge case in the Crewe flower garden come from, and did it match the bullets in the heads of Harvey and Jeannette Crewe?

Forensic scientist Jim Sprott – more famous these days for his work on mattress liners to prevent cot death – was tasked in late 1972 with analysing the infamous Exhibit 350, the shell case from the garden. Everyone knew the bullets that killed the Crewes were Number Eights, so named because of the numeral stamped in the base of the lead bullet inside the cartridge. Ammunition maker Colonial Ammunition Company, later ICI, testified that Number Eights were last manufactured in 1962, some eight years before the shootings. While other farmers who used their guns once in a blue moon still had unused Number Eights, Arthur Thomas was a regular possum and rabbit shooter – once famously blowing a possum to bits inside the house when it disturbed him by scuffling in the fireplace one night. Thomas had no Number Eights and no boxes or cartridge containers of that vintage – his ammunition was much newer. Yet a Number Eight bullet had been found in a box of nuts and bolts in his garage, the day after Len Johnston had been at the house.

So far, so good. When the shell case was "found" in the flower garden, everyone assumed it could have contained a Number Eight bullet as none of the lawyers or Pukekawa farmers knew differently. As publicity grew about the trials and the controversial shell case, however, Jim Sprott made a public appeal for people to send him their Number Eight bullets to examine. Some 22,000 bullets eventually came in, but it took the eagle eyes of a retired police officer turned sporting goods retailer, Jack Ritchie, who'd realised when checking his own Number Eights that you could distinguish them from the newer bullets because the letter 'C' in the ICI logo on the cartridge shell base was typed differently on the Number Eights. Ritchie alerted Sprott.

For the first time, Sprott had a baseline to work from. Was it possible that Number Eight bullets only ever came in the cartridges with the smaller 'C' on the base? After examining the first hundred or so of his eventual 22,000 bullet haul, his answer was yes.[139] And guess what, the shell case police "found" in the flower garden had a new-style larger 'C', not one of the old Number Eight styles.

This, of course, could only mean one thing: the garden case could not have contained a Number Eight bullet, therefore it could not have been a cartridge case left in that garden by the killer of Harvey and Jeannette Crewe. It was an anachronism – something outside of the evidential timezone. The Crewes were killed with 1962 bullets, but police had actually "found" a mid-to-late sixties cartridge case. This proved to objective observers that the shell had been planted there.

Sprott wanted access to Exhibit 343, the Number Eight bullet allegedly "found" by Detective Stan Keith in Arthur Thomas' garage. If Sprott's theory was correct, the Number Eight would be carrying a small 'C' on its shell base. It was coming up to the second trial in 1973, and the exhibit was in the care of the Supreme Court. Sprott phoned lawyer Kevin Ryan at home, blissfully unaware that police were tapping Ryan's phone so they could keep one step ahead of Thomas' legal team. So when Sprott divulged what he had found, and that he needed to see the Keith case to check its base, he was also telling one of Hutton's hirelings listening in.

When Kevin Ryan rang the deputy registrar of the Supreme Court

---

[139] To be precise, he found four styles – three of which held Number Eight leads, and one which never did.

and arranged a meeting first thing in the morning to unlock the evidence safe so Sprott could examine the cartridge, Hutton's man was taking notes. So at 8.30am when registrar Ian Miller, Ryan and Sprott were taking the case out of its container, who should burst into the room but Detective Inspector Bruce Hutton, screaming blue murder about evidence tampering, something he was apparently well acquainted with. Hutton would later deny phone tapping and tried to convince people he just "happened to be walking past" the court and noticed a light on.[140]

Nonetheless, Sprott was right. The Keith case, the bullet that Len Johnston evidently planted in Thomas' garage, and where Stan Keith extensively searched one apple box and found it, but failed to search a box next to it containing Arthur Thomas' love letters from former girlfriends – that Number Eight bullet wore a small 'C' on its base, just as predicted, not the large 'C' on the base of the flower bed shell.

Sprott, just to make sure he wasn't confusing cartridges, made a tiny mark inside the 343 shell case in the court that day. Strangely, when the Crown presented it in trial a few days later, and invited him to peruse it in the witness box, the mark had gone. He was looking at a case which had been switched, apparently by police hoping he wouldn't notice.

The significance was that Detective Keith gave evidence on oath that the shell for Exhibit 343 had been "fired" by police to remove gunpowder residue, and that the firing pin hitting the base of the bullet could have caused changes to the 'C'. Yet the DSIR's Donald Nelson had given evidence on oath that the 343 shell had not been fired, and Dr Sprott likewise testified that the shell he had looked at earlier had not been fired. Thus, in their attempts to tip up Sprott, police unwittingly handed out more proof of the bullet 'switcheroo theory'. Clearly, the police had both a fired and unfired version of one bullet – a legally impossible situation.

Again, it should have been game, set, match. But because Hutton was tapping phone calls, he knew lawyer Kevin Ryan was on to ammunition makers ICI, and Hutton ensured police got there first. Nonetheless, in a drag race to the finish line, Ryan and Sprott secured evidence from ICI Australia that proved the planted car-

---
140 *Beyond Reasonable Doubt*, p264

tridge case could not have contained either of the bullets that killed the Crewes.

The battle of the expert evidence became clouded and flew over the heads of a bored jury. Crown Prosecutor David Morris, having leant on ICI's New Zealand branch, muddied the waters by declaring ICI NZ regarded the garden shell and the one found in Thomas' shed were "indistinguishable" and that there was "no reason whatever why the Charles shell [garden shell] should not have contained the bullet of Harvey or Jeannette."

Defence lawyer Kevin Ryan didn't have the evidence to hand that he needed to show Morris was wrong, so the jury ignored his protestations and found Thomas guilty regardless, and the Court of Appeal a few weeks later told Thomas' lawyers, "tough luck" – there were no grounds made for a retrial in the eyes of a full five bench court.

Chief Justice Sir Richard Wild inveigled himself onto the bench for that hearing, and during a trout fishing trip on Lake Taupo soon afterward was asked by a good friend what Sir Richard thought of the serious doubts about the cartridge case. Wild twitched his fly, inspecting the slow lazy rise of a rainbow to the surface and muttered, "Somebody has to go down for the murders".[141] Clearly, the head of New Zealand's judicial system needed a refresher course on the definition of the word 'Justice' in his job title.

"I was so down in the middle of the 70s, so down," continues Thomas. It wasn't just the divorce, it was a perfect storm of setbacks. When the Court of Appeal knocked him back on the cartridge evidence, he hadn't expected it.

"Five judges of the Court of Appeal, Sir Richard Wild was one of them. I thought, right, this is it. I need to pack my bags, I'm going home. There's concrete evidence that the shell case did not contain any of the fatal bullets, backed by the Melbourne Police. It was concrete, you know, so sealed. And they turned me down you know. And I went down like a sunken ship, you know, and the ex is divorcing me. The concrete evidence... I was shut in."

That's when he stopped seeing visitors. "I was shattered, I'd gone, I was absolutely blown away, you know. And I had nothing left but the grey prison wall, that's what I had, that's it. But anyhow, an

---

141 Arthur Allan Thomas, from conversation with Greg Newbold

act of God or something, I read a book written by Norman Peale, *Power Of Positive Thinking*. It was like reading the Bible. You know what happened on the end of that? I got another breath of air and see, this is the best of the lot. You know what? I'm gonna get to the top of this bloody mountain and win it. And something in it, an act of God, some power up there or something like that. I was a different man."

As part of re-taking control, Thomas later decided he would not accept parole, he wanted his convictions quashed, nothing less. "I sat up there in front of the Parole Board like King Arthur. I said 'You guys are not doing anything about me. I'm just staying up in the prison until my name's completely cleared. Now, I'm making it *very, very clear*'. I spoke loud like that."

Of course, there was still the minor issue of challenging the Crown evidence. There would have been further investigation of the cartridges, undoubtedly, but for the inconvenient fact that Crown prosecutor David Morris and Det. Inspector Bruce Hutton hatched a cunning scheme. "Bruce," said Morris down the phone, "It's probably a good idea to throw away any exhibits you don't need anymore." Hutton duly obliged, sending Stan Keith down to Auckland's Whitford Tip with 137 exhibits on July 27, 1973.

Those exhibits ditched – thrown – far and wide into the landfill, before being bulldozed over, included all the disputed cartridges and the bullets from the Crewes' bodies. "The Minister of Justice, Dr Finlay, said today he was 'desolated and deeply troubled' to find that all the exhibits in the Arthur Allan Thomas case have been disposed of," reported the *Auckland Star* in its lead story two months later, when news of the disposal finally broke. "Among items irretrievably buried at Whitford Tip are cartridge cases which were crucial to the defence case in the Crewe murder trials."[142]

The Justice Minister said he'd asked police to dig the items up, but they refused, saying it would be impossible. For the record, in 1994, Wellington's main landfill was closed for a week while police searched for and eventually found a Czech CZ-27 pistol which businessman John Barlow was accused of using to shoot Wellington property developers Gene and Eugene Thomas (no relation to Arthur Thomas) with.

---

142 *Auckland Star*, 14 September 1973

Regardless of the disposal, the genie was out of the box already. The cartridges had been forensically photographed by manufacturers ICI and their base impressions compared under a microscope – images of which remained for all time for anyone to see.

After further testing, ICI's Australian operation changed its tune and senior executive Ian Cook swore a new affidavit rejecting the company's earlier court testimony in favour of police: "Only since I have provided the information have I appreciated that there are significant differences, as well as similarities, between the embossed impressions on the cartridge cases produced by IMI [the Australian division] in the relevant period."[143]

In short, the company confirmed the cartridge case found in the garden came from a production run at least a year after the last Number Eight bullets were produced, and possibly much later – as that particular production design was ongoing from 1964.[144]

Dr Jim Sprott threw down the gauntlet at one point, saying very simply: "If anyone can produce a cartridge like the one police say they found in the garden, and it contains a pattern 8 bullet like those that killed the Crewes, then our argument fails. I challenge the police, the DSIR and anyone else who still believes that Thomas is guilty to produce such a cartridge."[145]

For the record, no one ever did. No such cartridge existed anywhere in the world.

As momentum built for yet another Thomas trial, the man was becoming a media celebrity from behind bars. When a rubbish basket in his prison cell was discovered aflame, newspapers ran front page banner headlines that someone was out to get him. When the Retrial Committee needed funds, newspapers ran stories on how Thomas had turned to basket-weaving to raise money for the appeals. And in the end of year, *Best of 74* news round-up, he shared star bill-

---

143 *Auckland Star*, 20 September 1973
144 According to one of his lawyers, Gerald Ryan, Thomas greeted news of a breakthrough in the cartridge cases this way: "He has become religious and considered this to be in answer to his prayers. He was very hopeful that right will be done," said Ryan in the *NZ Herald*, 2 November 1973. Although he couldn't have known it then, the cartridge case evidence turned out to be the key that unlocked his cell, and it was, said journalist Pat Booth, "a freak combination" (*Auckland Star*, 20 September 1973) of events that gave him the key. Had it been virtually any other bullet used to kill the Crewes, it would not have been possible to prove Arthur's innocence based on bullet manufacture. It just happened that this particular bullet went out of production after a 13 year run and a new case design was slipped in. It took another six years to secure Thomas' release, but this was the last major piece of evidence needed.
145 *Auckland Star*, 4 Feb 1975

ing with a young popstar:[146] "Elton John and his manager John Reid appear in the Auckland Magistrates Court on an assault charge after giving New Zealand's largest concert at Western Springs. John (26) is discharged without conviction after admitting assaulting a journalist outside a nightclub. Reid is jailed for one month for assaulting the journalist and a model, Judith Baragwanath." Judith, incidentally, was the wife of deputy Crown prosecutor David Baragwanath. Of Thomas the newspaper simply wrote alongside his photo: "Thomas Appeals Again". Said it all, really.

One of the other important developments to emerge in this time behind the scenes concerned the mysterious axle that had allegedly been used to weigh down the body of Harvey Crewe. Five men – Robert William Hills, David Edgar Brewster, Bruce Richard Eyre, Trevor John Salmons and John Lyall Martin – came forward to the Thomas Retrial Committee to confess that they'd been involved to varying degrees in taking an old axle from the Thomas farm in 1965 – a year before Arthur Allan Thomas moved onto the property.

David Yallop, in a letter to Prime Minister Muldoon in 1978, enclosed copies of these affidavits, but their contents and names have never been published in a book until now, after they were passed to me by Arthur's oldest brother, Ray Thomas.

In one affidavit sworn in 1976, Bruce Eyre explains how he'd been working on restoring an old 32 Ford in 1965. purchased from some locals known as the Pellow brothers for the princely sum of 30 pounds. Eyre says he'd hoped to get it up to road standard, but soon realised this was an impossibility.

"So I decided with one or two of my friends that we would fix it up to the stage where it could be used for driving around the countryside, but not on the road...for shooting expeditions and things like that. My friends included John Martin and Richard Thomas, my younger brother Desmond Eyre and there may have been others but that was the main group that was interested in the Ford."

The car was initially on the Eyre property, then moved across to the Thomas property for more work, but it was forced to remain there for a month because "it conked out there and that's where it stayed."

Eyre's affidavit states that Dave Brewster then volunteered to help

---

146 *Auckland Star 8 O'Clock Edition*, 28 December 1974

fix the car but only if it was towed to his place, which was duly arranged. The boys packed the car full of odds and ends they'd found at the Thomas farm, including an old axle.

"I noticed," said Trevor Salmons in his affidavit, "that Bruce Eyre was looking around for any other bits that might be handy and I saw him drag an old axle from under the hedge on the Thomas farm and bring it to the front of the Ford. It was then that I overheard Bruce say that he was going to try and make this axle fit the Ford."

"I cannot remember whether the axle was too short or too long, although I can remember Bruce Eyre laying it out in front of the Ford to see whether it measured. I can remember him saying something about 100 years with a sledgehammer making anything fit," recalled Salmons.

Bruce Eyre also remembered discussing the axle with Salmons. "I said the axle...could be made to fit the front of the Ford. He said that it couldn't."

One thing Salmons clearly remembered about the axle found under the hedge was "in particular, the shape...it is depressed in the centre piece and the end pieces come up."

Partway through the towing, the boys stopped off at Trevor Salmons' place, where Robert Hills was working on a car in the Salmons' garage. Seeing a tractor pull up with a 32 Ford behind it, Hills sauntered over to join the debate.

"They had an old axle lying in front of the old Ford car. Bruce Eyre at that stage was saying how he was going to make this axle fit into the old car to lower it down. I myself, being a motor mechanic, realised how difficult or even impossible this would be."

Hills took a long hard look at the axle, and a long hard look at the Ford, but didn't have the heart to give Bruce Eyre his blunt assessment or get directly involved in the Eyre/Salmons argument. Instead he walked away, shaking his head. Eyre and his mates ummed and ahhed for a while longer, then continued towing the car to Brewster's place behind Brewster's truck, but only after dumping a lot of the junk in the car on the roadside because it was too heavy to get up the hill. Amongst that junk was an old axle, depressed in the middle with end pieces that rose up – just like the 1928/1929 Nash axle that had coincidentally been disposed of by Arthur Thomas' father Allan a few weeks earlier in July 1965 when he took it to local mechanic Rod Rasmussen.

It is almost certain that the axle Bruce Eyre took was the Nash axle. The likelihood of the Thomas farm containing two similar but different axles at that precise moment in time – end of July, early August 1965 – is so remote you'd have a better chance of winning lotto. The Royal Commission would later hear from vintage car enthusiasts who'd been scouring the Thomas dump in March 1970 for car parts and found no axle or stub axles, so clearly the axle had been taken long before and five men have confessed to doing so in 1965. The axle was never on the Thomas farm when Arthur Thomas lived there. He never knew it existed.

It is highly likely the boys also took the stub axles because, as Bruce Eyre says on oath, "We were gathering any bits of material together at all that may have been used in the reconstruction of the Ford."[147]

Most of the five men who testified 11 years after taking the axle off the Thomas farm were not mechanics, but one in particular was. Let's look at his expert testimony in regard to whether the axle he saw matched the axle presented in court:

"I can definitely say that Exhibit 293 is very, very similar to the axle that was outside the Salmons' house...I would point out the following similarities," swore Robert Hills in his affidavit.

"(1) No stub axles. (2) One king-pin still intact and not removable. The reason I remember the king-pin feature is that when Eyre said that he was going to make the axle fit the old Ford it was obvious to me it was impossible to refit a stub axle on because the king-pin had been welded into position in such a way that it could not be removed and I recall Bruce Eyre saying he could weld another eye onto that axle, that is, Bruce Eyre was going to weld another eye onto the axle that had the king-pin permanently attached to it."

What is the probability of two different vintage axles being on the Thomas farm, both with one king-pin permanently welded into place on the same side? While you mull that over, let's continue the mechanic's testimony:

"The general shape of Exhibit 293 is the same shape as the axle

---

147 There is no explicit reference in the five affidavits to the stub axles, but they certainly fit the description of the type of gear the men were looking for. More to the point, we can't escape the reality that Detective Len Johnston somehow found the exact two stub axles that had been on the main axle. If the stub axles were not in Arthur Thomas' farm dump – and they weren't because Johnston had to plant them there – and the axle wasn't on the Thomas farm because it had been taken five years earlier, we can draw a clear inference that the junk must have been together, otherwise how else did the stub axles eventually turn up?

at the Salmons house. I can [also] say that the spring-bearings on Exhibit 293 are similar to the spring-bearings that were on the axle at the Salmons house because I remember noting at the time that they would be in the wrong position to attach springs to the Ford car.

"Again, I want to emphasise that the main point of identification in my mind is that the king-pin on the right hand side of Exhibit 293 is attached in such a way that to my mind it is immoveable, and that is exactly the way the one king-pin was attached to the axle at the Salmons house, and it is this point above all that makes me very, very sure that the two axles are very, very similar. Indeed, I would say that the two are indistinguishable.

"Today, 7th August, 1976 is the first time that I've had a careful, leisurely look at Exhibit 293 and the more that I look at it the more certain I become that it is indeed the axle that was placed in front of the Ford car at the Salmons' residence as described above," testified Robert Hills.

Trevor Salmons, the other mechanic to examine the axle – the man who was also sceptical it could be made to fit the Ford – remembered the shape of the axle was very similar to the court exhibit, and that it was "just the bare axle, similar to Exhibit 293 although I cannot say it was identical. On Exhibit 293 the spring bearings are on top of the axle and I can remember that that is another similarity...I would further add that there is no feature about exhibit 293 which is dissimilar or inconsistent with the axle that Bruce Eyre removed from under the hedge."

Now, as I've said the other three men were not mechanics and didn't look at the axle with the expert eye of Hills or Salmons. When push came to shove, Bruce Eyre said "I cannot say beyond all doubt that it was the [same] axle," but he added, "I can, however, remember that there was an axle which was lower in the middle and which would have the effect of lowering the Ford car down if the axle were attached and therefore it would have been an axle similar to the Exhibit 293."

David Brewster didn't appear to recall the axle specifically, but John Martin did:

"I believe that this was the same shape and type of axle as the one we removed from the Thomas property in 1965. It was a front axle without stubs."

This is the first time the contents of those crucial affidavits have been revealed in a book. They lay the final circumstantial evidence ghost to rest. So it is now certain, at least to me, that in 1965, a year before Arthur Thomas moved back to the district, the axle from his father's old trailer had ended up under a hedge at the property after apparently being reclaimed from a workshop by a young Richard Thomas, apparently because he knew it might be useful for a car restoration project. It was picked up by Thomas and his mate Bruce Eyre just a few weeks later for use in the 32 Ford, then jettisoned in a ditch beside Trevor Salmons' house a couple of miles up the road from the Crewe farm with a bunch of other car parts.

Presumably, it languished there in the weeds until a passer-by with the eye of a trained observer decided it might become useful for weighing down bodies.

Remember this, it will become highly relevant in the final chapter.

All of this was happening behind the scenes. Publicly, Arthur continued to languish in a kind of phony war. In 1977, Thomas was in the news because a 76 year old "prophet" from the Auckland suburb of Three Kings told a major daily that Arthur would be released on March 3 1978. The same prophet, Harold Thompson, an active Rotarian and JP, also foretold, "Don't make any plans for July 4, 1982. The outlook is for earthquakes, tempests and tidal waves. Death and damage will be colossal, worldwide. Luckily, the Auckland Harbour Bridge will not be destroyed but most of its approaches will be." For good measure, he also predicted that on September 3 1986, "Russia and Arab allies will attack and destroy Israel without warning, in four days."[148]

He told the newspaper he'd only recently stumbled upon his ability to prophesy, by holding a pendulum on a piece of string, and was testing it out. It was, after all, the 1970s.

Needless to say, on a track record like that, Thomas would have had a better hit rate throwing darts at a calendar. Things, however, were moving in the heavens. Well, at least the political equivalent. Prime Minister Rob Muldoon took a massive swing at the judiciary over the way they'd handled the Thomas case.

"I don't think anyone who has followed the case as closely as I have can be satisfied,"[149] he said, sparking fury from newspaper editorials that accused the Prime Minister of meddling in judicial

---
148 *Auckland Star*, 15 June 1977
149 *NZ Truth*, 17 May 1977

independence. Some called the Muldoon comment on the Thomas verdict "unprecedented".

Mid 1977 was an interesting period. Although Muldoon was getting gung-ho on tackling the courts over the Thomas case, he appeared fearful of police. Thomas Retrial campaigners Jim Sprott and Pat Booth had built up a dossier, which I'm sure they still have safely tucked away, detailing other incidents where police had planted evidence and fabricated testimony to gain convictions. That dossier was sent to Muldoon but a request for an investigation of the allegations in it was declined by Cabinet.[150] The fear appears to have been that opening up police to full scrutiny in 1977 might drag all sorts of things out, including possibly the misdemeanours of politicians.

Muldoon, however, was gearing up to hire Robert Adams-Smith QC to independently review the evidence against Arthur Thomas. He wanted a second opinion, and he didn't trust the New Zealand courts. When the Adams-Smith inquiry was announced in 1978, newspapers reported Thomas as "unhappy", because the initial terms of reference – the possible identity of the mystery woman – were so narrow.[151]

Former Auckland CIB chief Graham Perry dug a figurative grave for both himself and a cow, when he came out swinging in defence of Bruce Hutton that year. "I was abreast of proceedings throughout the [Crewe] case," Perry told journalists. "One of the points I consider most important is the fact that Thomas' rifle was allegedly used by him to kill a cattle beast, immediately prior to the suspected dates of the shootings," said Perry. "That beast has never been found or exhumed."

For a Detective Chief Inspector claiming to have been "abreast" of the case, Graham Perry was remarkably badly informed. Pat Booth in the *Auckland Star* did him the disservice of publishing a police evidence photo of the dead cow beside an exhibit marker.[152] It seemed the police establishment realised their rear-guard defence against overwhelming evidence of corruption in the Thomas case was starting to fail.

Muldoon's man on the spot, Robert Adams-Smith initially appears to have been wary of police interference in his investigation. Despite being appointed by no less a figure than Prime Minister Muldoon

---

150 *NZ Herald*, 3 May 1977
151 *Auckland Star 8 O'Clock Edition*, 18 November 1978
152 *Auckland Star*, 15 November 1978

directly, the Auckland QC never identified himself to the people he interviewed, nor did the Papers of Authority provided by the Prime Minister on letterhead identify him by name. "He carries letters identifying his task," reported Pat Booth, "but not naming him. And he does not give his name when he calls."[153]

He didn't get identified until his first report was released on 26 January 1979. It was reprinted verbatim, albeit censored by the Prime Minister's office on one matter still under investigation, in at least one major daily newspaper. In that report, Bruce Roddick's positive identification of any woman is shot down. The QC says Roddick admitted he had not seen the woman's face because she was too far away.[154]

"I inquired of Roddick," writes the QC, "as to how, if he could not distinguish facial features, he could put the woman as being 'in her thirties'. I said that not being able to see her face, surely it must have been difficult for him to put an age on the woman. He replied that he was able to do so 'partly by the way she held herself'. I then asked how he could tell without seeing facial features that it was a woman in her thirties, as opposed to someone in her twenties. His reply was that it was because the woman had a more mature figure than one would expect with that earlier age group."

So again, as I've spelt out earlier, the debate was over whether the woman was in her twenties or thirties, not whether she was approaching 50. For all those who say Roddick has positively identified this woman, the QC writes:

"Roddick advised me that at no stage has he recognised any person in a photograph as being one and the same person as he saw on the Friday morning, June 19. At no stage has he said other than that the women he has indicated are *similar* to the woman he saw."

North & South magazine this year made much of the "four sightings" of the mystery woman, which included Roddick seeing her twice at court. Robert Adams-Smith nails the mythologised evolution of this theory well and truly to the wall, saying it began with the December 1970 depositions hearing at the Otahuhu Magistrates Court, and a room where witnesses and supporters of the victims and the accused had gathered to wait.

"All he said was that he remembers noticing a woman with fairish

---
153 *Auckland Star*, 24 January 1979
154 *The Dominion*, 6 February 1979

hair in this group [of Crewe family and supporters]. At that stage Roddick did not say to himself 'that looks like the woman I saw at the house', or even 'that woman looks familiar', or even 'I wonder if I have seen that woman before?'. He merely noted the woman as being with the group and that she had fairish hair.

"He did not link in his mind at that stage the woman with the woman whom he had seen on the Friday morning. He frankly admitted to me he did not take much interest."

It's absolutely certain then that in December 1970, the closest time to the first sighting back in June that year, Bruce Roddick did not recognise the woman sitting across the room from him, Norma Demler, as the mystery woman. He told the QC that thought did not occur to him until he saw her again at Arthur Thomas' first trial at the Supreme Court in March 1971, and even then there was no flash of recognition to that event, but back to the depositions hearing.

"The thought process," writes the QC, "was, (a) 'I have seen that woman before at the Otahuhu Court'. (b) 'I wonder what she is doing here again?' (c) 'Could it be she is just listening to hear my evidence?' (d) 'Or could it be that she is the woman I saw at the farm?'"

There you go, proof of the power of suggestion in a step by step demonstration.

The QC also extracted more information from Queenie McConachie, the woman who had seen a child playing in the front paddock of the Crewe house at 1.30pm on the Saturday after the murders. The child was dressed in clothes later identified by police as those worn by Rochelle Crewe on the Wednesday her parents were killed.

The McConachies were driving to a rugby game, and as they drove past a pregnant Queenie noticed Rochelle playing, and starting to run towards the house.

"There's Jeannette's little girl!" she remarked to her husband who also turned his head to look.

Robert Adams-Smith QC said he was in no doubt that both original sightings were genuine. However, he expressed concern at the embellishment of Roddick's memory.

"It could well be Mr Roddick now considers that a woman whom he saw at the courts on those two occasions is one and the same as the woman whom he saw on Friday morning, but that opinion has not been reached on any recognition basis but rather on a thought deduction basis as detailed in my summary of my interview with him.

"The frank admission by Roddick that he was quite unable to distinguish facial features means he is not in a position to positively identify any woman as being the woman whom he saw on that Friday morning, nor is it correct to say that he has recognised the woman in photographs or on other occasions.

"Roddick cannot and does not say that the woman he saw on the Friday morning is one and the same person as the woman he saw driving the Crewe car approximately a fortnight before the crime."

All of which means the mystery woman remains a mystery, despite what other people think they remember.

You might think this report was bad news for Arthur Thomas. David Yallop certainly blasted the QC's report. But Adams-Smith recommended more investigation be done, and Muldoon approved it. His second, confidential report was handed to Muldoon in mid December,[155] and its findings, that the murders were more likely to have been committed late on the Wednesday afternoon or early evening, and that there was no evidence to support a late evening killing as claimed by police, would be enough for the Prime Minister to determine that Arthur Allan Thomas was the victim of a set-up.

The choir was assembling, the Fat Lady was testing her voice. Very shortly, Arthur Allan Thomas would walk free. He just didn't know it yet.

---

155 "The Ordeal of Arthur Allan Thomas", special liftout published by INL Newspapers, December 1979

CHAPTER 12

Escape From Prison

You would think, having read this far, that Arthur Thomas would be a bitter man. Surprisingly, he isn't. Sure, there's the occasional expletive if you allow him to dwell too long on some nefarious police trick, but the secret to Thomas' happy life is actually not to dwell on the past. Wife, and partner of 30 years, Jenny Thomas deserves most of the credit for that equilibrium. Early on she realised that part of learning to cope with trauma in your life is learning how to move beyond it.

There was no shortage of people who wanted a piece of the Arthur Allan Thomas story, from speculative media or family members still seeking closure, to wider groups in the public who identified with the iconic nature of the struggle for justice and wanted to use it as a rallying point for wider change. But as Vivien had found out to her cost, those who live by the sword of truth can perish as collateral damage. Jenny knew that if Arthur Thomas, the gentle simple farmer she'd come to know and love, was to have a chance at rebuilding his life, it had to be done at an increasing distance from his past. Objects in the rear view mirror were much closer than she wanted them to be.

Then Jenny Cresswell, she was a child of 11 when the Crewe murders burst into her family living room via what people then referred to as 'the goggle box' in the corner. Television was in its infancy, and TV news equally so, but nonetheless grainy black and white images of the Crewe farmhouse and missing occupants captured the attention of a nation which had only one TV channel to watch.

Throughout her teenage years, Jenny followed, off and on, the developments in the Thomas case, as did we all, and like most she too wondered what had really happened that June 17 night. The last photo taken of Arthur and Vivien together – a constant media favourite – struck a chord.

"The pyjama photograph that's in the *North & South*. I thought, what a lovely couple and how sad that was. That was my initial feeling. Sadness, and yeah, a nice young couple."

She didn't, however, join the Thomas Retrial Committee or become an activist in his case.

"No. Not at all, no. I'd just turned 21 when Arthur was released. My birthday was in November so I'd just turned 21. I was painfully shy. I still am quite a shy person I think outside of my little group of friends but I was painfully shy and that's why I had never written to Arthur prior to him coming out, yeah."

Thomas himself had no idea he was coming out. It was December 1979 and he'd been shifted to the prison farm at Hautu, attached to Rangipo, at the start of that year. As a farmer it was an ideal kind of prison cell, low security, working with the hands, feeling the soil and sunlight again. He was there as a familiar face strolled up the path towards him.

"Des Thomas came down for a pre-Christmas visit and on that Saturday (15 December), he said, 'Well, is there anything you want?' And I said, 'Well, I wouldn't mind a bottle of whisky', cos it's Christmas coming up and if there's a little bottle of whisky I could put it in my room and pretend it's Christmas time. I told him, 'You can even put it in the flower garden because I'm weeding the gardens and things so I'll be able to pick it up and put it in my room'.

"So on the Sunday – because he visited two days of the weekend – he put that bottle in the particular place we'd secretly arranged, down the back, and no worries, no one else knows about it."

As the morning of Monday, December 17, 1979 dawned, Des Thomas was already back at Pukekawa. Down at Hautu Prison Farm, Arthur was waiting for his garden roster to begin, and the opportunity to dig up his Haig Whisky from its hiding place. He had literally only just finished squirreling the mini bottle on his person and scurried back to his hut to hide it under his mattress when a voice suddenly called out.

"Thomas!"

Arthur froze like a possum in the headlights. Surely he hadn't been sprung already! Sheesh, what a grim start to the Christmas week.

And he hadn't even had lunch yet, he thought, looking wistfully in the direction of the canteen.

"Superintendent?" Thomas tried to inject just the right amount of innocence into his response, eyes flicking rapidly to his hut and back, looking for some sign of his room being turned over. There was none.

"Come with me."

Arthur followed, like a lamb to an obviously impending slaughter, to prison superintendent John Todd's office.

"When I walked in," says Thomas, "I see the phone off the hook on the desk. It was the Minister of Justice, see. Anyhow, Superintendent Todd says, 'Look. I've got a Christmas present for you'. And of course I say, 'Oh, what's that?' He said, 'You've been pardoned'. And he stood up and stuck his hand out and shook my hand.

" 'But hang on', I said. 'Do you mean my conviction has been quashed?' Because this is important, as sometimes there's a reprieve or you're released but the conviction stands, see. I wanted to know. And he said, 'Yes, conviction quashed'. He looked at me for a moment. 'Well, where do you want to go?'

" 'Where do you want to go?' I should have said England, you know, it'd be nice to have a holiday [laughs] I think of it sometimes and sometimes I do joke about it."

For Thomas, it was too much to digest on an empty stomach. After nine years in custody, the jailer was asking "where do you want to go" of a man whose every step had been controlled by guards for so long it was second nature.

"Well, look we'll head probably towards Pukekawa," said the superintendent after a moment. That's when Arthur found his voice.

"The Shaws in Tokoroa. That's one of my cousins."

Superintendent Todd picked up the phone off the desk. "He wants to go to relatives in Tokoroa, the Shaws." A moment passed, then a nod. "Sorry Arthur, no one's home."

Welcome to the Hautu California: He could check out any time he liked, but actually leaving was proving more problematic. The Minister of Justice on the phone wanted another name, and Arthur gave up one of his Aunts in Hamilton.

This time the call from the Minister's office in Wellington struck paydirt, and they broke the news to a surprised elderly woman that her prodigal nephew was being released into her care that very afternoon. Suddenly, the superintendent was clasping his shoulder and calling him "*Mr* Thomas".

"It wasn't just 'Thomas!' anymore. It was 'Mr Thomas' and 'Do you want a cup of tea and bikkies?' and oh it was just as quick as that, man," remembers Arthur. "I would have preferred lunch," he mutters.

"Look, don't talk to any of my officers or any inmates," explained Todd. "Just throw all your stuff out of your room, it belongs to the prison."

As Arthur began clearing his mementoes and personal items from his hut under the watchful eye of a guard, he suddenly remembered he had contraband under the mattress.

"The officer has to be in the room checking everything's alright, things are going out and the right stuff's going in the box, you know. Oh and this – and I shouldn't even have worried about it because I'm now a free human being – but I've got this bottle of whiskey and I thought righto, so I lifted up the covers of the mattress so quick, right in front of his eyes, you know, lift it right up – whrrr – in the box, you know. Quick as a flash."

By now the inmates realised something was up – and as Thomas returned to John Todd's office for the tea and biscuits, the superintendent switched on the midday news.

" 'Arthur Alan Thomas pardoned'. That's all it said."

Todd went to grab his keys, then stopped. "Blast! It's my carless day".

For those too young to have experienced the oddity that was a carless day, let me briefly explain. In the late seventies, in response to skyrocketing fuel prices caused by tensions in the Middle East, the Government decreed that every motorist in the country would have to nominate one day a week they couldn't drive their car. Coloured stickers allowed traffic police to quickly spot offenders.

For Superintendent Todd, he had a dilemma. The prison vehicle he should have been using this day was in for repairs, and the only other car was officially on its carless day.

"If it's good enough, Arthur, for the Governor-General to pardon you; it's good enough if we use the car, eh?"

Fresh out of jail, but travelling illegally. Thomas was experiencing mixed frissons of excitement and anxiety, and the superintendent's demeanour was adding to it. "Well, he actually said about having a whiskey in Taupo. And I didn't believe him but then he said, 'Oh, somebody will recognise you'."

There were no cellphones in 1979, but Arthur Thomas didn't make any calls to his family from the jail. "No. Nothing. Not to anyone. No way, I was just gone. My backside had to be out of there so fast – so fast, the car was ready, it was ready with fuel; everything was so quick. Governor-General's orders, you see."

One of the first things his aunt asked when the car pulled up in Hamilton was, "What's it like to be free?" Arthur threw a sideways glance at the jailer seated next to him. Somehow he didn't quite feel free yet, not with 'Guv'nor' driving him around. Nonetheless he invited John Todd in for a cuppa with his aunt. "It wasn't his fault, he had nothing to do with it all," explains Thomas.

News of the release, of course, had travelled fast. The general media assumption was that Thomas would head back to Pukekawa, so newspaper photographers with their huge flashbulbs and journos with notebooks in hand swooped on the Thomas farmhouse there. Thomas, meanwhile, was phoning Pat Booth from his aunt's house in Hamilton, offering the scoop. Booth headed down to pick him up. Somebody, however, had evidently forced a Ministry of Justice official in Wellington to cough up the destination address.

"Someone knocked on me aunty's door, so I stuck my head down too and listened. She talks very quietly. 'I understand Arthur Allan Thomas is here?' 'Oh, *no*. I don't know where he is.' She was such a good actress. 'Thank you, bye bye.' Shut the door."

Thomas and Booth waited a few minutes, then Arthur was smuggled out the back door, through "a good neighbour's property" to Booth's car. From there they drove to Pukekawa – not to the main house but instead to Des Thomas' place. Arthur still wasn't sure how to handle freedom.

"I had to unwind all that has built up in my mind over the years, and it's all getting released. The fact is I'm a free man – I just can't believe I can have a drink. Do my thing. I can stand on my head. No worries, you know?"

One of the first readjustments he had to make was sleeping in an ordinary bed. "I asked Kaye – that's Des's wife – 'Hey Kaye?, have you got any sheets?' And she said 'Yeah, on the bed'. But her sheets were coloured sheets – I didn't recognise they were sheets! I'd become used to taupe or white sheets you know. Coloured sheets!" He shakes his head in disbelief.

There were other changes he'd seen on the way in. The familiar farms he'd grown up around had in many cases been converted to market gardens, livestock replaced with neat ploughed fields and vegetables.

As Arthur stared out the window at the sun going down across the paddocks, the household was abuzz with people sharing a beer, discussing the next move.

"There's got to be a public inquiry into this!" exclaimed Des to earnest sounds of agreement. "There has to be." The big decisions would have to wait until morning, however – Arthur's mother and father were confined to barracks over at the family farm, distracting the media while Booth got his exclusive story out.

That next morning, December 18 Thomas returned to the farm he'd been arrested at nine years earlier, to greet a horde of news reporters, all wanting to know, "How does it feel?" They were patsy questions, but Thomas knew and appreciated that public support for his case, via news media pressure, was a crucial ingredient in the mix of things that caused his release.

"Did you commit the murders?" one TV journalist asked. Thomas eyeballed the camera lens directly as a hush descended on the crowd. "I am innocent of the Crewe murders."[156]

"Do you swear you are telling the truth?" a voice cried out.

"I am a Christian, and I swear my innocence before God...There is no way I did it. My name is clear and I'm innocent of the crime. I came pretty near being mental there during part of my imprisonment. I didn't know if I'd end up in Lake Alice or in Kingseat. I just didn't know where I'd end up.

"But I didn't blame God for the situation. I knew it was caused by man-made greed and corruption. I've lost 10 years of my life, my farming career and my marriage – I'm washed out. If I hadn't been wrongly imprisoned I'd be well off now with a farm, a wife and possibly a family. I feel sad about not having all that. But I've just got to start as a new man as from yesterday – pick up what I can and take it from there.

"It's a challenge after ten years and I've got to meet that challenge, or I'm nothing."

The *Dominion* newspaper wrote of a man caught by circumstances in a time warp. "His narrow-legged, cuffed suit – the same one he wore at his wedding in 1964 and his second trial in 1973 – is now

---

156 *The Dominion*, 19 December 1979

the only decent clothing he owns. Outmoded pointed shoes and a slicked-down hairstyle marked him as someone who's been out of society for nearly ten years."

Asked about his romantic chances, Thomas was circumspect, saying he'd like to meet someone and start a family. "I'll be taking things slowly. It depends on what fish I can hook out. I've got to get the fish and bait and see what's going on – check the scene." Little did he know, but the fish was baiting the hook to catch a Thomas.

One of the people watching all this unfold on the TV news was that "painfully shy" young woman from Blenheim, Jenny Cresswell. When she saw he'd been released at the end of 1979, she plucked up the courage to send 41 year old Arthur a letter at Pukekawa.

"He replied to me!" she laughs, still sounding surprised.

"I got a lot of letters," interjects Arthur, "I think it was about 1500 letters from people around New Zealand and overseas, with the pardon." But Jenny was determined to be noticed, and her letter had accompanied a huge bunch of roses – "One red rose for every month I spent in prison!" says Arthur. The gesture was almost wasted, as Thomas and his parents had left for a holiday at Paihia together, but Arthur's aunt had collected the mail, and while she'd given away the roses to a rest home she made sure her nephew knew about the letter from a girl who'd sent 112 red roses.

"Now that is ..." says Arthur, his voice choking a little, "I'll tell you what that was, to me, to my heart...Ohhh," he sighs.

Jenny steps in to save him. "As Arthur puts it, that gave me 'the edge'."

"Oh, I was talking to me old man, and said, 'I've gotta have a little close look at this because this is the heart business of a lady'. You know, that's *really*, really, you know, she's bloody good. Oh, Jenny. Oh yeah you know." The couple laugh as he gets lost for words again.

"I came up to visit and I walked in on his mother's 70th birthday party at Mercer. So I pretty much met Arthur in front of all his family and friends and well wishers and..."

"The first time," nods Arthur, remembering.

"Absolutely daunting, it was," she continues. "And when I got to the little sign that says 'Pukekawa' by Rangiriri, and it sailed on past I thought the bus had actually forgotten about me." Extremely shy and fighting a huge case of nerves, Jenny wondered if it was fate telling her to 'stay on the bus, forget about us' and head through to Auckland. "I thought the bus driver had forgotten. I thought okay, cool, I'll go to Auckland for the night. I'll stay in Auckland the night and then I'll go back home. I really got cold feet."

She needn't have panicked. The coach shuddered to a halt a few minutes later just outside the Mercer shops. "Pukekawa, Mercer passengers, this is your stop." Waiting at the bus-stop was Arthur's youngest brother, Des. He looked like a Thomas, the resemblance was unmistakable.

"When I look back I wonder how I'd had the guts to do that at that age," Jenny reflects. "Because in the ensuing years after that I lost a lot of confidence because we went through quite a bit didn't we, really together, and I lost a lot of confidence."

When they first got together, some of the Thomas Retrial supporters believed Jenny had been planted by police as a spy leading up to the Royal Commission hearings. "So they didn't trust me – they didn't trust to talk to me…We had the baby, we had Bridgette and that was a wonderful time but there was a lot of… yeah, it wasn't easy. So I look back at it and I think how did that work all out? It was like there was, like it was meant to be sort of… it was a…"

Arthur points his finger skyward, smiling and saying nothing.

"A guiding hand?" I ask.

"Yeah, a guiding hand," Jenny concedes. When you hear their story, you start to understand why. While the entire Thomas family had rallied together to help secure his release, ironically his freedom blew the family apart. They were the best of times, and the worst of times.

"They were really tight. They were a really, really tight family until the compensation got brought up and then everything changed," explains Arthur. "I know my father really wanted me to split up my compensation money to all the family and carry on fighting for more money. And Peter Williams, my QC lawyer said, 'Arthur, the New Zealand tax payers paid this money through the Royal Commission to put you on the land where you were when you were arrested'. So that's why I bought this farm. But my father and some members of the family said, 'We'd like a bit of a, you know, something out of it.' And there is some bitterness there."

The problem was that the compensation was only enough for one farm, and it was Arthur who'd been locked away for nine years, imprisoned with killers and sex offenders, his name blackened. Even now, in the writing of this book, people have ventured theories as to how Arthur Thomas killed the Crewes. Mud sticks no matter how much you can prove it's just mud.

Thomas didn't have to push very hard for his Commission of Inquiry. Not trusting local judiciary, Prime Minister Muldoon appointed an Australian, retired NSW Supreme Court chief judge Robert Taylor, to lead the inquiry. I've covered a lot of Commission evidence during the course of the book, but it's worth seeing how they summed up some of the main points.

Among the findings, the Commission discovered the Thomas rifle left a "distinctive scoring mark" on bullets when it was test-fired, but that distinctive mark was not found on either of the two bullets that killed the Crewes.[157] Evidence of this, one of the "striations" I mentioned earlier, was never revealed at any of the court trials or appeals. Additionally, the Commission discovered the DSIR knew other striations on the Thomas rifle test bullet did not match anything found on Jeannette or Harvey's bullets. In other words, it was likely Thomas' gun did not fire the fatal shots, based on the evidence police had but chose never to tell the juries.[158]

"Dr Nelson gave no evidence relating to them at either trial. His evidence was so incomplete in the light of all these matters that it presented to the jury a false picture of his examination and findings and which of itself could have resulted in a miscarriage of justice."

Another gun cleared by the Commission was Mickey Eyre's – the DSIR had made some mistakes in its ballistics analysis and the Eyre gun could not have fired the fatal shot because its barrel only had five landing grooves, not six. Because the bullet fragments gave only limited data, there were likely to be thousands of guns in New Zealand that could have provided similar firing marks.

The Commission found that the DSIR's Dr Nelson was an unreliable witness because he let his pro-police bias get in the way of the evidence: "a tendency on the part of Dr Nelson, manifested in other areas in far more serious ways, to shape the evidence to fit his own theories rather than to shape, and if necessary abandon his own theories in the light of the evidence."[159]

The Commission found exhibit 343, the number eight bullet found

---

[157] Royal Commission report, page 14
[158] Ibid, page 61
[159] Ibid, page 36

in Arthur's shed, had indeed been switched at the court hearing with a different bullet. "In our view, the substitution must have been a deliberate one, carried out by some person aware that Dr Sprott had found a significant difference between the headstamps of exhibit 350 and the cartridge case of exhibit 343. That difference is, as we have already stated, obvious even from a careful visual examination."[160]... An unfired category 4 shellcase was deliberately substituted by the police to the knowledge of at least Mr Hutton."

The destruction of evidence by throwing away exhibits at the Whitford tip was also found to be an attempt to conceal a crime.

"Hutton's statement that he was present with Keith when they were taken to the dump and distributed was false. His description of the manner of their destruction was false to his knowledge. Hutton had both these exhibits destroyed because he knew exhibit 350 had been planted, and exhibit 343 was a suspect exhibit for which an unfired shell had been substituted.

"We find the disposal of these exhibits and the reasons for it has an added significance. It strongly supports the case against Hutton of planting 350 to procure the conviction of Thomas. The destruction of exhibits 350 and 343, and the telex report from Hutton, constitute impropriety on the part of the police. The telex sent by Hutton to Assistant Commissioner Walton was in part false, and intended to misrepresent the position so that a further search for exhibits 350 and 343 would not be undertaken by the police."[161]

The Commission found the Nash axle found under Harvey's body had not been switched with a different one, but that the axle had been altered by someone and used after mechanic Rasmussen last worked on it in 1965.[162] The Commission also stated that 45 other trailer parts that should have been found on the Thomas dump, if the trailer assembly had indeed ended its life there, were not found in that dump.

"Mr R. A. Closey, a vintage motor cycle enthusiast, gave evidence of searching the Thomas farm in company with a group of likeminded persons about 3 months prior to the time the murders occurred, namely in March 1970. Despite searching the tip area closely, they located nothing but model 'T' parts," reported the

---
160 Ibid, page 52
161 Ibid, page 90
162 Ibid, page 64

Commission.[163] No stub axles were found or visible, and neither was an old Nash car axle. Of course, we now know the axle had been taken by a group of youths in 1965.

In regard to jury tampering allegations, the Commission heard that police had thoroughly vetted prospective jurors through their own intelligence files, and that one of the police heading the operation told them "he had never before engaged in such a thorough vetting of a jury panel."[164]

"In our view, the thoroughness of the checking of the jury by the police was excessive, improper and calculated to prejudice the fairness of the subsequent trial."

The upshot of all this was a decision to pay compensation to Arthur, and also his family and lawyers. The Royal Commission paid out nearly $19,000 in 1980 dollars to Arthur's father Allan Thomas, reimbursing legal fees he'd paid to support his son's appeals. Vivien Harrison was awarded $10,500, Des and Ray Thomas each received reimbursements of $5,400, brother Lloyd $5,300 and various other siblings $10,700 between them. Dr Jim Sprott was paid $50,000 for his professional forensic work and various lawyers took the bulk of a further $49,000 allocation. Journalist Pat Booth, whose work had led to the cartridge case discovery and overturned the conviction, was singled out for honourable mention by the Royal Commission:

"We draw attention to the immense labour of Mr Patrick Booth in the field of investigative journalism. This was carried out as a private enterprise and at some considerable sacrifice to family life. He has formally claimed only a token $1."

As Arthur tells it, his father wanted the $950,000 compensation split between the whole family. "The whole lot of them; yeah that's what my father wanted." With nine kids, plus the parents, that's not a lot to restart your life on. "Yeah, I'd have nothing left. Nothing left. I'd be on the dole now, no farm, and I'd be on the dole now."

Thomas remembers the moment, sitting across the kitchen table from his father at Pukekawa, when it all just got too much to bear. "He was pressuring me to split up the money, and I was thinking, you know, this is getting out of hand a bit. I didn't want these sorts of problems, I'm supposed to be all happy. But money's terrible bloody stuff," he sighs.

---

163 Ibid, page 70
164 Ibid, page 108

Arthur remembers rising from the table, staring at his father, anger flashing between them like an electric storm. The younger Thomas pushed past his dad.

"Where are you going?"

"North, I've had enough of this, I need to get out of here."

The elder Thomas watched as his son's silhouette disappeared down the driveway. Things would never be the same again. That initial falling out with the family, at the end of 1980, came as a shock to 22 year old Jenny, who'd spent several months that year living at Pukekawa while the movie *Beyond Reasonable Doubt* was made, before returning to Blenheim while Arthur took a trip to Australia.

"They'd been very tight and Arthur's dad was, to me, in those days he was a lovely, wonderful guy but I'd never understood why it went to crap in the months after that. And it seemed when I came back on the scene, when Arthur bought the farm and we came back here, it'd had just turned around. It had gone a 180. Things would've been so much different if they'd got even half of what they wanted from the Commission. Things would've been so much different," reflects Jenny.

Sensitive to his father's wishes, Thomas nonetheless made one final try on behalf of the wider family for compensation, while arranging to visit Prime Minister Sir Rob Muldoon at his Chatswood home in Auckland. Arthur wanted to thank him for taking the time to investigate his case, and the pardon that followed.

"I drove there and knocked on the door, it was Sir Rob – short fella eh," he quips, holding his hand about a garden gnome's height above the seat of the couch. "Shook my hand and everything, 'Come inside, Arthur', – I come into his private house and he was sitting like this and everything..."

"Well Arthur..." began Muldoon, "I thought you were guilty."

Thomas just blinked as Sir Robert gave one of his trademark cackles. "Then I had a visit from your ex wife."

Thomas blinked some more. He hadn't known about that.

"And she told me exactly where you were when the murders happened," explained Sir Rob. "I looked her in the eye and I changed my mind. Then I got Duncan McIntyre and a few other MP's; these are executive council Cabinet Ministers on our side and then that's how the ball started to roll."

Thomas couldn't believe his ears. The woman who'd walked out of his life in 1975 had given a parting gift he knew nothing about, and according to the Prime Minister it was Vivien's insistence that her husband had been right beside her all night that persuaded Muldoon to investigate.

Arthur remembered what he'd said about Vivien at the Pukekawa news conference: "I'm disappointed for the fact she didn't carry on the fight. She just walked right out and left me." He winced. Apparently he owed his release to his ex.

"I never knew," he confides in me, wide-eyed, across the coffee table. "Muldoon told me: it was the ex that turned him around. Put that in the book".

He only had a few minutes with Muldoon, but there was one other piece of information he found grimly amusing.

"One of Muldoon's first decisions had been to go and see the retired judge, old McGregor, who butchered the review of me case. The Prime Minister says he knocked on the door and McGregor opened it, took one look at Muldoon and said, 'I don't know who you are, go away please'. I mean, Muldoon was the Prime Minister and this retired judge didn't even recognise him."

Before leaving, Thomas raised the plight of his father and siblings. Surely, he asked, it might be possible to look at wider compensation for the hurt and stress they'd all been put through?

"It cost them a lot of money, a lot of running around, a lot of worries and things and is there any chance of giving a bit of extra money to the family. And he said, 'I can't promise anything. I have to leave this to the Minister of Justice'. That's all we heard; didn't hear nothing more. So I did that, that little bit for the family."

On one of the last occasions Arthur and his father spoke, when Arthur's mum Ivy was confined to a wheelchair, the subject of money came up again.

"I like to talk to my mother a wee bit, she's in a wheelchair and she's never had much chance to talk to people – she'd always get talked over all the time you know and I didn't like that. Anyhow when I said goodbye to my mother and then walked out the door, my father escorted me out and he wanted to talk to me without my mother knowing. And he said, 'I wanna know if I could have…' – how much money for the racehorse, Jenny, $30,000 wasn't it or something? For a silly racehorse, yeah."

Arthur and Jenny had already spent nearly $70,000 on one of the siblings to help them buy a property, so buying a racehorse while his mother was in a wheelchair wasn't top priority. "Well I don't know where else I can get the money from to buy a racehorse," complained the senior Thomas. For Jenny, it was the last straw.

"Arthur had talked me into taking Bridgette, because Bridgette was only about, I don't know, three years old at that stage. I hadn't wanted to, as we'd had a policy of 'no contact' practically since she was born, but we had a lovely visit with them and it was sort of a little bit like old times for me. And then to come out and for him to have another go at Arthur over the money, I just said to Arthur 'that's the last time I'll ever come here', and we've never been back."

It was possibly a version of 'Curse of the Lotto Millionaires', only this was more tragic. It poisoned family relationships and while Arthur and his wife and daughter made regular trips to see mum Ivy Thomas in the rest home, there was a gradual slide in contact with the rest of the family.

"If that visit had gone well and that hadn't have happened we would've had a far better relationship with them. But no, he had to go and mention money again," says Jenny, shaking her head.

Arthur says that for their part, the rest of the family tried to cut him out of his inheritance after Allan and Ivy died. "My dad's logic was that the prison compensation was all I needed, whereas I'd put my blood sweat and tears into that farm, just like the other siblings, it was my birthright." Their parents' farm and property had been placed in a trust, but Arthur only found out through a chance encounter with a former worker on the Pukekawa farm at an end of year do, and he let slip that the farm was up for sale.

"When I spoke to the guy, he said, 'Oh your farm's being sold.' and I said, 'Well hang on, there's two other Thomas'; there's me uncle up the road and the uncle down the road, it might be their farms.' He said, 'No, it's your farm. The family doesn't want you to know'."

Thomas hired a lawyer, who discovered his father Allan had cut him from the Will completely shortly after the racehorse argument. Remembering back to his years of unpaid labour on the farm instead of going to high school, Arthur Thomas decided to contest. It was settled out of court and he received four percent as his share. His eight brothers and sisters were left with 96% of the estate to split between them — an average of 12% each.

Arthur Thomas lowers his voice and sighs, the money issue dragging him down. "It's a shame. Damn shame. My family worked their backsides off for me, and we lost each other over the compensation issue. Money is an evil thing."

Ray Thomas puts his own perspective on it:

"Do these people in [parliament] realise how much pressure it puts on innocent people and their families? To have gone through every legal court in New Zealand twice or more and getting no good honest justice. Not having anywhere to go. Not having the backing of major news. Not having enough money to fight corruption with the backing of taxpayers' money.

"It seems as though the Crown engaged top lawyers and QCs to look into major cases at taxpayers' expense but 'please find in the Crown's favour'.

"Does the system know how they disrupt the lives of families and innocent personnel? It's absolute horror, pain, disbelief and sheer frustration of the system we were brought up to believe in. It's put there to protect the Crown, not for the truth.

"All I wanted to be was a husband, father and farmer, instead of being a detective chasing up leads and wild goose chases. Then also dozens of trips of 200 miles each way to retrial committee meetings and getting home in time to do the morning milking.

"After 10 years fighting for justice in the Thomas case we came out of it mentally, physically and financially exhausted. Looking back, I find it hard to believe just how naive I was. The cost of proving one's innocence is too high," laments Ray Thomas.

Jenny's words were right: if only the Crown had compensated the family for the pain and humiliation and hurt caused to them, "things would have been so much different."

Perhaps, with the revelations still to come in the final chapter, the wider Thomas family will get their day of reckoning after all.

But to a younger generation of Thomases, this is all academic. Arthur and Jenny's daughter, now Bridgette Rowe, is in her late 20s, and the events of the 1970s may as well have come from the dinosaur era. She says her life has remained more or less untouched by her father's history. "I haven't seen the movie or anything, but I've just seen what's written in the papers recently."

Bridgette was born in 1982, just two years after Arthur's release. It was, says Arthur, a magic moment. "Absolutely proud, it made me very proud, this little girl in my arms, after all the crap I'd been through and here's this little wee baby in my arms. It's a great feeling, yessirree." It was symbolic of the fresh start he'd sought, and the plea he'd put out at his Pukekawa news conference the day after his release.

Equally symbolic was turning the first clod on the Orini farm he bought with the compensation money. "I remember digging my boot in the dirt on the farm – "This is *my* bastard." Because I'm a farmer, like this is my farm, my farm. I kicked the dirt, you know, I just had the feeling I was home."

For Jenny, there wasn't really a shadow hanging over them nor was she concerned about people who questioned the 20 year age difference. "I never looked at Arthur like that. It was just our life was going to start and he'd got out of prison, that's the end of it. It was quite separate in my mind. I never really thought of him as being greatly older than myself. So no, as far as what other people thought, it didn't feel wrong, it didn't feel weird. It was just going to be the beginning of our lives forward. I wasn't going, that was it."

Arthur and Jenny had not hidden the events of the past, but naturally it would have gone over the head of a five year old. However, it surfaced quite starkly when she started school. "I told Bridgette when I was at the beach, told her the story, she was only young, and she said she'd heard about it at primary school, that I'd been in prison. The other kids had told her that her dad had been in jail." She'd only been at school for a week.

An ordinary person might find such things difficult. Arthur, however, found in Jenny a rock he could anchor to, someone who could lighten the mood. She still does. In the late 1990s when new firearms licensing was introduced, Arthur applied for one of the new gun licences. As a condition, he had to personally front up to the Ngaruawahia Police station for a good character check.

"They called Jenny, my wife, in see, and I was outside and I heard them laugh like hell. And of course the lady asked her 'Has Arthur ever threatened you with a gun?' 'No, never.' And then Jenny told them, 'Yeah, but there is the small matter of the Crewe murders'."

"Well," starts Jenny in her own defence, "yeah, she said, 'Has Arthur got any criminal convictions?' Of course she has to ask it, doesn't she. And I said, 'Well there was a small matter of the Crewe murders.' And we just looked at each other and she…"

All Arthur could hear were gales of laughter emanating from the police station as the two women enjoyed the irony of the moment.

"She laughed first," insists Jenny, "and I couldn't help but crack a smile then... I was very, very serious before."

Not all dealings with officialdom were so easy. When they wanted to travel to the United States, Arthur's visa was held up because of confusion over his criminal status. In American law, a "pardon" meant the criminal had been forgiven for the crime, not declared innocent of it. Under s407 of the New Zealand Crimes Act, however, it means something entirely different:

"Where any person convicted of an offence is granted a free pardon by Her Majesty, or by the Governor-General in the exercise of any powers vested in him on that behalf, that person shall be deemed to have never committed that offence."

US Immigration Service agents are cynical types at the best of times. Far easier to tick the box marked "Murderer" and chuck him out.

"I was going on an aviation tour, I think it was 1990 to America, Oshkosh. Big show. When I put the application in on the entry form for Customs like everyone has to do, under US law even if you have been pardoned you have to tick the box as to whether you've been in prison. That's the wording that actually stuffed everyone up. Big problems getting that visa," says Thomas.

Thomas' tour group was held up "for hours" at Los Angeles airport while US Immigration debated what to do with him. A similar problem hit the family when Arthur took his wife and child to Florida in 1993, and this time the delay forced them to overnight in LA because they'd missed their connecting flight. Arthur and Jenny actually married in the US on that trip, but even that had a documentary hurdle they needed to overcome – proof that Arthur's marriage to Vivien had ended in divorce. It required a frantic call to lawyer Kevin Ryan's office, who faxed across the divorce papers to Arthur and Jenny at their US hotel with a personal cover note: "Good luck mate, I'd like to be your best man!"

Sick of the harassment at the US border, in 2000 on the eve of another trip, Arthur asked Auckland law professor Bill Hodge if there was a long term solution. He suggested a multi-year, multi-entry visa, but as they researched they found the New Zealand Police had retained one final sting in the tail for Arthur Allan Thomas – a red flag against his name on the Wanganui Computer.

"Jim Bolger was in charge of our embassy in America in those days, and he was the right man to have on the spot because he'd been involved in the pardon. And that's how I found out police had put a warning flag on my name and the Americans now had that flag on their system as well. So we had to apply to get that flag removed. Jim Bolger, David Lange, all the top guns were involved in helping persuade the Americans to remove the flag."

Jenny was left tying up the loose ends as departure time neared. "I spoke to David Lange on the phone, and he told me he'd had to write, and it was actually talked about on the floor of the US Senate. I was worried because it was all up to the last minute that Arthur's flight would have to leave without him, and I suppose I got quite waspish with David and said, 'is that all you can do?'. He sort of chuckled and said, 'Well, I could go out and lie down on the runway in front of the plane to stop it from taking off, I believe that would be quite effective, but I'm not prepared to do that!'"

The warning flag was, finally, removed and as a result of Arthur's case, the wording on US Immigration Service forms has changed to reflect the British meaning of the word "Pardon".

Little did Arthur know that he would soon be cheating death.

CHAPTER 13

The Icarus Agenda

Many people have heard the story of the Bird Man of Alcatraz. He kept canaries while doing a life sentence in America's highest security jail. Arthur Allan Thomas, on the other hand, kept a cat during part of his prison stint. He dreamt, however, of flying, and had done so ever since the day his uncle Ivan invited him to watch a topdressing run at Patetonga in May, 1955. Arthur was 17.

"I can still see this particular plane because it was fascinating in those days. Fred Sawyer, flying a Cessna 180. It was the last load and he said, 'do you want a ride?'. I kicked my gumboots off and hopped in beside him. He took me for a ride and did two runs – I never forgot it, eh. Low and fast, up, around, steep turns and back down again. Lord I was hanging on."

The adrenalin rush from joining the paddock jockeys on their leaps from farm to farm stayed with Thomas and played a big part in his career in topdressing. From behind bars he could only stretch his wings in his mind, but when he was released Arthur Thomas decided to do it for real: not just as passenger but as a pilot.

His choice of aircraft wasn't a Cessna or anything so safe. Instead, Thomas felt his destiny lay in those glorified lawnmowers with wings: microlights. As one who chartered a single engine Cessna to fly through a thunderstorm the day of the Edgecumbe earthquake in 1987, I appreciate the limits of aircraft. As one who saw his life, and large chunks of a grass airstrip, flash past his eyes on an almost-crash landing of a TV3 twin engine aircraft, I appreciate the small protections that an actual cabin provides. Thus, when Arthur Thomas looks me in the eye and tells me he flies microlight aircraft as a hobby, he probably senses I think he's barking mad.

"He's had a very interesting life in microlighting," smiles Jenny knowingly. Although as you'll see, she didn't know the half of it until well after the events in question.

"It's only a problem when the engine stops," explains Arthur without a hint of irony.

Oh really? My raised eyebrows invited him to explain.

"I was so close to death. I was flying a Bantam over to see a friend by the name of Rex Scott – the late Rex Scott – and I was just gonna head over towards the hills and all of a sudden there's a thump and the craft starts wanting to fly higher! And then I had to put the stick hard forward to fly level – you should go down see when you give it hard stick. Oh crap!"

As Jenny would later describe it, Arthur was experiencing a perturbance on his event horizon. Loose translation? Too much event and a rapidly shrinking horizon. Arthur wrenched the joystick but he just couldn't control his aircraft.

"What's happened? What the heck's gone wrong? And I thought, I'm bloody dead."

There were a few other choice expletives running through his mind too, as the Waikato river loomed large. The engine was still running, its huge propeller blades beating the air but largely uncontrollable.

"I can't carry on, there's the Waikato river, there's Huntly coming up, thumping into the hills in front of me – I'm going to be in the proverbial."

Faced with a choice of the river or the hills, Thomas went for plan C. He still had rudder control, if not elevation control, "So I just kicked the rudder round quietly," he laughs, "I'm shaking like a sheep I'll tell you."

Over to the right were paddocks, and one of them, Thomas knew, was used as a training strip by microlight instructors. As he turned his head to get better bearings, he caught a glimpse over his shoulder of why he'd lost control – an elevator on the tail-fins had jammed and it was trying to force the microlight higher. Normally forcing the stick forward would bring the machine down, but in this case it was merely flying level. Thomas deduced however that throttling back at strategic moments would allow him to lose altitude.

"I did a 747 let-down. I saw the airstrip way down there, so I did slowly, slowly descend – cut the power, see. And slowly turned this plane right round and had everything lined up for the landing on this paddock, it was a rough landing, but I kissed... I got out shaking and this thing here —" Thomas breaks off thumping his chest with his fist, "just nearly stopping, and I kissed the ground."

Arthur thought he would spare his wife the finer details of his flight that day.

"How did it go?"

"Oh, up and down, really. Nothing special."

But as any husband knows, a wife will always find out. Arthur hadn't factored that particular law of nature into his calculations. "Oh, I'll be grounded. If I told Jenny, I'll be grounded," he tells me nervously.

And find out she did. "Because," says Jenny, "the people that he landed his micro light on, the lady, her mother lives opposite my dad in Blenheim."

To paraphrase Humphrey Bogart in *Casablanca*, "Of all the paddocks in all the farms in all the world, he flies into mine."

Mother just happened to be visiting her daughter after Arthur Thomas crash-landed in her daughter's paddock, and of course she was terribly excited to find out someone as famous as Arthur Thomas had dropped out of the sky for a visit, and of course when she got a chance to visit Jenny for a chat over tea and scones the subject inevitably came up.

"Arthur!!!"

You can imagine Arthur's surprise to walk in the living room and find his flight mishap the subject of considerable discussion. "Arthur got the tail end of that when they left," admits Jenny.

"Yeah, I got stick alright. I didn't want Jenny..."

"He got caught out majorly," Jenny interrupts.

"I didn't want Jenny to ground me. She'd ground me over that."

He didn't lose his wings but he did lose some tailfeathers. These days, Arthur reports to "Jenny Traffic Control", and she's engaged a local "bush radar" to keep tabs on her wayward pilot. "He's been very lucky," she says, "but I think that he's got a guardian angel sitting on his shoulder."

"Yeah, yeah I've always said that, right from the day I was pardoned," agrees Arthur, who then explains the reason for the comment. Another microlight flight, this time through the rugged Waihi Gorge.

"We were flying real high, to go over the mountain ranges – the

Kaimai-Coromandel range to Whitianga. There was another guy – my old topdressing pilot Keith Christie – flying way ahead of me, and it was a beautiful flight, really, really high. I was so relaxed, just enjoying the scenery way below. Suddenly, the engine just stopped. The motor shuddered and the blinkin' propeller, the wooden prop, just stopped."

All Arthur could hear, as Simon & Garfunkel made famous, was the sound of silence, and the eerie "shhhhhhhhhhhhhhhhh" of the wind hissing past his ears. It turned out that the crankshaft had a manufacturing fault but, at 1,500 feet and dropping fast, this was a bit of an academic issue for Arthur Thomas right then.

"I put the nose down see, because I had to maintain airspeed or the machine would stall. I thought I can't go any further, because that's the hills in front of me, so I turned around and there was the Paeroa Golf Course.

"Righto, I'll pick an area of the golf course, nice paddock somewhere."

Fat chance. The closer he got to the ground, the more trees seemed to fill the paddock. Trees and sandtraps. Suddenly Arthur realised he wouldn't make the 19th in one piece if he touched down there. And all he could hear was "shhhhhhhhhhhhh" in his ears as his microlight swished ever nearer to terra firma. "Next thing I saw some long paddocks, a dairy farm, you know long, narrow paddocks, so I thought here we go, I'm gonna come into this particular paddock and I come in steaming fast – much too fast! No brakes. These things have got wheels but no brakes, eh. It's coming too fast, I'm gonna go right through the fence next door."

Faced with a choice between trees, fence or impersonating a bug on a windscreen by slamming into the ground too fast, Thomas made a split second decision to violently turn his craft from side to side, "might wash some speed off, see?" It worked, he says, "slowing it down a bit for the next paddock. Piece of cake – on the ground!"

The woman who owned the farm wasn't too impressed to see a city slicker in his magnificent flying machine tearing strips out of her paddock. "But I said 'I'm very, very sorry. I'm a farmer', and when I told her I was a farmer, 'oh, very good… 'Come and use my phone',".

Arthur called the engine suppliers who expressed surprise that a client had dropped out of the sky and lived to lay a complaint. That's not usually how it works in the microlight business, and there was nothing in the company manual explaining what they should do. "Why don't you let her cool down for a bit, then start her up again?" said a mechanic over the phone, helpfully.

"Start her up and just see what happens, and I did. And I got full power and I held it for several minutes – full power. Oh, that's odd – nothing wrong." After talking to the mechanic further Arthur decided it must be safe enough to fly home. "Took off, see, and I climb, climb... I thought the higher I go the better so I can... you know, if I got a problem. Next thing, it didn't stop, it just started to play up. I thought okay, not gonna go any further than this, I'll look for a paddock with the engine going and land it again, and then I'll eventually put it on a trailer and bring it home and pull it to bits. I pulled it to bits and found the crank had cracked. When they're put together they freeze one and heat the other – that's how they make the crank. And one bit split and they didn't pick it up when they were manufacturing."

You would think, after two near misses like that, that Arthur might throttle back on his Icarus ambitions, but apparently not. He upgraded his microlight and: "I've been down to Invercargill in it, yep."

I have to reach up and pull my eyebrows down from where they've stuck to the ceiling.

"I'm sorry, you've *what!?*"

"Yep, I've flown to Invercargill, although with stops on the way down. And been to Warbirds in Wanaka."

"You flew a microlight across Cook Strait?"

"Oh that's nothing for this plane. It's like my car; it's got an engine like my car."

"This one he's got now is like a little plane," says Jenny. "But he has flown across Cook Strait in the Bantam...which is all struts and wires and fabric and..."

"You're kidding me!"

"Old danger man here! Old danger man," she laughs.

"So", I ask, "you're riding a motor mower across Cook Strait, you know, full of great white sharks, the whole lot, you know..."

"I wouldn't do it now," admits Thomas. "But 15 or 20 years ago, I did it two or three times."

People back then told him he must be a few spark plugs short of an engine, but Arthur assured them, "You don't know microlights – I do, she's a piece of cake."

He admits to me however that he was quaking on the inside. "I do get a bit nervous when I first leave the North Island or South Island coming back. But then I thought, oh, this motor doesn't really know it's crossing the Cook Strait."

The trick, he says, is to shadow fishing boats or the Cook Strait ferry, so that if he has to ditch someone will rescue him. I can see now why he believes his guardian angel rides pillion.

When I ask Arthur what it is that drives him into the sky, his reply is simple: "Freedom. It's the complete opposite of my time in jail, and the world looks great from up there." He frequently flies these days with friend and son-in-law William Rowe.

But even in his upgraded microlight, the tiny little plane he helped build in 1994 with the much more reliable four stroke engine, he hasn't escaped mishaps. On one occasion, sunstrike as he came into land carrying his teenage daughter as a passenger caused him to clip a fence and flip the plane. Both of them walked away unscathed, but this crash captured news media attention.

"She's a great little aeroplane that. Hey remember when I had that little accident with Bridgette? How many fire engines... was it three fire engines? How many cop cars? Three or four cop cars... ooh was heaps."

When police found out it was their old mate Arthur Allan Thomas, they breathalysed him. He came through it clean. He wasn't so happy about running into a policeman at a cafe in Pukekohe ten years ago, however.

Jenny and Arthur had decided to order lunch, and a beer, when a man from a table nearby sidled up to Thomas at the bar.

"This guy says, 'How are you?', and then gestures over his shoulder and says, 'Do you know this guy over here?' And I looked at him and couldn't recognise him. It was pretty dark, but then he said, 'Don't you recognise me Arthur?', and ooh, the voice. I picked the voice. Oh, struth!"

The "voice" belonged to a retired Detective Inspector, Bruce Hutton, and the man at the bar was former policeman John McKenzie.

"There was one thing we were not going to be talking about was the murders, because he's verballed me before and I wasn't going to give him a second chance," mutters Arthur. "Bruce Hutton spoke about my father and the Pukekawa farm, and how my father got a licence for training racehorses. The conversation went on for about two minutes."

Arthur went to pay for his beer but McKenzie insisted he'd take care of it.

"We would have walked out," remarks Jenny, "but we'd already ordered lunch. We didn't feel very comfortable having our lunch there but we were too cheap to buy it and then leave it," she laughs.

The *Herald* this year claimed the two men "chatted away like long-lost school pals"[165] – a description that mightily annoyed the Thomases. "The article made it out to be a reunion of old friends! It's a bit of a stretch of the truth there!"

His life, since release, he assures me has been largely uneventful, mainly centred around farm, family and friends. One of the highlights was meeting his idol Johnny Cash, the man whose music he'd listened to since the early sixties and through his prison years. The meeting was arranged by concert promoter Ian Magan when Cash toured with The Highwaymen in the early 1990s.

"I like Johnny Cash. I told him I'd been in prison," says Arthur. But what came next stunned him. "June Carter, his wife, had seen the movie *Beyond Reasonable Doubt*. Yeah. She told me. She told me, 'I seen the movie about your case'."

It is, indeed, a small world. But if the next couple of chapters are anything to go by, the old movie needs a new ending.

---

165 "'Have a beer' – pub yarn breaks ice in Crewe-case clash" – *NZ Herald*, 29 May 2010

CHAPTER 14

The Mystery Man

There's a question which remains unanswered in this ultimate cold case. If the killer was not Arthur Allan Thomas, nor Len Demler, then who was it? That's the question that's been haunting Pukekawa for decades.

"People think we're doing all this for Arthur's benefit," grimaces younger brother Des Thomas over a cup of tea on a rustic wooden table in his cozy Pukekawa farmhouse. "It's not for Arthur. Arthur's a free man who's been out for years. I'm doing this for Jeannette and Harvey. A young couple were brutally, brutally murdered in front of their baby, and the killer is still at large. The Crewes deserve justice. So does the community."

The years hang off Des like the fur on a shaggy dog. The 18 year old stripling who dropped everything to help Vivien run the Thomas farm after Arthur's arrest, and whose own marriage later imploded under the pressures of the case, has morphed into a 58 year old truthseeker, who makes his living selling water deliveries in summer and firewood in the winter.

For Des, a possible suspect remains Mickey Eyre, although he admits few of his siblings believe that any more. When you talk to the Eyres, they remain deeply hurt at the suspicion surrounding one of their own after all these years.

"I know he's utterly wrong," barks Mickey's brother Joss Eyre at me, "because I was 16 when the Crewes were murdered, and I'll say this to the Thomases, they should look in their own backyard. I've never believed that Arthur Thomas did it, but the evidence points to a member of the Thomas family. The axle, the dump, everything. The Royal Commission cleared the gun Mickey had.

"Richard Thomas, him and his father came to see us and we were quite prepared to help the Thomases because we couldn't believe that Arthur did it. Now my mother turned around, because mum used to go where angels fear to tread, and said to Allan, 'Allan, I don't believe that Arthur did it, but whoever did it, hanging is too good for them.' With that, Richard Thomas stood up, he went white as a sheet, he clenched his fist, he looked me daggers in the eye and said to his father, 'Come on Dad, we've got to go'. And from that day on they went after my brother."

I remembered the words of the petrol pump attendant who'd told me how some people cross the street when they see each other in Pukekawa. I think I now know who he meant. The feud between some of the Thomases and some of the Eyres runs long and deep, each blaming the other for the Crewe murders.

By the time you've finished reading the next two chapters, I think you'll agree there are people with far more motive than either a Thomas or an Eyre, and more technical prowess. The thing everyone seems to forget, particularly Pukekawa's Hatfields and McCoys, is that the killer was clinical, deadly and highly efficient at erasing all trace of their identity from the crime scene. The killer was someone who knew exactly how to evade detectives and beat them at their own game.

It was always assumed the killer was a local because the murderer appeared to have known the Crewes well enough to be welcomed in the door (assuming we discard the thoroughly discredited shot-through-the-open-window-on-a-stormy-winter-night theory). But what if the murderer wasn't a local – at least, not directly?

We, all of us, move within circles: immediate family, neighbours, suburb, workmates, social clubs. Those circles, particularly the latter two, can be widely spaced, geographically. And the circles interlink, so "family" can visit regularly from far away, or table tennis players can meet once a month from miles around. You get the picture. 'Local' is not confined to the village itself.

A misunderstood rendering of the "it must be a local" theory is precisely the reason Pukekawa was torn apart by fingerpointing; 'if it's not me, it must be you'. But there are others who can have local knowledge without necessarily living in the area and being part of the immediate community. Right at the start of this book I told you the dualistic, one-or-other approach to this case was fatally flawed. Sometimes you have to step outside the box to appreciate the wider situation. If the police investigation had not been so utterly incompetent and corrupt, four decades would not have been wasted battling over whether it was Arthur, Len or, to a lesser extent, Mickey. Maybe, just maybe, it was someone else altogether. In these next two chapters, you are going to meet a few potential candidates.

Len Demler's discovery of the key in the outside lock of the back door suggests the murderer may have let himself in with prior knowledge of where a spare key was kept. Ordinarily that might mean either relative, close friend or lucky guess, but it could also mean illicit lover. David Yallop, in his foraging around the Crewe family, came to the conclusion the Crewes were married in name only by the time of their deaths:[166]

"A baby's bedroom, barren as a prison cell, not one colourful poster or painting on Rochelle's walls. A lounge, equally devoid of those little things that make the statement 'Harvey and Jeannette live here'; no paintings, ornaments, those little nicknacks that we all clutter our homes with, none are in evidence.

"Windows that are curtainless. Floors that are bare. I have seen more homeliness in a motel room than I can find in those photographs of the Crewe farmhouse. Clothes slung everywhere. A woman's dressing table devoid of any femininity.

"The place – I cannot refer to it as a home – reeks of apathy. It reeks not only of the deaths that undoubtedly occurred there but also of a dead relationship, dead long before 17 June 1970," wrote Yallop.

Is it possible that Jeannette had been having an affair, perhaps that had now turned sour, and that the third person in this triangle ended up in that house, on that day, armed, jealous and angry? He might have had little to be jealous about – police found no anniversary presents in the house for either Jeannette or Harvey, nor anniversary cards – their fourth anniversary was apparently not being marked by either of the Crewes.

"The evidence of Harvey's mother Mrs Marie Crewe drew a picture of Jeannette the perfect mother, the perfect housewife," wrote Yallop as he launched into a spot of 1970s male chauvinism. "If that was an accurate picture, then either Jeannette Crewe had a

---

166 *Beyond Reasonable Doubt*, by David Yallop, p41

complete nervous breakdown in the days that preceded her death, or her house was subsequently ravaged by an army of sluts!"[167]

There is a very telling admission in the police files, where Bruce Hutton tells his team he's focused on Demler or Thomas because, "At no stage during the enquiry to date has there been the slightest indication of any other person being involved or having a grudge against the Crewes."

Not the "slightest indication"? I wonder how Hutton will respond to this next piece of information.

In 2008, I was approached by a retired businessman who'd worked an agricultural machinery sales beat in the South Auckland/Pukekawa/Tuakau districts in the late 1960s and early 70s. This man explained to me that he'd been sitting on a dreadful secret for 38 years, too scared to tell.

"Dear Ian

"About June 1970 the Crewe murders took place at Onewhero. As you are aware, as at today's date no one has been convicted for this horrendous crime since Arthur Allan Thomas was released from prison with a pardon.

"What would genuine new information about this mystery be worth, providing it is not absorbed, some idiotic fantasy or clairvoyant rubbish but indisputable facts, such as the name of the blonde woman who fed baby Rochelle? As you are aware, this has been the most asked question and one of the conundrums of this most infamous murder mystery, and I firmly believe that I know who she was.

"I have had information since 1970 that I have been far too frightened to release. I made an effort to inform the police in 1970 and spoke to a Sergeant Johnston (I shall never forget his name) and outlined what I knew about some people that should be interviewed. Imagine my surprise when he went right off the rails and told me that if I ever rang the police with that information again or made any attempt to have it made known, then I would be the next bastard found in the river. Further, now he had my name and I was to shut my bloody mouth forever over this matter.

"Sergeant Johnston is now dead, however, with the information that I have I am still a threat because all of his buddies are not dead.

---

167 *Beyond Reasonable Doubt*, p101

The main threat is [name suppressed] and what I believe I know about him could see him jailed for the rest of his miserable life.

"I approached Mr [John] Carter our local MP about 18 months ago [around the end of 2006 or start of 2007] and he has been made aware of a snippet of my information. It was enough for him to send me the name of a certain Police District Commander, however I will not devolve [sic, divulge] any information unless I am 100% assured that anything I disclose will be given absolute confidentiality and my name, etc, is to also be 100% confidential. Something I was not given by the Police Commander at the time.

"I still have genuine concerns for my safety."

After receiving that message, I quickly made contact and promised confidentiality until we had discussed it further. We then met to discuss the revelation in greater detail, and he agreed I could run a story on the issue as long as I kept his identity confidential. He gave me both a written statement and a verbal interview, the gist of which is this:

"During my many visits to farms in the Tuakau area," says the new witness, "I became aware of [an agricultural contractor] by the name of [who we'll call "Mr Ex"] who was actively engaged…[visiting] many dairy and other farmers in Tuakau, Onewhero and the surrounding areas relating to their farming needs and problems."

The witness says he came to know Mr Ex, and his blonde-haired sister, through their mutual work in the farming sector covering the greater South Auckland and North Waikato areas. At one of their meetings, the man named as a new person of interest in the Harvey and Jeannette Crewe homicide investigation confided "about how the farmers' wives often made advances towards him when their husbands were out working on the farms when he called, and [he] seemed happy to be able to talk or boast about this.

"However, on one of my last visits, he was very agitated over some woman by the name I thought sounded like 'Gee-net' – he pronounced it as Gee-net – who was not happy with him for some unknown reason and had evidently threatened to tell her husband about that matter.

"This obviously had infuriated [Mr Ex] as he stated that a woman like her could ruin his business and his reputation, and if it became public it would cause further alienation of his relations (that I had already sensed were not great) between himself and his family, and he wouldn't let that happen. [Name suppressed] went on to mention that he would finally 'get her' – I presumed from past discussions that he meant he would win her over. However, at this time it was no concern of mine and it appeared to me he was letting this matter consume him, and the rejection of his advances (whatever they may have been) were definitely not appreciated."

The witness describes the person of interest as a man quick to anger, with "a very vehement nature" and prone to "violent, verbal" outbursts – although surprisingly he never swore.

"Although he discussed his farm meetings and meeting farmers' wives openly to me, I cannot recall him swearing and can't remember him doing so during any of his conversations with me, and I thought that was rather odd at the time given the nature of his ramblings."

The witness told me he paid no further attention to the man's exploits, until Jeannette and Harvey Crewe were found to have been murdered at their farm in June 1970, a little while later.

"As I had worked in the area and down the same road as the murders, I took an interest in the proceedings. I personally never visited the Crewe's farm and I could not honestly say if they were milking cows or running dry stock.

"However, I was more than surprised to learn that Arthur Allan Thomas had been charged with the murders. I had met briefly with Mr Thomas on two occasions, once…in Warkworth when I visited a neighbour of his [father's] and once when I called at his farm… On each of these meetings, although brief, I found Mr Thomas to be an extremely polite and quietly spoken man, and if anything a little naïve, but in no way would I have ever expected him to be a man capable of murder.

"As the information started to roll in over this case it was public knowledge that a blonde woman was seen at the Crewe's house, and it was openly reported that she had possibly been the person who fed the baby Rochelle.

"Who was she? This has been one of the most-asked questions and one of the conundrums of this most infamous murder mystery. The 18 month old baby was found in her cot at the Crewe's farm, and there was evidence that she had been fed and had had her nappies changed during that time.

"Mr Ex's comment to me about a woman named Gee-net threatening to tell her husband about some matter…came chillingly back to me, especially due to the fact I had seen [his] previous violent verbal outbursts."

The man's sister, a woman who doted on her brother despite his status as "black sheep" of the family, was fair haired. The witness, who knew her personally as well, has exceptionally good reason to believe the woman agreed to help her brother after the fact, because of the shame it would bring to their prominent family name. He believes the sister was undoubtedly the woman who fed baby Rochelle Crewe, and who has never been identified by police, at least publicly.

"Having thought about this matter," the witness told me, "I then phoned the police. I asked to speak to the senior officer in charge… and I relayed my suspicions to him and the names I had.

"Instead of showing any interest, I was shouted at over the phone – told 'never to ring the f**king police again about this matter, and if you do you'll be the next f**king person to be found in the river!'.

"I was also told that the police knew who the murderer was and to 'butt out completely, or else!'.

"To say I was s**t-scared over this reaction would be an understatement," records the witness.

Which is why it took him 38 years to come forward with the information.

A key question surrounds the police reaction to his tip-off: why was it so vehement and threatening? It turns out the man our witness spoke to was Detective Len Johnston, a key figure on the murder case and a man later implicated by the Thomas Royal Commission as helping to frame Thomas for the murder by planting a cartridge case in the flower bed that had already been extensively searched three weeks earlier without success.

Johnston, as I've previously noted, had miraculously come up with a theory about how the Crewe's were killed, which is recounted in the Royal Commission report.[168]:

"It is said that on 11 October, Detective Johnston had noticed in photographs taken at the scene as discovered by the police on 22 June 1970, that the kitchen louvre windows were open. He thought that possibly the murderer had fired his first shot from outside the house, with one foot on the parapet beside the back door and his

---

168 The Royal Commission report, www.investigatemagazine.com/thomascommission.pdf

other foot on the windowsill beneath the louvre windows. A reconstruction on the evening of 13 October showed that a shot could be fired into the head of a person sitting in the large armchair known as 'Harvey's chair' by a rifleman in that position. *However, the evidence establishes that a shooting in this manner is so unlikely that this possibility can safely be disregarded.* (See paragraphs 200 to 202.)"

The Royal Commission also notes that it was Johnston who uplifted rifle cartridges from Arthur Allan Thomas' farm:

"On 13 October, Detective Johnston picked up from Mr Thomas's farm a box of .22 ammunition, uncounted, which was to become exhibit 318. He appears also to have visited a tip on the farm that day, searching for parts connected with the axle."

As the Royal Commission notes, Johnston found the axle parts he was looking for at Thomas' farm as well, "located, after a cursory search of one of the three tips on the farm, two stub axles on which broken welds matched welding at either end of the axle itself. Wire samples, to be analysed and compared with the wire taken from the two bodies, were also taken by Mr Johnston on 13 and 20 October. On the latter date, Mr Thomas's rifle was again uplifted by the police."

But the circumstances of the axle "finds" on Thomas' farm seemed incredible to the Royal Commission:

"Inspector Parkes gave evidence that they collected their wire samples and that Detective Johnston then borrowed a spade and began foraging around on the tip. He said that, of three tips on the farm, Detective Johnston was concerned to search only *one*. After only a few minutes, to use Inspector Parkes' words, 'Detective Johnston located two stub axles. One was probably partly uncovered, but the other was buried.'

"Inspector Parkes said that Mr Johnston knew what they were, and seemed quite excited by his find. He did not search the tip any further that day. Inspector Parkes very fairly agreed that it was an extraordinary piece of luck that the two stub axles, which were to become such significant exhibits, just fell into Detective Johnston's hands."

For those who doubt Johnston was a corrupt cop prone to making death threats, consider this information given to me by a former police officer – now a senior lawyer – who worked alongside Johnston at the Otahuhu police station in 1963.

"I reported on one occasion to the supervisor Murray Jeffries that the CIB team were reeking of liquor on duty," the lawyer told me, when he heard I was writing a book.

"The next day, Len Johnston grabbed me in the corridor, up against a wall with his arm across my throat, and threatened me that if I ever made a comment like that again I'd 'better watch out on a dark night'.

"Later at the old Otahuhu Police station when it was the old wooden building, I noticed smoke coming from a sparrow's nest, so I climbed up to try and put it out. Len Johnston then told my superiors I had lit a fire there – he tried to fit me up for arson.

"Johnston's nickname in the office in those days was 'the Fitter'. He was the guy you went to if you'd decided who did a job and you needed to fit the evidence to that person."

It is clear that police framed Thomas, but no book or news report has ever explained 'why?' Why would police go out of their way to plant axle pieces and cartridge cases to frame an innocent, somewhat naive farmer nicknamed "Hayseed" by his fellow prisoners? And what motive might Detective Johnston have for threatening to kill a man offering the names of potential persons of interest in the Crewe murder investigation, especially one harbouring a grudge against Jeannette – the exact scenario Bruce Hutton had said was missing from the case?

When we ran this scenario past former Crewe homicide detective Ross Meurant, he was stunned at the threats and the refusal by Johnston to follow up the lead.

"The police should have looked into it. That should have been put to the Clerk and then it would have gone through the records system and gone out on a jobsheet for some Detective Sergeant and two guys, to go and look at it. That's standard procedure – anything that goes in, no matter how piddly-looking to begin with, is important in a homicide because you just never know.

"I mean, one of the things I was required to do at the scene of the homicide was to record the number of stitches that Jeannette Crewe had clearly dropped when she obviously dropped her knitting as she fell to her knees from the sofa near where Harvey was shot and went to his aid.

"Now, what the hell is the relevance of how many stitches she'd dropped? But we recorded evidence as minute as that, yet clearly information coming in as you've suggested is clearly more significant than how many stitches she'd dropped, so you'd assume it should have been investigated," says Meurant.

And yet, it wasn't.

What has never been revealed until now, is that the names given to Detective Len Johnston in 1970 by the now-retired businessman – and never entered in Johnston's official notebook – belonged to a wealthy Auckland family with strong ties to a senior New Zealand police officer.

Allow that one to sink in for a moment: a witness tips off the Crewe homicide chief's right-hand man with names of potential leads who turn out, as a matter of public record, to have friends in high places.

Did Arthur "Hayseed" Thomas get quickly framed by Hutton and Johnston because the woman who allegedly fed the baby was the love interest of a senior cop, and the revelations could not only have embarrassed a socially powerful family but also the police?

As Ross Meurant – who didn't know the senior cop's identity – told me, the pressure on officers to toe the party line, and even lie on oath to protect the image of the police, is immense.

"That culture was, and remains, part of the police. When you are 'deep in the forest' as I call it, or inside the tent, the objective is to preserve the police at all costs, rather than the rule of law. Once upon a time I did think preservation of the police was more important than preservation of the rule of law; I don't believe that anymore.

"And so there are an enormous number of subtle and not so subtle pressures that are applied to encourage people to toe the party line. The party line is always set further up the tree."

As Meurant tells it, the "party line" by the time of the Thomas Royal Commission was to suddenly testify that police had been careless in searches of the Crewe property, which is why they had 'missed' discovering the cartridge case first time around.

"The police had supposedly clearly been negligent and careless and we'd missed things. I remember one cop saying he'd flicked a cigarette butt into a tarpaulin which caught fire, and the Commission clearly didn't believe him. I didn't change my evidence because I'd already given evidence previously [in court] that I was methodical and careful, and I had no intention of perjuring myself at the Commission.

"But by that stage of the Commission, the person in charge was Bob Walton, and I was left with the clear impression that the objective was to preserve the police at all costs. And I think that's probably the reason why police, to this day, have not re-opened the case. I mean, Western police departments don't 'close' unsolved murders; this is an unsolved double murder because the Commission have told us that Thomas did not do it.

"Now I accept unequivocally that the ballistics evidence was fabricated as a demonstrable fact. I accept that Thomas didn't do it, as an article of faith, because the Commission told me he didn't do it. So we've got an unsolved murder but we've got police who won't go and find out who did it. And the question goes back to, in my opinion, this overwhelming culture of preserving the police at all costs. Because the costs of really analysing the implications of that fabrication of evidence and how far up the tree it went, is horrendous.

"The decision didn't start down the bottom, it was up the top.

"There are some dominating personalities in the police, and in my time they were Walton, who was chief monkey, there was [Graham] Perry, [John] Hughes, Hutton and others, these are the glory boys with profile and enormous egos, they are also the bastion of this culture that I talk about. They are the leaders of men, they lead thinking, they lead practices, practices which in my view deviate from time to time.

"As I look at the manifestations of the bad side of it, such as avoiding scrutiny by the courts when serious things happen like a police killing, that's just like the police operate in the countries where I now live in Eastern Europe. All these things we take for granted here – I think the public, it's disappointing that they're so gullible that even people like my mother, for example, think the police can do no wrong.

"New Zealand is saturated with, particularly, working-class conservative people who have this blind faith in the police," Meurant murmurs quietly, waiting to make sure it sinks in. It does.

Let's take a closer look at these dramatic new leads in the Crewe cold case. We've already tested the motives of Thomas, Demler and others, but what about the brother and sister named by the new witness?

Apart from the witness testimony, there is no obvious forensic evidence left that would link the couple to the scene. It is possible that the Crewe's business records might disclose commercial transactions involving the male, but it is almost certain that Harvey and Jeannette Crewe's business papers were destroyed decades ago. Even the Inland Revenue Department, which might have kept some information, probably destroyed it after seven years – possibly sooner given the murders and the winding up of the Crewe estate.

Bruce Hutton arranged for the bullets from the heads of Harvey and Jeannette to be thrown in the Whitford tip where they could never be found again, so any direct evidence linking to the genuine murder weapon has gone, and that's assuming the real murder weapon itself still exists after all this time and wasn't dismantled and thrown away by the killer.

The issue of motive for this prominent couple, however, is stronger than that advanced for either Thomas or Demler. In this case, there is the suggestion of an illicit affair between the man and Jeannette Crewe, or perhaps even simply ongoing rejected advances which she was threatening to tell Harvey about, who in turn might have warned other farmers whose business Mr Ex relied upon. There is also an iconic Auckland family name involved, with all of the associated possible reputational damage.

Could this man have been jealous of Jeannette's ongoing loyalty to Harvey? Was he, in fact, the one responsible for arson attacks and break-ins loosely coinciding with the Crewes' wedding anniversaries and baby Rochelle's birth in the years 1967 through 69?[169] The murders, of course, took place on the night of the 17th, the eve of their June 18th wedding anniversary in 1970, and exactly a year to the day after the haybarn on the Crewe property went up in flames during an arson attack.

An itinerant working loosely in the wider farming region, and living 50 or more kilometres away, could be seen at a property but not recognised. Yet if he or his vehicle were vaguely familiar because he was known to do business in the region, he wouldn't raise the instant suspicion that a total stranger might.

---

169 The Crewes were married on June 18, 1966. On July 29, 1967, their house was burgled and jewellery stolen. On 1 December, 1968, Rochelle Crewe was born at the Pukekohe maternity unit, and her birth duly announced. On 7 December, 1968, an arsonist used some of Rochelle's baby clothes, stored in her new bedroom, to set fire to that room of the house. Harvey Crewe found the fire when he arrived home from visiting Jeannette and his new daughter at the hospital. The blaze damaged the bedroom, but it was repairable. On 17 June, 1969, precisely a year before the murders, they suffered another arson attack when the haybarn went up in smoke. It was completely destroyed.

Likewise, his sister's appearance to feed Rochelle – as an out of towner no one would recognise her, and yet there's nothing threatening or suspicious about seeing a woman and child loose on a property. The assumption is that they're either the occupiers or guests.

Bruce Roddick, of course, went to his grave believing the woman he saw was Len Demler's girlfriend and subsequent wife, Norma. But his identification was based initially on seeing the woman from across the road 75 metres away for only a moment. Remember, he initially believed the woman was Jeannette Crewe. Fleeting glances at distances can give us the basics – short, tall, blonde, brunette – but not the finer detail.

For reasons already canvassed, I don't believe the woman he saw was Norma Demler. The idea that the new girlfriend of a murderer would stick around to help him shift bodies – including the bashed remains of his own daughter – and clean-up the blood, teeth and brain tissue left behind, is as absurd as believing that Arthur Thomas stove Jeannette Crewe's face in with a rifle butt, shot her through the head, then drove back to his wife Vivien in the marital bed where he confessed to slaughtering his secret love and asked his now also-ran wife to help come and carry the bodies away, clean up the mess, then lie for him to police and lead a public support campaign for the rest of her life.

The same logic that supports Arthur's innocence likewise makes it impossible for Norma Demler to be the mystery woman, no matter how much it seems an easy fit. And without Norma Demler, the circumstantial case against Len Demler becomes even weaker, for it now requires yet *another* mystery woman linked to Demler to have assisted in the clean-up and then melted away – without Norma Demler's knowledge.

This scenario is, of course, bordering on impossible. Which leaves us then with our new candidate – a woman who was both close to a top cop, and was a blood relative of the man named as a possible suspect. Blood being thicker than water, she does indeed have a genuine motivation to help after the event regardless of the revulsion she felt, not so much for her brother's sake but for her elderly parents whose world would be torn apart if the good family name was attached to a double murder.

And it leaves us, for the first time in 40 years, with a possible motive that explains why police desperately framed Arthur Allan Thomas in a bid to shut the case down. We all accept the evidence was fabricated on the basis of what the Royal Commission found, but no one has ever ventured an explanation as to why police went to those lengths. Did someone in the police stumble on her involvement and, knowing who she was, decide to steer the inquiry away from her?

In running this flag up the flagpole, I'm probably required to at least offer a hypothesis as to why the alleged killer/and or his accomplice chose to look after Rochelle and try and clean up the bloodstains. Guilt. I'm picking the killer's family were of generally strong moral character (hence the need to protect the family name from scandal), and that the sister in particular felt a moral obligation to help the innocent child. A random home invader would probably have left Rochelle to her fate, but the killer in this case had two problems – he needed help after the fact to dispose of the bodies, and he had a crying child to deal with. I'm picking that the killer initially drove home soon after the shootings, agonised over what to do, possibly regretting that his temper had led to murder, and asked his sister to help move the bodies and secured her assistance because the baby needed feeding. They clearly needed some time to get rid of the Crewes, which is why they couldn't just abandon the scene.

While there, the mystery woman's own maternal instinct may also have been the driving force behind cleaning up the blood. You see, we know baby Rochelle was allowed to roam around the property because witness Queenie McConachie saw her playing outside. The woman would have found it abhorrent to allow Rochelle to play in her mother's and father's blood or even see it in large pools, and probably cleaned it up not to cover her tracks but for Rochelle's sake or even that of family of the dead couple. Remember, the sister was a reluctant helper, after the event. She wasn't the killer. The pools of blood may also have offended her own sensibilities.

That's my hypothesis. In contrast, the best reason police could come up with for cleaning the scene was this:

"You have heard me consider these other people [known vagrants, peeping toms etc] who may have committed this crime," said Bruce Hutton at one internal briefing session, "and you cannot convince me that any of those were going to clean up the scene. If you let them commit the crime, I can't see them cleaning up the scene – taking pots of water back and forwards to the kitchen. Demler – certainly."

But why? What could Demler possibly gain from trying to wash bloodstains out of the carpet? The Hutton explanation that follows appears nonsensical to me:

"He is living on the adjoining farm knowing that evidence is here that a third person has committed this and it can't have been murder suicide. This would be the thing," says Hutton, "whether a third person – Demler – came in and gunned both or put the injuries on the body, we would know then it was murder...if he moved the bodies and the weapon and cleaned up the scene there would be nothing to point to him."

Personally, I would have thought if Demler wanted it to look like a murder suicide he wouldn't have cleaned the floors; dead people generally don't get up and clean the house after the event. And Hutton fails to come up with one convincing reason for Demler to mop the floors, whereas I think a guilt-ridden female accomplice, wanting to protect Rochelle from as much of the horror as she could, is far more plausible.

It's probable the woman, at least, kept a watching brief on the house over the next few days, popping in occasionally to feed and change Rochelle, until the alarm went up. It's quite likely the mystery woman drove back to the house on the afternoon or evening of June 22, saw the police activity, knew her job was done and just drove on past, never to return.

She may, in fact, have been there earlier on the very day Rochelle was found. The first trial heard evidence from police that the clothes dryer was running when police arrived at the Crewe house.[170] Thermostat controls had been added to clothes dryers from about 1946 onward, and by 1959 moisture sensors had been added which turned machines off when they sensed the clothes were dry. The Crewes had moved in after their marriage in 1966, so it's a pretty good bet the clothes dryer – a 'mod con' in those days – had a thermostat. If so, it can only have been on for a few hours. If it was an older style machine, I'd still argue the killers put it on, not the Crewes.

I remind the reader, before we all get excited at speculative scenarios of the kind that have dominated previous books on the Thomas case, that while this new overall hypothesis is much more plausible in its totality than the others, it remains unsupported by any hard evidence beyond a few basic facts:

---

170 *Beyond Reasonable Doubt*, p135

- A playboy-type itinerant who allegedly fancied himself with lonely farmers' wives as a perk of the job and who boasted about it to a colleague, including discussing one woman named "Gee-net" who was allegedly threatening to tell (these comments made before the murders)
- A phone call made by our witness to Len Johnston on the Crewe homicide team, offering the names of the brother and sister as persons of interest to investigate
- Alleged death threats made by Johnston in response
- The non-appearance of their names in Johnston's notes, and a failure by police to follow up the lead (a matter of public record)
- The link between the mystery blonde woman and a senior police officer (also a matter of public record, but not disclosed here for identification reasons)

It is always possible, and the reader should remind oneself before harshly jumping to conclusions about an individual's guilt, that the itinerant playboy may have been all puff and wind and never killed the "Gee-net" he was worried about.

It is always possible, on the same basis, that the mystery blonde woman's connection to police was a freakish but innocent coincidence.

But in light of all that, we are still entitled given the enormous public interest in this case to ask why Detective Johnston hit the roof when the names were given to him, and why the lead was never explored, never entered in Johnston's notes. In contrast, Norma Demler's name *does* appear in the Johnston notebook.

The reaction – "he told me that if I ever rang the police with that information again or made any attempt to have it made known then I would be the next bastard found in the river. Further, now he had my name and I was to shut my bloody mouth forever over this matter" – strongly suggests not only that Johnston clearly recognised the names, but that he well and truly understood their significance to the case. It also shows he was worried that the witness might attempt to phone another police officer with the information.

Why was that a concern? Because Johnston, as we know from the Commission testimony, was a corrupt cop. He fabricated evidence against Arthur Thomas in an eyeblink. It was within his power on the Crewe homicide team to quietly remove evidence from the police file tracking back to the powerful family. It was not necessarily within his power, however, to rescue the situation if another cop somewhere else wrote an entry in his own notebook and followed it up independently of the tightly-controlled Crewe investigation team. That, for Johnston, would clearly be a nightmare scenario.

There is a certain irony here, because in August 1971 inquiry boss Bruce Hutton complained to the media that some of the police witnesses had been threatened:[171]

"According to Mr Hutton a suggestion has been made to one witness that bodily harm might come to him if he did not change a statement he made to the police."

"Several witnesses and their families have sought the advice of the police and I can assure them publicly that we will not stand by and see them intimidated and their families embarrassed because they saw fit to come forward to give their evidence in the cause of justice," said Bruce Hutton.

How noble. Yet in this book you see a witness being threatened with death if he made *any kind of statement at all to police*, and that threat came from a police officer! It seems the police interest in protecting witnesses, evidence and 'justice' was very selective.

For the sake of completeness, there is another possible reason for Johnston's violent threats: having faked the case against Thomas already, it was he and Hutton who would go down if the real killer was eventually found. Having put the corruption ball into play, Johnston had no choice but to run with it to the end, otherwise his career, and Hutton's, would be over.

We know, from the physics involved, that the person who murdered the Crewes had to have an accomplice – 16 stone Harvey was simply too heavy for an ordinary person to manhandle as a dead weight. We know as a matter of record that a woman was seen on the property, and that Rochelle's nappies had been changed and she'd been fed. We know that such a woman would need extremely good reasons to remain silent and not blow the whistle – the kind of reasons that in my view only a direct biological tie to the killer might provide.

The chances of the accomplice being male appear, to me, remote, unless they too were blood kin of the killer reluctantly pulled in after the event. The crime itself appears to have been a crime of passion – either sexual jealousy or some other kind of personal relationship gone wrong. Such crimes don't normally involve sidekicks, and a

---
171 *NZ Herald*, 3 August 1971

male accomplice would take the 'conspiracy' to three, because we still know there was a woman on scene as well, thanks to Bruce Roddick's original testimony to the police in that very first week of the murder inquiry:

"There was a woman standing just inside the fence from the gateway. She seemed to be looking in my direction. She would be in her 30s, and about 5'10" to 5'11". I am 5'10" and she looked very tall to me. Her hair was not blonde, but light brown, her hair was cut short but curled up at the bottom."

A description which, according to the new witness who approached me, matches his personal memory of the woman he knew. Incidentally, this new mystery woman would have been in her late 30s at the time of the Crewe murders.

Chris Birt, who obtained the first of the two confidential investigation reports into the Thomas case written by the late Robert Adams-Smith, QC, for Prime Minister Muldoon, recounts how when Roddick was interviewed by the QC he recalled that the woman he'd seen had a "more mature figure" than a girl in her 20s.[172] This led Birt to speculate that 49 year old blondish Norma Demler was the one, but the new mystery woman's age, late 30s, fits with both the maturity Roddick recalled *and* his initial belief close to the time, that the woman was "in her 30s".

We also know the killer had to have been familiar with the movements of the Crewes and quite possibly the whereabouts of the spare door-key – either via quiet observation or direct knowledge. We know the killer reserved some special punishment for Jeannette – not a mere push away – and that the attack happened on the literal eve of her fourth wedding anniversary.

The police quickly assumed the killer had to be a local because of their necessary familiarity with the locale. The killer, however, could equally have been an obsessed stalker, which better fits with the pattern of previous attacks on the property, or someone who knew the wider area because of his work, not because he lived there.

It might be that the new witness' evidence has identified the wrong people (if we leave Johnston's otherwise inexplicable death threats to one side), but of one thing I am sure – the real female accomplice to the killer will definitely be either a sister, or a mother

---

172 *The Final Chapter*, Chris Birt, Penguin, p198

of the offender. Someone for whom the family bond, and willingness to forgive, goes deeper than a mere wife or girlfriend could ever muster when confronted with the carnage, or someone that the offender had a major hold over.

If the pattern of previous attacks is relevant, and I believe it is, the killer is someone who carries a serious vengeful streak – someone who felt wronged by Jeannette or Harvey as far back as 7 December, 1968, when news of the baby's birth inspired them to set fire to the baby's bedroom, and then to mark the eve of the wedding anniversary the next year with another fire, before choosing the same night a year later to storm through the door and actually shoot them.

The person of interest named by the new witness is someone who fits that personality profile (a long-standing sense of having been wronged in other matters, and prone to anger) but to make the leap required here, one would have to prove he had contact with Jeannette or Harvey as far back as soon after their marriage.

It is plausible, on the face of it, that with the Crewes moving into the district in mid 1966, this could conceivably have brought them into the orbit of this new person if it can be established he was working his rounds in the area at that time. I simply don't have that information.

I ask the reader not to jump to conclusions of guilt or innocence in regards to individuals who might fit the descriptions outlined in the chapter above. Don't, because there's a 99.99999% chance you've guessed wrong, and also because the skeleton of strange facts underpinning it might have an innocent explanation somewhere. What you can take out of this, however, is that the police were put on notice about a valid lead whose subjects were connected to the police, and they never, *never* followed it up. Instead, the witness had his life threatened.

More circumstantial evidence in support of the police trying to protect someone close to one of them is provided in Chris Birt's recent *North & South* article.[173] Bruce Roddick was the key witness who could put a woman at the Crewe farm between the time of the murders and the time of discovery. You'd think the police would welcome his evidence, but instead it was inconvenient and Roddick became the victim of massive police harassment, as Bruce's brother Graham told the magazine.

---

173 "A Life Sentence", Chris Birth, *North & South*, July 2010

"The cops would turn up all the time looking for Bruce, asking my parents where he was and what he was doing. Once, Inspector Hutton turned up in the middle of the night and wanted to haul Bruce out of bed for questioning. My father refused to allow it.

"They'd be phoning two or three times a day, too. Always the same – where was Bruce? My mother tired of this and stopped answering the phone."

According to Roddick, on one occasion police broke in while the family were out. "After one trip, [the family] came home to find all the drawers had been pulled open and the contents left lying around. The house had been searched – trashed. It was a hell of a mess. My mother was really upset."

Roddick told *North & South* a similar search happened soon after, only this time two pigs were unleashed inside the house and left to do their thing. "My parents had lived in Pukekawa since 1951 and had never had anyone entering their house in their absence. They felt at that time the police had done this to put pressure on Bruce. It upset Mum no end and she complained, but nothing was ever done about it. The police didn't seem the slightest bit interested."

Up until now, the Roddicks and everyone else have assumed the police were pressuring him in order to protect Norma Demler, but most of the harassment happened long before Roddick had nominated Norma as the mystery woman (and he never told police her name because he didn't trust them). I suggest the police were in fact fearful that Roddick might be able to eventually identify the real mystery woman – a woman connected to one of their officers – something much closer to home. Why else would Roddick's mystery woman sighting bug them so much? They worked the mystery woman angle into the trial of Arthur Allan Thomas with veiled implications that it was Vivien who Roddick had seen, so obviously the danger was not that a mystery woman had been spotted, per se. It all hinged on who she was.

That Bruce Hutton chose to so closely utilise corrupt cops like Len Johnston says something, in my opinion, about Bruce Hutton's character as well. Evidently the Royal Commission reached the same view.

If you think you know a person of interest in this case, email me at confidential@investigatemagazine.tv with the name and reasons, and I'll follow it up.

To briefly recap, we've had presented essentially three possible offenders.

Arthur Allan Thomas. Naive, gentle, trusting, handed himself to the police on a plate and didn't even realise he was doing it. Yet even so, police still had to fabricate their smoking gun evidence against Thomas, knowing they didn't really have enough to charge him without faking it.

Lenard William Demler. Uncouth, rough around the edges, but failed to wipe away a Jeannette bloodstain on the front seat of his car, had a very panicked reaction to discovery of bloodstained house, drew enormous police attention to himself through strange actions, supposedly confessed to a neighbour that he possessed a .22 gun capable of murdering the Crewes at a time when the whole country knew police were searching for that gun, and not only supposedly knew his girlfriend had been seen taking care of baby Rochelle, but then had no qualms about sending the same woman to court where she might be recognised.

Mr Ex, a third party from outside the district from a prominent family, whose sister was very affectionate with a senior cop, and blondish. Despite conducting regular business on Pukekawa farms Mr Ex's name appears in no police notebook in regard to the Crewe inquiry, and he has done nothing since to draw attention to himself in regard to that case.

Now, having looked at those suspect profiles, let's take a look at how FBI criminal profiler John Douglas, of *Mindhunter* fame, describes the three different types of crime scene he's come across, and what they tell us about the offender:[174]

Organized. When I say a crime is organized, I generally mean it was premeditated. Little evidence is found at the scene. The subject carefully planned the crime to minimize risk and apprehension. Generally, the organized criminal is the anti-social personality. Someone who knows right from wrong. Someone who is not insane, who will show no remorse over his criminal acts.

Disorganized. In contrast, when I say disorganized, I'm referring to a crime or crime scene that shows little, if any, pre-planning on the part of the Unsub (unknown subject). The disorganized

---

174 http://www.johndouglasmindhunter.com/articles/030214.php

Unsub has a high risk of being identified and apprehended. Evidentiary items such as fingerprints, blood and semen are often found at the scene. In cases of rape and homicide the Unsub often utilizes a "blitz" style of attack that renders the victim unconscious or dead. The disorganization of the crime may indicate any or all of the following conditions: a youthful offender, the influence of alcohol and/or drugs, difficulty controlling the victim or mental illness.

Mixed. When I say mixed classification, I mean a case such as that of O.J. Simpson, where the crime scene appears to be very premeditated. The subject brings to the scene the weapon, gloves and a hat – premeditated. Yet the crime scene appears disorganized. The subject had a well-planned idea but did not expect to be confronted, as the subject was, in this case, by Ron Goldman. So he – O.J. – basically lost control over the situation so the crime's ultimate appearance shifted from organized to disorganized.

When you look at some cases in the mixed category, you may be able to pick up more than one offender at the scene. For example, one part of the scene may appear to be very sophisticated and very organized, while other parts are in total disarray. This may indicate that two people participated in the act, operating in concert with one another.

Clearly, the Crewe murder scene fits the "organised" profile with a "mixed" overlay in the sense of taking care of Rochelle after the event – suggestive as Douglas writes of two people being involved. In this case, a very careful killer and a remorseful helper. I suggest to you Arthur Allan Thomas definitely doesn't fit the profile of someone capable of an organised murder scene, and Demler's actions suggest he wasn't the one either. Neither of these men could be accused in their subsequent behaviour of "minimising risk and apprehension" – quite the contrary. Thomas betrayed absolutely no understanding that he ever really appreciated he was a suspect until the handcuffs went on, whereas the careful killer would have been acutely aware the police were on to him. Len Demler was too set in his cantankerous ways, and again lacked the mental flexibility to see himself as police were seeing him. The real killer, again, would have been much more street-smart.

Maybe it wasn't Mr Ex. But it had to be someone like him. Maybe there's a fourth potential suspect and, just maybe, perhaps I've saved the best till last:

CHAPTER 15

The New Prime Suspect

What if the killer of Harvey and Jeannette Crewe wasn't the brother of a police officer's girlfriend? What if the killer was a police officer himself? Who would be better placed to commit the perfect crime than one of the investigating officers?

When I first received that tip-off you read in the last chapter, two years ago, I thought perhaps we'd finally nailed the Crewe murder mystery. But as I dug deeper into it, the background role played by a particular police officer nagged at me. At first, I thought his reaction in that case unique, but then I found out more, and more, about him. And slowly but surely this police officer's profile grew in significance in the investigation. Everywhere I turned, there he was,

Detective Sergeant Len Johnston, based at the Otahuhu CIB, was a dirty cop. His colleagues have admitted as much, and the Royal Commission found so. We know he was physically violent, and prone to making death threats – even to fellow police officers who crossed him. He matches the FBI profile of an "anti social" personality. He knew how to stage evidence to make other people look guilty – his nickname in the force was "The Fitter". We know he intimidated his colleagues when he didn't get his way, and started a fire at the old Otahuhu police station as part of that intimidation.

More significantly, we know he had met Harvey and Jeannette Crewe previously, when tasked to investigate the burglary at their property in 1967. He would have known the layout of their house, and had details on his file. It is highly likely, as investigating officer, that he asked Jeannette where she kept the spare key to the house, and possibly he may even have suggested a new hiding place. Did he in fact begin stalking Jeannette and was he responsible for all the fires in 1968 and

1969 after that initial burglary he attended? Is that why Jeannette was terrified of being in the house alone, the year before she was murdered?

I knew a woman who'd been stalked and violated by an obsessive and violent police officer. She was too afraid to report him, for fear police would close ranks on her and it would become worse. Was Len Johnston cut from the same cloth? Essentially bulletproof?

Did he go there that night because she'd finally threatened to tell Harvey, or simply because he was jealous and he knew it was the couple's wedding anniversary the next day? Was he the one who tried his luck on Jeannette? Did he shoot Harvey first then, when Jeannette rejected him, smash her in the face with a rifle butt, knocking her out? Did he then rape her and then execute her afterward?

We know he was desperate to frame someone for the Crewe homicides and close the case down.

In the second trial, Crown prosecutor David Morris ladled on the innuendo, virtually accusing Arthur Thomas of rape, and burning the mat on the floor to cover his sins.

"A long hearth mat and cushion were at some stage burned by the murderer…Whether it was done to conceal…marks traceable to the killer or his treatment of Jeannette we do not know…The evidence is equally consistent with a desire to get to Jeannette, even if this entailed first killing her husband and later Jeannette herself…there is nothing to suggest any alternative."

It was a horrendous allegation, but one that Len Johnston's boss, Bruce Hutton, claimed he was entitled to raise:[175]

Hutton: *I'm convinced in my own mind that she was raped.*

Yallop: *But she had all her clothes on when you found the body. Even her pantyhose were intact.*

Hutton: *Oh yes, but look at the injuries she had, though.*

Yallop: *The broken nose, the lacerations?*

Hutton: *Yes. Now you tell me why that mat was burnt then? Decent-sized mat in front of the hearth. Why burn it?*

Yallop: *It's a good question.*

Jury foreman Bob Rock later said the rape allegation was compelling to the second jury. "As foreman of that jury I believed the reference to a sexual assault to be fact. Why was the carpet burned if not to get rid of seminal fluid?"[176]

---

175 *Beyond Reasonable Doubt*, p67
176 *Beyond Reasonable Doubt*, p268

What's good enough for police to ask is good enough for me to throw back at them. Len Johnston, as a detective, would know exactly how to cover his tracks at a crime scene. He could have carefully undressed an unconscious victim, and dressed her again afterward. If she was unconscious, she could not fight off a sexual violation and there would be no evidence of a struggle in that regard.[177] He had to kill her because she could identify him, and he had to move the bodies because forensic evidence could personally tie him to Jeannette. Ask yourself this, what possible reason could there be for burning a cushion, other than that it might be left with traces of something that could link back to the killer? Evidence was burnt in the Crewe fireplace. Why?

As a father, Johnston would have taken pity on Rochelle. But how do I explain a female presence? In his case I don't think even a relative would step up to the plate. I could only surmise that a female criminal acquaintance over whom he exercised power – common enough in police corruption cases – was drafted to assist. She may ultimately have been killed by Johnston to maintain her silence. It would be useful if police or the newspaper libraries still had records on any South Auckland prostitutes who disappeared in 1970 or 1971, or any women found dead of "accidental" causes or even suspiciously, who might fit the mystery woman description.

An alternative motive for Johnston could be blackmail. We know that Harvey Crewe avoided discussing whether insurance had paid out on the burglary Johnston was called in to investigate, and that Harvey was short of a few quid. Is it possible that Johnston, a dirty cop, sussed out the burglary was an inside job and was blackmailing either Harvey or Jeannette and it all came to a head?

Curiously, at least one commentator on the Crewe murders floated the idea 30 years ago that the burglary was fishy, and quoted Len Johnston's evidence on the point:[178]

"On the 30th July 1967, I went to Pukekawa to the house of Jeannette Lenore Crewe, who is now deceased, as a result of a burglary she reported. Among the items that were alleged to have been stolen were her handbag, a row of pearls, her watch, engagement ring, two brooches and a brush and comb set.

---

177 Jeannette's autopsy revealed bruising in her armpit, which pathologists could not explain in the context of the shooting and bashed face, but I venture it might be consistent with a rough and rapid sexual assault by a large male leaning on his prone victim.
178 Johnston's testimony to second trial, 1973, commented on by Robert Coombridge in "The Crewe Murders at Pukekawa"

"The house showed no signs of being searched. The property itself was stolen from the dressing table drawer of her bedroom. Alongside or near the door of her bedroom was a dressing table which contained money and other valuables and these were not taken. Entry apparently had been gained to the house through the back door which apparently had been left shut but not locked."

Firstly, Johnston's testimony doesn't exactly endorse the reality of the burglary. He refers to the stolen items as "alleged" stolen items. He says burglars "apparently" entered via the back door. He expresses surprise there was no sign of a search, and that actual cash in an adjacent drawer wasn't taken.

There's no mention in his testimony that he saw Arthur Thomas' brush and comb gift, but it is almost guaranteed he did. He is bound to have looked around, bound to have asked what it looked like, and I'm betting if he looked in the wardrobe and found Arthur's one he'd have asked about its history, just to satisfy himself it wasn't the stolen one. Yet there appears to have been no mention of it in the burglary report that appears in police files.

We know Len Johnston would have seen Harvey Crewe's rifle. "Harvey's gun was also there," Crewe family friend Beverly Batkin said back in 1977.[179] "In the lounge. I don't know much about guns, but apparently it was quite a good one. That was not taken."

That gun, which may have been a combination .410/.22 shotgun/rifle, as we've previously seen, wasn't taken in the burglary but disappeared by the time of the murders and has never turned up. In today's money, vintage models of those guns can sell on the international market for more than US$20,000, so the phrase, "apparently it was quite a good one" might be apt. Curiously, there's no reference in the police files to its existence, yet Johnston went to the trouble of referring to other expensive items in the house that were not taken by the burglar. Why did he not mention the gun in his original burglary report? Or did he later alter the file and his own file notes to remove mention of it because he was in fact the killer and he used that gun, and he wanted record of it erased?

So here's what might have happened. Dirty cop investigates burglary and quickly realises it was an insurance job probably instigated by Harvey (hence the cash wasn't taken because it was cash Harvey

---

179 *Beyond Reasonable Doubt*, p33

needed[180]). Perhaps taking a shine to Jeannette, he confides at some point that he knows Harvey did it to claim the insurance, and that if Jeannette doesn't do him some favours or pay him some money he'll arrange for Harvey to be arrested and maybe even her also. Jeannette caves in to avoid the scandal, leading to her increasing fear of being in the house alone.

We know police came to the burglary, and to both the arsons – three visits in three years. Johnston may have been the attending officer for the fires, but we aren't told in the documents released to date.

"On the day after the haybarn fire in June 1969," writes Yallop, "Owen Priest called at the Crewe farm to see if he could help clean up the mess. 'Jeannette refused to open the door to me. She would not even open the fly-screen door even though she knew it was me. She was scared for some reason'."[181]

As Yallop tells it, "Jeannette became very nervous. She refused to stay in the house on her own. She would rather sit in the car with Rochelle in the fields waiting for Harvey to finish his work." To me, that speaks of a woman who's been getting visits while her husband is out on the farm, consistent with allegations about either Mr Ex or Len Johnston.

For Jeannette, the horror is two-fold. Not only is she being blackmailed, but she's doing it to protect a husband who effectively took away her engagement ring – a supposed token of undying love. One is reminded of David Yallop's observation after examining photos of the Crewe house: "The place – I cannot refer to it as a home – reeks of apathy. It reeks not only of the deaths that undoubtedly occurred there but also of a dead relationship, dead long before 17 June 1970."

Perhaps Johnston, realising Jeannette is actually loaded, even fancies his chances of formalising the relationship and replacing Harvey, and he starts upping the ante. The arson using her new baby's clothes was Johnston sending her a message, as was the fire

---

180 When investigators checked the net worth of the couple, they found Jeannette had assets totalling more than $150,000 in 1970 money (enough to buy seven houses in Auckland or Wellington at the time, equivalent to as much as $2.8 million in today's money). She had $4,640 in her own bank accounts. Harvey had a total of $34 in his. It's possible Harvey staged the burglary precisely because he didn't want to use his wife's money to run the household with. Jeannette's friend Claire MacGee told David Yallop the dead woman had once confided in her about the money issue: "She told me it would have been better if she had not had any money. Better for the marriage if they had had to rely on Harvey's income. He resented the fact that she was wealthy." *Beyond Reasonable Doubt*, p31
181 *Beyond Reasonable Doubt*, p34

on the eve of the Crewes' 1969 wedding anniversary. He might well have argued, "Harvey got rid of your engagement ring, he doesn't really love you", but he needed Jeannette to be a willing participant if he was going to leave his own wife. Jeannette, increasingly scared, tries to find a way out of the terrible rut she finds herself in, and that rut manifests itself in those familiar signs of depression – the messy, uncared for house that isn't a home, the lack of wedding anniversary presents for each other.

Then, in the lead-up to her 1970 anniversary, something snaps. Either Jeannette threatens to tell Harvey, or finally she tells Johnston to get lost, and he confronts the couple and kills them to shut them up and protect his own career and reputation. Being a cop he can create the perfect crime scene, and the only weakness was the woman he brought in to assist afterward – although this actually is another piece of evidence pointing to Johnston as the killer: whoever did it had to clean up not just their own involvement, but also that of the accomplice. Would Len Demler, Arthur Thomas or the disabled Mickey Eyre have had such a skillset?

With a reputation for planting evidence, clearly the man has skills at accessing properties unnoticed. After all, he managed to plant the axle stubs on Thomas' farm and the Number Eight bullet in his shed, and no one saw him or his car. You don't get a reputation as "The Fitter" by being unsuccessful at it.

Again, this is entirely speculative on my part (although no more so than Pat Booth's murder suicide theory), and Johnston's surviving family will undoubtedly hate me for raising it. Nonetheless, as an officer who deliberately and knowingly framed an innocent man to support equally speculative theories, Johnston is a valid target as to motive and opportunity, even in death, particularly as he had in fact committed crimes, whereas Thomas had not.[182] I'm entitled to throw the same questions at Johnston as he did to the Thomases, and Johnston would appear to have had more opportunity, more contact with the deceased and more prior form than the man he framed.

Here are the baseline facts again:
- Detective Johnston had previously met Jeannette,
- He had been at her home,
- He knew the layout well because of his previous inquiries there

---

182 Lenrick James Johnston died in 1978

- He probably knew where the key was kept,
- He was violent,
- He was corrupt,
- He had previously started a fire at the Otahuhu Police Station to try and frame a whistleblowing colleague (showing prior form for arson),
- He framed someone else for the Crewe killings and, as a detective with responsibilities in that district, he had local knowledge of the farms, roads and residents – perhaps even more knowledge than most residents would have,
- He most likely had previously searched local waste dumps or ditches as part of routine investigations into other matters, and therefore knew where to find things like old axles and fencing wire,
- As someone with a reputation for fitting people up he could easily have picked Arthur Thomas as the fall-guy even before the murders happened,
- Like all good Type-A killers, he kept an extremely close eye on the police investigation and returned to the scene of the crime under cover of his job.

It may be significant that the inquiry lurched heavily in Thomas' direction only after Len Johnston became involved. It was Johnston who came up with the inane theory of the shot through the window from the gunman on the windowsill, forcing police to re-evaluate their construction of the crime and lead detectives away from further digging into the real circumstances.

It would be interesting to see if Johnston's whereabouts for June 17th through 22nd 1970 could be verified, even after all this time, and I wouldn't trust his police notebook or jobsheets for that period as definitive at face value. Unfortunately, mere memories of Johnston's whereabouts on that night will be useless by now – police themselves in their case against Thomas doubted he could remember his whereabouts on the night, only a fortnight or so after it happened.

Something else to consider: earlier in this book I flagged the possibility that if Johnston knew where the bodies were, he could arrange for them to be found with incriminating items like axles. The axle turned out to be the crucial piece of evidence, along with the cartridge case in the Crewe garden and the number eight bullet in Arthur's shed that Johnston had planted, against Arthur Thomas.

Johnston was brought into the homicide inquiry specifically to work on the axle investigation, but *virtually every major piece of evidence against Thomas, right down to the brush and comb set controversy – had Johnston's fingerprints on it.*[183] Fortuitously, Harvey's body was found by a police colleague of Johnston's, floating at the Waikato riverbank. Of all the places in the world, how did police know to look there? Fortuitously, an axle was found underneath it by Bruce Hutton. And fortuitously, Len Johnston knew exactly how to procure the two stub axles for this ancient 1929 shaft[184], and he knew exactly where to find them on Arthur Thomas' farm even though they had not been there during a search just a few days prior.

It's at this point that a crucial deduction can be made. We know the axle and other car parts were removed from the Thomas farm in 1965 by Bruce Eyre, Trevor Salmons and friends wanting to use the parts to restore a 1932 Ford. They've sworn affidavits that the axle and other useful car parts were dumped on the side of the road near the Crewe farm.

Clearly Johnston, in his police work in the area, had noticed the old axle and parts at some point. It's a given: he's a nosy detective constantly being called in to track burglars (who frequently jettison unwanted goods on the side of the road).

When police officer Len Johnston reached a decision to kill Harvey and Jeannette, he knew exactly where to get weighty objects for his grisly task. *Only the killer could have known where to find the matching stub axles for the exact axle used to hide the body of Harvey Crewe.*

Johnston's guilt might have gone unnoticed, but for the affidavits from five men who all testified about their roles in the taking of an axle from the Thomas farm. Those affidavits destroyed the police fabrication that Arthur had ever possessed the axle. They put the axle back in the wild where the killer found it and used it. Yet Johnston's "find" of the stub axles back on Arthur's farm now looks impossibly out of place. Those stubs would have been with the original axle, dumped on a roadside.

There are only two possibilities. Either Johnston was a corrupt cop

---

183 Even the missing Chennells estate firearm went through Len Johnston.
184 Further evidence of suspicious police activity around the axle came in 1979. Vintage car restorer David Crewes told journalists how police had taken a 1928 Nash car axle away from him for a long period of time. Police denied this to the media, which in itself is strange. What's even more strange is that the axle, when returned to him, had a slight bend in it in exactly the same spot as the alleged Thomas axle. *South Waikato News*, 10 May 1979

looking for evidence to plant against Thomas and fluked it by finding the same ditch the killer had taken the axle from, and the cop just happened to find the exact stubs for it; Or, Johnston was the killer all along. Which is the simpler and more believable explanation?

In finding those stubs so quickly and conveniently back on Arthur's farm, Len Johnston provides the best circumstantial evidence yet that he killed the Crewes.

Why then, you might ask, did Johnston get so hostile over witnesses naming people like Mr Ex and the police officer's girlfriend, or Kawerau mill worker Sandy Fletcher when he reported seeing two people acting suspiciously on horseback with two bundles? If police officer Len Johnston was the real culprit and they in fact had nothing to do with it, why did he threaten to hurt them? Probably because, according to criminal profilers, sociopaths like to maintain control of the crime. If Johnston was the killer, and in fact had stolen some things from Arthur's farm before the killings to help set him up (perhaps inspired by the gift card he'd seen during the burglary investigation that he knew could put Thomas in the frame if needed) then the last thing the detective wanted was his carefully constructed deception whistling off in a different direction, outside of his control and perhaps endangering his own efforts to hide his tracks.

He probably was content to maintain a watching brief while it looked like his boss was going to charge Demler; Johnston wouldn't have cared who got pinged as long as they went down for it. But when the case against Demler died Johnston was right there steering Hutton's investigation towards Arthur Thomas.

We know that Johnston inveigled himself onto the inquiry when the axle turned up underneath Harvey – the axle he put there. Now we know why he was keen to join the inquiry. Because he had the rest of the axle parts and could use them to frame the most convenient suspect.

Many writers and journalists have made reference over the years to similarities between the Crewe murders and the murder of Sidney Seymour Eyre at Pukekawa in 1920, where the accused Samuel Thorne fired his fatal shot from outside the bedroom window of the Eyre farm house, killing Eyre as he slept. Thorne was convicted after police found a "rare type of ammunition" at Thorne's property. Thorne allegedly escaped on a horse named 'Mickey', and Mickey was the name of the murder victim Sidney Eyre's grandson, who was seen by some in the Thomas family as a possible Crewe murder suspect.

There is, however, another case on police files for the district, long forgotten by the media, the double murders of the Lakey couple in 1934 by William Alfred Bayly just south of Pukekawa. In this case, police searched a flower bed outside the house and found a .22 rifle cartridge. On the table inside the Lakey house, detectives found a dining table set with three plates where the evening meal sat prepared but uneaten, similar to the Crewe crime scene (half-eaten, three plates).

"Christobel Lakey (wife of Samuel Pender Lakey) was knocked unconscious by heavy blows to her chin and jaw" before being killed.[185] An old axle with two wheels attached was used to transport the bodies, and Christobel's body was wrapped and tied around with sackcloth and hidden submerged in a pond on the farm.

Coincidence, or the work of a detective who knew his local history and was leaving a sardonic signature?

Remember how the Crewe murderer fits the "organised" crime scene profile developed by the FBI's 'Mindhunter' John Douglas? Here's how Douglas described it, and to my mind it's a close match with what we know of Johnston:

"Organized. When I say a crime is organized, I generally mean it was premeditated. Little evidence is found at the scene. The subject carefully planned the crime to *minimize risk and apprehension*. Generally, the organized criminal is the *anti-social personality*. Someone who *knows right from wrong*. Someone who is not insane, who *will show no remorse* over his criminal acts."

Another expert on FBI profiling says organized crime scenes reflect people of average or *above average intelligence*, involved in *skilled work* and *very self-controlled*.[186] Some experts say brutal facial injuries, such as those delivered to Jeannette, are delivered by *someone known to the victim*.[187]

Hawkes Bay lawyer Pete Carver wrote an analysis of the Thomas case in 1972. In it, he speculated that the trail pointed to whoever had planted the evidence as being the real killer. "Let us, for a moment, assume it was not Thomas but a certain person, X, who wished,

---

185 *The Crewe Murders At Pukekawa* by Robert Coombridge, p38
186 "Criminal Profiling: an introduction to behavioural evidence analysis" by Brent E. Turvey
187 http://www.criminalprofiling.ch/introduction.html

understandably, to make it appear that it was Thomas. X takes the rifle and the axle. After the crime, there is certainly some most damaging circumstantial evidence as far as Thomas is concerned.[188]

"It often happens in detective fiction that the real murderer makes but one mistake. It may be, with the cartridge case X has just made that mistake...In fact, if X had not planted the cartridge case he may well have got away with the crime," wrote the barrister. How prophetic those words might turn out to be. We know Len Johnston planted the evidence and created the theory that Hutton went with. If it looks like a duck, if it quacks like a duck...

The big question then: did police, in fact, have the killer of Harvey and Jeannette Crewe on their own payroll? If so, it was the ultimate case of gamekeeper turned poacher, a Jekyll and Hyde life, a man who spun the Crewe murder inquiry right from day one. It would require a "Cold Case" team with Commission of Inquiry powers to dig up all of Len Johnston's old files and look for similar fact evidence of corruption and foul play. If he pulled this kind of stunt once, he may have pulled it again. Of one thing I'm certain: whether he was the killer, or merely the one who covered it up, all roads in this investigation ultimately lead back to Len Johnston, and the question I posed early in this book. Why did police frame Thomas? There always had to be a reason.

The judge in Arthur Thomas' first trial, the late Sir Trevor Henry, once said there were a couple of aspects of the case that always worried him:[189]

"It was, to my mind, a local murder. No stranger could have gone on to that farm, committed a double murder and carried out the various acts that were unquestionably carried out. How all that was achieved by the murderer I will never know. No one saw or heard anything. It defies belief.

"It was truly extraordinary that there was no forensic evidence to link Thomas to the murders. No prints, no hair, no blood. They usually leave some trace somewhere. But in this case not a single thing anywhere. No clothing of Thomas destroyed, and whoever did it must have been covered in their blood at some stage. It defies belief."

Indeed it does, unless you look at it this way: The audacity of the

---

188 *NZ Truth*, 14 March 1972
189 *Beyond Reasonable Doubt*, p192

killer returning to the crime scene apparently multiple times has astounded investigators for 40 years. Who could be so bold? Len Johnston, as a police officer, was perfectly placed. He would always know if the balloon had gone up because his CIB team had responsibility for that area. He could monitor police radio traffic. He could have arranged a special phone ring code to alert his accomplice if she was in the house and the whistle was blown.

If he was there himself and disturbed at the scene by visitors he could flash his police ID and say he was an officer responding to an anonymous phone tip-off, giving him the perfect cover to move around the scene, shift visitors back from his crime scene, and call it in, "on the record" to base confirming his "discovery" of a murder, if it came to that.

Only a police officer, I suggest, could be so uniquely placed to be so bold.

I venture to suggest that the Crewe murder inquiry became the ultimate detective story, precisely because a detective was ultimately responsible. Who else but a cop could hide their tracks so well? Who else but a cop could so neatly frame an innocent cow cocky? Who else, but a guilty cop, would want to?

And what of Bruce Hutton? Hutton and Len Johnston's corrupt practices cost taxpayers something like $50 million. Nobody has relieved Bruce Hutton of his freedom. Solicitor-General Paul Neazor in 1981 found any reason he could clutch at not to prosecute Hutton, and said so in a confidential report. That's merely his opinion. As you've seen, I've spelt out sections of the Crimes Act that might permit the arrest and prosecution of Hutton, even today.

Ray Thomas told me, "The Solicitor-General in his report, December 1981, says there was not enough evidence to justify a prosecution against Hutton and Johnston. As far as I am concerned we had more on Hutton than the police had on Scott Watson and look what happened to him," says Ray.

Readers can reach their own conclusions on whether police should leave 81 year old pensioner Bruce Hutton alone, when other pensioners are are threatened with prosecution for lesser alleged crimes:

"A Wanganui pensioner who sparked an armed police callout when he confronted teenage vandals with an air rifle may face charges..."[190]

---

190 *NZ Herald*, 19 March 2009

In another case, Crown prosecutors recently argued for the right to try a pensioner for sex crimes committed in 1954, despite the "antiquity" of the charges.[191]

When companies go bad, and particularly when there is fraud involved, the directors are charged and frequently sent to prison. In a police investigation where there is fraud, no one ever gets charged. But what if Hutton's guilt is limited to planting the empty cartridge case in the garden? What if he only authorised *that* because he genuinely believed Thomas was guilty? What if he only believed Thomas was guilty because Len Johnston had, for his own reasons and without Hutton's authority, planted the other evidence like the live bullet found in Arthur's shed, and the stub axles found on Arthur's dump? The more Hutton distances himself from Johnston, the more guilty Johnston begins to look in regard to the murders.

If Hutton did not order Johnston to plant the stub axles, that's more proof Johnston had gone rogue for reasons of his own.

So here the story ends. Two years after I first approached Arthur Allan Thomas offering new information on his case – a contact that led to the invitation from Arthur for me to tell his story – and forty years after the mysterious deaths of Harvey and Jeannette Crewe at Pukekawa on 17 June 1970, a new suspect now emerges.

This man stands head and shoulders above any name previously put forward. The case must be re-opened. If police officers were not just restricting their activities to investments in brothels and drug rings[192], or pack raping 16 year old girls in the name of Friday fun, but instead had extended the corruption just a little further to double murder, the public has a right to know.

All archived police and court files involving cases Johnston worked on should be re-examined by a specialist cold-case team independent of the New Zealand Police, and former colleagues and contacts of Johnston interviewed.

For Ray and Des Thomas and their siblings, the opportunity for a civil action against the Crown on the basis of negligence, misfeasance in public office, breach of statutory duty, and a breach of the Bill of Rights Act may be possible. The test is only on the balance of probabilities, not the higher beyond reasonable doubt test for criminal trials, and I suggest most people presented with

---

191 "Rape charges against pensioner too old for court – lawyer", *NZ Herald* 5 March 2008
192 *Investigate* magazine, June and July issues, 2007

the evidence and argument in this book would find a higher than 51% likelihood that the police acted corruptly, and further, that Len Johnston probably killed Harvey and Jeannette Crewe whilst employed by the Crown, and that he played a material role in the framing of Arthur Thomas with all the resultant damage to the Thomas family. I would imagine they could get a court judgement with many zeroes on the end of it.

That's something for the family to consider, but there is of course a bigger reason to re-open the investigation. Perhaps the last word belongs to Arthur Thomas himself:

"Sometimes in my microlight I fly to Auckland or Pukekohe, and occasionally I'll go over Pukekawa. I look down at the Crewe farm and wonder what really happened down there. It makes me think, what the heck happened there that night, or the next day? If only we could turn back the clock and look at people's movements.

"What about Jeannette and Harvey Crewe? It's very important. This is what the whole case was about. Jeannette and Harvey were murdered, brutally murdered, and it's more than one person that done that. The issue seems to have gone away by jailing me, but what about the real killers? Let's get back to the truth and facts of the matter. They were murdered, and dumped in the Waikato river. In death they deserve the truth, and New Zealanders deserve the truth."

As Arthur wipes his eye, and I turn off the recorder, I can't help but agree.

APPENDIX

The Jennifer Beard Case

The following bonus chapter first appeared in *Investigate* magazine in late 2008. The Jennifer Beard case was the other big murder mystery of 1970. I've included it here because the Crewe murder inquiry has often been compared to the Beard case. Additionally, the story I uncovered opened up substantial new leads on this cold case as well, and repeating it here might jog someone's memory.

In the words of the Bryan Adams song, it was the summer of '69. Astronaut Neil Armstrong had just walked on the moon, and on the rugged West Coast of New Zealand an Australian schoolteacher was entering the final 24 hours of her life. Tuesday, December 30, 1969 had brought her to the foot of New Zealand's southern alps. Tomorrow would be New Year's Eve, 1970 was just over the horizon, and the attractive blonde in what witnesses described as "tight shorts" was preparing her pack for another day of hitch-hiking the following morning.

25 year old Jennifer Beard – born in England but working in Tasmania – had just checked into the Franz Josef Motor Camp. Around her, the sounds of children playing as other carloads of families checked in for the evening.

But there are two others who arrived in tiny Franz Josef that evening whose movements would come to dominate the later police investigation. One was the man later admitted to be the prime suspect in Jennifer Beard's murder, a Timaru man named Gordon Bray. The other was an itinerant worker known only as "Dave".

Bray, at almost six foot tall with "a powerful build in the mould of a wrestler or a circus strongman", according to journalist and author Mark Price in his book *Getting Away With Murder*, was a truck driver by trade and reasonably well known on the West Coast routes. This particular Christmas, his Austin A40 car had broken down at Tekapo and he'd been forced to abandon it along with some of his camping gear and clothes. Returning to Timaru, he purchased a 1954 Vauxhall Velox, blue in colour, and started his summer holiday drive all over again on December 29.

Arriving on the West Coast, Bray did not stop at the Franz itself, choosing instead to camp in the grounds of his regular haunt, a hotel named "The Forks" 18km north of the settlement. In other words, he didn't spend the night at the same motel, or even the same town, as Jennifer Beard.

"Dave", on the other hand, was a different kettle of fish. Close to the Franz Josef Motor Camp was a hostel run by Fay Percy, and catering mostly for workers employed by the Papanui Sawmill Company. On the afternoon of December 30, a rough looking, possibly drunk, character calling himself "Dave" was knocking on the door of the sawmillers' hostel, looking for a room for the night.

"His speech tended to be a little slurred and I thought he had difficulty standing up," Percy later told police. "He was about 5 foot 6 inches in height and tended to be fat. His stomach protruded well over the top of his trousers.

"He was bald on top of his head with his hair receding at the sides. His hair was dark coloured with grey streaks. It was greased down to the sides of his head. It was not curly."

In her police statement, Percy described Dave's face as "roundish" and "weather-beaten". There are a couple of other crucial pieces of evidence in Percy's statement however. One is that "Dave" was driving a 1950s Vauxhall, coloured green.

"A dull green, cabbage green would best describe it. It was covered in dust ... I can't really recall anything else about the car except to sum it up as an old 'bomb', you know the sort of car you would expect young louts to run around in."

Jennifer Beard was last seen alive in a green, 1950s Vauxhall Velox.

The second piece of evidence is that "Dave" had spent time in Invercargill, or so he said. Fay Percy detailed her conversations with him for police:

"He then went on to talk about his having been camping but I can't remember what exactly he said.

Man: I'm buggered. It seems that I have been driving for days and days. I've come up one coast and down the other. How long have you been here?
Me: A couple of months.
Man: Where do you come from?
Me: My parents live in Bluff and we have a house in Invercargill.
Man: I have worked and lived around Invercargill for a few years.

"I am not sure whether he said for years or for a few years," Percy said in an aside to police. She added that he appeared to be looking for work in a sawmill, and she told him about a mill further south, in Haast. He replied that he'd worked in sawmills since he was 11.

"I must say that by his general appearance I believed him," Percy is quoted in Mark Price's book, *Getting Away With Murder*. The book also records that "Dave" wanted directions to the nearest hotel, and stated a preference for Southland beer to West Coast beer.

That hotel was the "Franz Josef", just opposite the motor camp where Jennifer Beard was staying. A man matching Dave's description, with a "prominent" belly, was seen at the bar that evening, and Fay Percy positively identified him when she arrived to join her husband for a drink.

Dave had paid 60 cents for his room instead of the usual dollar, pleading poverty to Percy. So it was with an innkeeper's cynical eye that she watched him slugging back drinks. It was the last she saw of him, however. When morning came, his car had gone.

That morning, New Year's Eve, was to be the last day of Jennifer Beard's life. At around 8.30am she was seen climbing into a car by Glenys Kindley, one of the women whose families had arrived at the motor camp the previous evening, and who had met Beard there.

"We'd had breakfast," Kindley is quoted by Mark Price, "and we were all just going out of the camping ground gates and I saw her getting into this, I thought, green car, into a car. I saw her getting into the car with this guy and I said to [husband Don] 'I don't like the look of that guy. I don't want her to get in that car'...It was an old car and I thought it was dark green. Sort of a green colour... It was just a feeling – 'I don't want her to get in that car'. And of course I started off on Don: 'I don't want her to get in there. I don't want her to get in there. Look, she's sitting in that old car over there, y'know. Don't fancy that much'."

Was it Dave's green Vauxhall, the "old bomb" as Percy described it? We don't know.

Many of the families were taking their kids to see the Fox Glacier, 24 k's further south. At 10am, the McIlroy family, who'd also been at the camp, pulled into the Fox Glacier carpark. In front of them was what both Peter and Pauline McIlroy described to police as "a dark green" car having trouble starting, and Jennifer Beard was in it.

"I only noticed that it was a green coloured car and it was rough-looking," Pauline McIlroy told police. McIlroy was also the only police witness to get a good look at the man driving the car, while he stood outside the vehicle.

"I only had a side view of him…His hair was dark and roughly combed. The hair was not short cut. I think that his hair was receding."

Her statement to police guesstimated a height of 5'6" or 5'7", and she added that the man had "a very large stomach. That is the thing that I remember most. It was that noticeable that it took my eye. He was not broad-shouldered. For a man with that size stomach I would have expected him to have broader shoulders."

The McIlroys didn't see the green car leave, but other families on the road south from the Franz Josef Motor Camp that day did catch up and overtake a green, mid 50s Vauxhall Velox with Jennifer Beard inside. Don Kindley described it as "mid green" with a dull finish and a 1954 Velox, when he saw it in the vicinity of Lake Paringa, halfway between Fox and Haast to the south. Pauline McIlroy, not far behind in the convoy, also caught up to the Velox there and made her last sighting of Jennifer Beard.

"She was sitting in the front seat of the car."

The Vauxhall was only going around 40 mph (70 km/h) according to the witnesses, whose own vehicles were cruising at up to 70 mph (116 km/h). Both the McIlroys and the Kindleys overtook the Velox, but a few k's further south they came across a minor car accident and stopped to assist. While they were helping, the Velox lumbered into view and stopped before reaching the accident scene after being waved down by two teenagers who'd been passengers in the car that crashed. Sixteen year old Pamela Wildbore told police "I knew that it was a Vauxhall because my old boyfriend owned one. The colour of the car was dark green. It was in rough condition."

The other teen, 14 year old Stephen Bailey, also confirmed it was a green Vauxhall, and both claimed to have seen patches of primer paint on the car. Pamela Wildbore saw a man and woman in the car. The driver got out briefly and exchanged a few words, but drove off after hearing no one had been seriously hurt.

Both teens described him as around the 5'11 or six foot mark. Heights are a difficult thing to get right in witness statements, because the heights of the witnesses can add nuances to their own perceptions of other people.

As the Velox drove off, Glenys Kindley recognized Jennifer Beard in the front passenger seat. The Kindleys caught up with the Velox and overtook it further south at Lake Moeraki – the last time Beard was seen alive. Don Kindley told police the driver appeared to be chatting Beard up, and Glenys remembers Beard did not look impressed. She also remarked, again, on "how rough the car was", and Don Kindley told police he remembered his wife turning to him and remarking, "What an evil looking bugger he is".

That was the last any of the Franz Josef camp families saw of the Velox. The story is picked up by a family heading north, who came across the massive Haast River bridge at 1.30pm. When the Crossan family reached the northern end of the bridge (ie, the other side), they saw a green Vauxhall Velox parked in the rest area carpark with its bonnet up, and a man tinkering with the engine. Being good, honest kiwi folk in 1969, the Crossans stopped to offer help.

Bill Crossan's police statement says the Vauxhall driver asked if he knew anything about gearboxes. Crossan replied that while he wasn't a mechanic, he was familiar with cars. A spring in the gearbox linkage had broken and the car was having difficulty changing gears. Crossan and his teenage son Peter assisted, and eventually makeshift repairs were completed.

Another car, driven by the Wadsworth family, arrived on the scene just as the green Vauxhall Velox sped off in a hail of gravel.

Although neither family realized, Jennifer Beard's body was just metres away from them, directly under the bridge. Both the Crossans and the Wadsworths continued heading north, while the Velox disappeared across the bridge heading south.

Another family stopped in the rest area a little later and their eight year old daughter went to relieve herself on the riverbank. She came back up and told her mum there was a woman lying on the gravel with "no clothes on" and she looked "asleep". The child's parents, fearing their daughter had interrupted a lover's tryst, bundled their daughter into the car and drove off. Jennifer Beard spent New Year's

Eve mostly naked, alone and very dead on the riverbank below the Haast River bridge's northern end. It would be three summer weeks before her decomposed body was discovered.

THE MAIN POLICE SUSPECT

Although Jennifer Beard was reported missing on January 9 when she failed to rendezvous with her boyfriend in Milford Sound, her disappearance did not hit the media until Tuesday January 13. That was when Glenys Kindley picked up a paper, saw Beard's photo, and contacted police. The hunt was on. Police collected separate statements from a number of the witnesses detailed above, and all talked about the green Vauxhall. For their own reasons, police initially chose not to release that information publicly. In turn, this means the initial witness reports are unlikely to have been tainted by later media reports.

Police widened their appeal for anybody who had been on the road between Wanaka in the south to Franz Josef in the north to come forward. One of those to respond to the plea was Timaru man Gordon Bray, who'd been holidaying at The Forks 18 km north of Franz Josef. Bray jumped in his blue Vauxhall Velox and drove to the Timaru police station. According to police records, the initial statement they took suggested he had not seen any hitchhikers on the coast side of the southern alps. When police search inquiry head Emmett Mitten read this it struck him as strange, given the number of hitchhikers on the road, and he flagged Bray as worthy of further attention.

As anyone who has ever given a police statement can testify, however, answers to questions can depend entirely on the direction the police officer is leading them, and how much the transcribing cop edits the answers. He might have asked whether Bray had seen any lone, blonde female hitchhikers, but recorded the question more generally. This indeed seems to have been the case because when asked to give a more detailed statement the following day, Bray wrote that he'd seen a number of hikers, either in couples or groups, "but I did not see a solitary girl hitchhiker. I gave two lots of hitchhikers a ride."

Those two included Christchurch man Dave Viney, and a couple of young women. All reached their destinations safely with Bray.

Mitten's attention was again drawn to Bray when police interviewed management at The Forks Hotel and discovered Bray had stayed there.

On January 19, the country's newspapers confirmed for the first time that police were looking for a mid 1950s green Vauxhall Velox and its driver. It was that description that tweaked the memory of Bill Crossan and his efforts helping the driver of a green Vauxhall at the Haast river bridge three weeks earlier. He told police, who immediately dispatched a search team to the area. A short time later, the body of schoolteacher Jennifer Beard was found.

The following day, as part of routine inquiries, detectives spoke to mechanic Ian Milner at the Fox Glacier garage. Milner told them of a man driving a "dark blue" 1954 Vauxhall Velox who stopped in on New Year's Eve at 3pm for repairs to his gear linkage. This was the first time anyone had talked about a "blue" Velox, but it was significant to police because Gordon Bray's 1954 Velox was coloured blue.

However, Milner, like some of the earlier witnesses, recalls the car being in rough condition with patches of primer paint.

"I remember some aluminium colour being on the car somewhere. This could have been on the wheels or the bumper, or it could have been patches of K16 on the sides of the car."

Another mechanic, at the Whataroa garage about 50 kilometres north of the Fox Glacier, and about 175 kms north of the Haast bridge, told police he recalled working on a 1955 Vauxhall Velox with patches of grey primer paint, and gear linkage problems. He couldn't recall the car's main colour, but gave a similar description of the driver to Milner's: both men recalled he had fairish, greying hair, about 5'8 with a largish stomach.

When police seized Bray's car for testing, however, they found no patches of primer paint, and no forensic evidence linking it to Jennifer Beard – no hairs, nothing.

As police murder inquiry head Emmett Mitten told journalist Mark Price:

"The car we had described to us was very dirty and rough…When we saw [Bray's] car it was very clean and polished and shiny and certainly didn't look like the type of car that had been described to us."

When police paraded Bray's Vauxhall in a lineup for the witnesses to choose from, no-one picked the blue Vauxhall as the car they had seen Jennifer Beard in, not even the Crossans who had worked on the mystery Vauxhall for 15 minutes at the Haast bridge.

"The car we saw at Timaru [at the identification parade] was definitely blue – almost a navy blue, royal blue, navy blue colour and the car we saw was definitely green," eyewitness Peter Crossan told Mark Price for his book.

Could Bray have painted the car? Apparently not. Police found evidence that the Vauxhall had received a new blue paintjob shortly *before* Bray purchased it on Boxing Day 1969. Therefore it was blue throughout his West Coast trip, not green. And being a new paintjob, there were no primer patches.

But adding to the confusion is that Bray, by his own admission, did experience gear linkage problems with his Vauxhall. For the record, 1950s and 60's Vauxhalls were notorious for strange mechanical faults – your humble scribe was a passenger in one Velox which suddenly lost one of its front wheels while driving past an Auckland police station in the 80s, and I owned another Vauxhall whose steering rod snapped in rush-hour traffic in downtown Auckland, bringing the car to a screeching halt with the front wheels pointing in different directions.

Is it possible that more than one 1950s Velox had gear linkage problems on the West Coast that summer? Indeed it may be so. Nearly 30,000 Vauxhall Veloxes were registered in NZ in 1969 from the relevant mid 1950s model run. Even a West Coast police officer owned a green Velox that had to be eliminated as a vehicle of interest. When Christchurch police put out a request for mid 50s Velox owners to come forward, more than 1,400 cars were lined up in streets around the Christchurch Central Police Station the next day!

Police put Gordon Bray himself in a lineup parade, but neither Pauline McIlroy or Glenys Kindley – the only two witnesses who definitely saw the suspect with Jennifer Beard – identified Bray as the driver of the green Velox. Nor were Bill or Peter Crossan, who'd been up close to the suspect when they helped fix his car, sure that Bray was the right man. They picked him based on his resemblance to the description, but not because he was definitely the man they remembered helping. For Peter Crossan, the clincher was Bray's hairy back, because he remembered the man he helped also had a hairy lower back.

Police, after much agonizing, decided they did not have enough evidence to take Bray to trial.

And so the case has languished for the past 38 years. Gordon Bray, the prime suspect, died in 2003, while 2005 saw the publication of Mark Price's wrap-up of the case against Bray, based on the police files.

But one of the reasons police did not charge Bray with the murder was the existence of the mysterious "Dave". It was clear Bray and Dave could not be the same man, but police never located Dave. The likelihood of a good defence lawyer being able to punch holes in the prosecution of Bray by pointing to another suspect was a risk police simply were not prepared to take.

Now, however, *Investigate* has obtained fresh information that may shed light on the possible identity of "Dave" – information that former top cop Emmett Mitten is stunned he was not told about at the time – even though Westport police were advised.

Enter Gordon Watts. Now retired and living on the West Coast, back in the summer of 69 Watts was the manager of the Hardy and Thompson Sawmill at Westport. In 2005 there was a brief media flurry when Watts advised that one of his sawmill staff, a man identified only as "Ron" might have been Jennifer Beard's killer. Today, we can take that story even further.

You'll recall earlier in this article how "Dave" had turned up at a Franz Josef sawmillers' hostel on December 30, 1969, driving a dusty, rough-looking green Vauxhall and claiming to be an experienced sawmiller. Dave's description, including his potbelly, and his green car, more closely matched that of the man last seen with Jennifer Beard than Gordon Bray's did.

In an interview with Investigate, Westport sawmill manager Gordon Watts says he's personally convinced a sawmill worker now identified as "Ron Hunter" needs to be found and interviewed over his actions and movements around the time of Beard's disappearance. Ron Hunter, he says, was a "broad, stocky chap, about 5'6 to 5'8, with receding hair at the front, and a pot belly".

"I was the manager of Hardy and Thompsons Sawmill. He worked for me. I reported this to the police in Westport and they took no notice of me, they said, 'oh no, it's not him'. The next thing, the [identikit] photo came out and our mill was the first on the paper run. His photo was on the front page and the next thing he was gone.

"The paper came in, I saw him. You see, when I heard the mill close down in early in the afternoon I thought, 'that's bloody funny, what's wrong?' I thought maybe there'd been a power failure, so I went out to have a look."

When he got to the machinery that Ron Hunter had been manning, other staff relayed the sequence of events.

"The guys told me 'he's gone, Gordon, he's vanished!'"

According to the *Westport News* newspaper, the identikit photo that caused Ron Hunter to flee was published on January 30, 1970. Somebody else in town had evidently recognized Hunter and contacted police, because four police cars swooped on the mill within an hour of Hunter's disappearance.

Ron Hunter had fled so fast he didn't even bother collecting two weeks' cash wages owed to him – a point mill manager made to Westport Police officers when they arrived. *Investigate* asked if Watts had rung the police himself on this occasion:

"No, they came looking for him. Because I'd told them a week earlier that he worked for me, so they knew where to find him.

"I told them they were too late, he'd gone. They asked 'where?'

" 'Could be anywhere', I said, because we had huts up in the bush in different areas, and I said, 'he could have gone up there because he's been up there before', and I said, 'he could see you coming. We've got clothes up there so he could dress up, walk down the road, catch a bloody bus and you'll never know'.

"It was definitely him, that photo, yeah. And he never got paid his wages. He just buggered off."

Gordon Watts is angry that police didn't take him seriously when he first fingered Hunter as a possible suspect in Beard's murder. This took place a week before the identikit was published, and it was sparked by the fact that Ron Hunter owned a green Vauxhall Velox, and he had earlier remarked [before anyone knew about Beard's disappearance] about being in the Haast area over New Year.

"I reported him when he first started there," says Watts, "because he told me at one point he'd been down the Haast, down that area, and we put two and two together, so my employee who's just died recently went down to the Westport cop station and reported it, and they said, 'Oh no, you'd be wrong, you've got the story wrong'. They said 'no, it's not him, this chap in Timaru is the suspect, not him'. So I just dropped it. They didn't take a statement off us or anything."

Instead, Gordon Watts and his second in command decided to do some snooping of their own.

"There's a chappie, the one who's dead now, one of my staff, but we went round and found him living on the beach a bit further along, and we saw the car parked in by the trees and we tried to get closer to get the number, but he had a bloody dog and the dog barked, and he yelled out, 'If you buggers don't eff off I'll shoot ya!'

"So what do we do? We had to back off, back away."

As an itinerant of no fixed abode, Hunter simply hut-hopped.

Surprisingly, there's no record of these incidents in Mark Price's book, nor is there any record that Westport Police alerted murder inquiry boss Emmett Mitten about the extremely suspicious behavior of a green Vauxhall Velox-driving itinerant sawmiller doing a runner when the identikit picture was published in January 1970.

"If what you are telling me is true," Mitten told *Investigate* from his Christchurch home this month, "I would be stunned and disappointed that this information was investigated by local police but not passed on to me. This is the first I've heard of this incident. Ever."

Of mill manager Gordon Watts' positive identification of his new employee Ron Hunter as the man in the identikit picture, former Deputy Police Commissioner Emmett Mitten virtually explodes down the phone:

"That makes more than just a casual observation, that's a valid observation!"

And the fact that the man owned a green Velox, had been down in Haast at the relevant time, had done a runner when the photo came out, had failed to collect a fortnight's wages, and had threatened to shoot anyone who tried to see his car – how does Mitten react to that?

"Well I tell you what, if we were back in January 1970 and you phoned me and gave me that story, I'd be very, very excited. Like I said, if it's true, then I'm hugely disappointed if these things happened and nothing was done about it."

Such information should have come direct to him, immediately.

"With the way that inquiry went, anybody with a green Velox rated more than a cursory glance. Nine times out of ten it would end up close to me, with senior staff coming to talk to me about it. In virtually no case would a possible suspect who had a green Velox have been written off by the local cop without taking it any further."

And yet, here in June 2008, this former top cop sounds shaken as the realization dawns that Westport Police may have had Jennifer

Beard's killer within their grasp, and failed to tell him or other senior staff about it because they assumed Gordon Bray was the main suspect.

"I've got absolutely no knowledge of any of the actors [Hunter or Watts] in this," laments Mitten. "The hard part now is, who is Ron? There were something like 50,000 people interviewed for that inquiry."

While the *Westport News* report in 2005 named the suspect only as "Ron", former mill staff were quick to confirm his last name was "Hunter".

"I had a staff of about 20 working for me, and they all knew Ron Hunter," growls Gordon Watts. "I can say it was him alright! They saw him looking at the paper, looking at his photograph, bang, he was gone."

According to Watts, Hunter is believed to have been born on the West Coast. Others we've spoken to claim he moved around the South Island taking seasonal work.

Investigate checked birth records for the 1930s. We found a "Ronald Hunter" born in Granity, near Westport, in 1936. We failed to locate him in the electoral rolls for the West Coast between 1956 and 1970, which could mean he was no longer living on the coast during that time, or alternatively that he didn't bother registering to vote.

There is no evidence that this particular Ron Hunter is the one who worked at the mill, but if he is he would have been nearly 34 when Jennifer Beard was murdered. Although that places him five to 15 years younger than the age estimates of the eyewitnesses, it is entirely possible that a weatherbeaten West Coast outdoorsman could look a decade older. Additionally, many men have already begun to go grey at the temples in their thirties, let alone suffer receding hairlines.

Watts believes Ron Hunter, who would be 72 this year, may still be alive and living in Australia.

"I've heard he turned up in Australia."

Murder inquiry head Emmett Mitten says the new lead should be passed to Dunedin Police (current custodians of the Jennifer Beard "cold case" file), and he urges detectives not to get hung up on Gordon Bray all over again.

In a confusing tangent to the original investigation, detectives had found a singlet and trousers folded in the bush not far from Beard's body. When they eventually examined the pockets of the trousers, they found a receipt belonging to Gordon Bray.

Slam dunk? Perhaps not. Firstly, the man with gearbox troubles on the Haast River bridge just minutes after Beard was murdered was definitely wearing trousers at the time, and when he later popped into service stations. Secondly, if you were the killer, would you leave your clothes behind at the scene with a receipt bearing your name?

Even Crown lawyers, when they reviewed the file for prosecution purposes, felt it was more likely that someone had nicked some of Bray's clothes from his abandoned vehicle.

"Whoever looks at the Beard murder has to put the Bray thing to one side," says Mitten. "There were, I think, about four men who we could never establish a) that they existed and b) where they were. The scenario you painted about someone taking some of Bray's clothing – that's a point he raised as well, that someone could have taken clothes from the car he abandoned at Tekapo."

But there's more on a character named "Ron", and his possible involvement in Beard's death. Former West Coast possum trapper Dick Stacey remembers a man named "Ron" who he reported to police as a possible suspect. Ron used to have a green Vauxhall Velox, but according to Stacey he got rid of it around the time of Beard's disappearance, citing "gear change problems". Stacey's brother Rua has been quoted in a document provided to police on the case as recalling that this particular "Ron" talked about having problems with the Vauxhall down at Haast.

Dick Stacey says the surname "Hunter" doesn't ring a bell with him, but the name "Ron" definitely does.

For Emmett Mitten, the testimony is tantalizing, but without a surname, not necessarily helpful.

"The other major problem you're going to be confronted with here," Mitten warns, "is so many of the witnesses have died. Even in the police, many of those who worked on the case have passed on."

A case in point may be the Dick Stacey testimony. While Stacey clearly remembers tipping off police in the company of a fellow possum trapper, he can't remember the precise identity of the hunting companion he did so with. One hunting buddy, "Boarhide" Templeton, is now deceased. The other, Vic Diack, wonders if Stacey is remembering another of their hunting buddies, Les Houghton from Invercargill, who was also in the Haast area in a green Vauxhall Velox around New Year 1970. Houghton was investigated and cleared by police.

"Les had a Vauxhall," says Diack. "Les was just up there for the Christmas holidays, but I wasn't with them when it happened."

INVESTIGATE: So you didn't go with Dick Stacey to make a statement to Invercargill police?

"No, no. Although the police did ring me. They wanted to know where Les Houghton was at the time. He had actually been at my house a couple of nights before he left to go up there, and they really questioned me where Houghton had been because it was a similar car to his. And I think Les did say to them, 'If you want to find the body, look under the Haast Bridge'. It was just one of those things. We all thought that at the time.

"New Year's Eve, I'm pretty sure Les spent with us down here at Invercargill. That's what the police wanted to know."

But there are differences in Diack and Stacey's stories that suggest they may be talking about two different men. Stacey remembers "Ron" getting rid of his Vauxhall in strange circumstances and replacing it with an old Landrover. This was one of the things that made Stacey suspicious enough to walk into a police station. Diack, on the other hand, says his mate Les Houghton drove Vauxhalls until the bitter end.

"He never owned a Landrover, no."

But Diack adds to the mystery by confirming he remembers the name Ron Hunter:

"I've heard the name, but I don't really know the guy. I have heard that name, Ron Hunter. I couldn't put a face to him, but I have heard the name."

Diack, Stacey and Houghton all hailed from Invercargill where they had seasonal work at the Alliance Freezing Works. They travelled to the West Coast on the off-seasons.

Police witness Fay Percy – who told of a mystery Vauxhall driver named "Dave" – says her suspect was an experienced sawmiller who'd spent a lot of time around Invercargill. Gordon Watts, the Hardy and Thompson Sawmill manager, says the Ron Hunter he hired was an experienced sawmiller.

The task of locating Ron Hunter now falls with the current police force, but Emmett Mitten agrees it will be a tough job.

"If anybody's looking at anyone, you've got to take 38 years off the person you're looking at. And as you will well know from interviewing people, witnesses are notorious for having different versions."

It's important to remember that locating a Ron Hunter who was on the West Coast in December 1969/January 1970 does not prove that he is definitely involved in Beard's death. Nonetheless, finding the Ron Hunter who was the spitting image of the identikit photo, and who drove a green Velox, and who fled the area immediately, could be the breakthrough police have waited 38 years for.

If you have any information on the whereabouts of this particular Ron Hunter, please email confidential@investigatemagazine.tv.

For an index to this book, please download the PDF index file from
www.investigatemagazine.com/thomasindex.pdf
For a fully text searchable digital copy of this book, please visit
www.ianwishart.com

www.ingramcontent.com/pod-product-compliance
Lightning Source LLC
Chambersburg PA
CBHW050553170426
43201CB00011B/1682